DAVID CARR is Professor of Philosophy at the University of Ottawa. He is author of *Phenomenology and the Problem of History: A Study of Husserl's Transcendental Philosophy.*

Time, Narrative, and History

Studies in Phenomenology and Existential Philosophy

Time, Narrative, and History

DAVID CARR

INDIANA UNIVERSITY PRESS
Bloomington / Indianapolis

Manufactured in the United States of America

Library of Congress Cataloging-in-Publication Data

Carr, David, 1940–
Time, narrative, and history.

(studies in phenomenology and existential philosophy)
Includes index.
1. Time. 2. Narration (Rhetoric) 3. History—
Philosophy. I. Title. II. Series.
BD638.C33   1986   901   85-45742
ISBN 0-253-36024-2

1 2 3 4 5 90 89 88 87 86

For

Elisabeth Carr

and

Stephen Carr

with love

Contents

Acknowledgments   ix

Introduction   1

I   The Temporal Structure of Experience and Action   18

  1. From Real Time to Real Human Time   18

  2. The Temporality of Experience   21

  3. The Temporality of Action   30

  4. The Melodic Element of Time   40

II   Temporality and Narrative Structure   45

  1. Configuration and Narrative Structure   46

  2. Complex and Extended Experience and Action   52

  3. Narrative, Narrator, and Audience   57

  4. Some Concurring Views and Some Clarifications   65

III   The Self and the Coherence of Life   73

  1. Coherence and Narrative Structure   73

  2. Self-Authorship and Authenticity: A Dispute   80

  3. Settling the Dispute over Authenticity   86

  4. Being in Time   94

IV   Temporality and Historicity   100

  1. The Problem   100

  2. Husserl and Heidegger on *Geschichtlichkeit*   102

3. Historicity and Narrative   110

4. A New Problem   116

V   *From I to We*   122

1. In Search of the Trans-Individual Subject   122

2. Moving beyond Phenomenology: Common
   Experience and Common Action   127

3. Hegel's Dialectic of Recognition   138

4. Group, Time, and Narrative   146

VI   *Time, Narrative, and History*   153

1. Individual and Community *in concreto*   153

2. Communal Narrative and Historical Time   163

3. From Historical Time to Historiography   168

4. Who Are "We"?   177

Index   187

Acknowledgments

I would like to express my thanks to the Ottawa *Eiskreis*. The members of that august body have probably heard more about this project than they ever wanted to know, but they have patiently listened and responded with probing questions, suggestions, and encouragement. I am especially indebted to my colleagues Hilliard Aronovitch and Andrew Lugg. The students in my recent graduate courses at the University of Ottawa, in which many of the ideas in this book were first exposed and tested, deserve thanks as well. Further advice and encouragement have come from my colleagues William Dray and Peter McCormick.

The Social Sciences and Humanities Research Council of Canada provided me with a semester's freedom from teaching and with a research assistant, the capable and helpful Thorsteinn Hilmarsson. Jocelyne LaCasse typed most of the manuscript; for this she deserves sympathy and many thanks.

Finally I would like to thank Leslie Carr for her encouragement and support while this book was being written.

Introduction

This study is intended as a contribution to the philosophy of history. I should explain right away, however, that the nature of my proposed contribution differs considerably from what is usually understood by philosophy of history. It is customary to point out that the term, as used today, has two radically different senses. What I want to do here corresponds, in fact, to neither of them.

What is usually called the substantive or speculative philosophy of history has addressed itself to the whole of human history and asked after its origin, the nature of its unfolding, and in some cases its ultimate destiny. Associated primarily with certain thinkers of the eighteenth and early nineteenth centuries (Vico, Herder, Hegel) and often debunked as a disreputable and fruitless enterprise, this approach has given way, in the late nineteenth and the twentieth centuries, to the so-called critical or analytic philosophy of history. Here "history," as permitted by the well-known ambiguity of the term, denotes not the historical process itself but the knowledge we have of it as delivered by historians, or, alternatively, the disciplined inquiry in which they seek for or arrive at such knowledge. The philosophical questions asked are basically epistemological and concern the concepts, modes of explanation, validity, and objectivity of the historians' claims about the past.

The development of this approach to history has been attended by a constant reference, implicit and explicit, to the sciences of nature. If the substantive philosophy of history can be compared to a high-flown "philosophy of nature," which speculates about the cosmos beyond the reach of our warranted scientific knowledge, the critical philosophy of history corresponds to the more modest "philosophy of science." This development became possible and inevitable in nineteenth-century Germany when history was institutionalized in university departments, dignified with the title of *Wissenschaft*, and

1

accompanied by pretensions to rigor and objectivity. Wilhelm
Dilthey proposed a *Kritik der historisichen Vernunft* and the neo-
Kantians followed suit, seeking to do for historical science what Kant
had done for natural science. From that beginning through its revival
at the hands of twentieth-century Anglo-American philosophers, the
critical philosophy of history has been concerned with whether
history can legitimately be called a science and, if so, how it com-
pares with the science of nature. Philosophers have answered these
questions in many different ways, some attempting to reduce history
to social and thence to natural science, at the one extreme, and others
arguing for history's radically separate and autonomous character at
the other. The latter are in effect arguing that it is inappropriate to use
natural science as a standard and are thus objecting to the comparison itself, but they are occupied with it nonetheless.

What strikes me about this development is not so much the appro-
priateness of the comparison itself as the fact that throughout, the
focus of philosophical reflection is on history as an established,
ongoing discipline with a strictly cognitive interest. Questions about
"our" knowledge of the past are really questions about the historian's
knowledge of the past; in other words, knowledge is portrayed as the
sort possessed or sought by someone with an interest in objective
and warranted claims, securely grounded in the evidence; and the
past is portrayed *as* it is known by someone with such an interest.
What is under analysis is exclusively the connection between the
historian and his or her object.

There is nothing wrong with examining this connection philosophically. There are good reasons for doing it. But this procedure
lends itself to a certain abstractness, which can be characterized,
somewhat exaggeratedly, as follows: Historians are assumed to enter
the scene, existing of course in the present, and equipped with all
the aims, interests, and skills of their profession. They are then
portrayed as coming upon some documents, monuments, or ruins;
and the philosopher then asks how, on the basis of this meagre
evidence, historians can reconstruct the events and persons of a past
they can never directly know. In other words, how does the historian
move from a total ignorance of the past to knowledge of it?

This approach thus suggests, without saying it in so many words,
that "our" only real connection to the historical past is the result of
historical inquiry, whether we carry it out ourselves or are provided
with it second-hand by reading the results of the historians' work,
whereas it seems to me obvious that we have a connection to the

historical past, as ordinary persons, prior to and independently of adopting the historical-cognitive interest. Or so I would like, in the following, to argue.

I will not call this "connection" to the past "knowledge" of it, since it is customary to reserve the latter word for what is at least warranted by some agreed-upon epistemic procedures. What I am saying is that in a naive and prescientific way the historical past is there for all of us, that it *figures* in our ordinary view of things, whether we are historians or not. We have what the phenomenologists call a *non-thematic* or *pre-thematic awareness* of the historical past which functions as background for our present experience, or our experience of the present. The historian has this experience as well, of course, prior to becoming a historian. In a sense it is what the historian seeks to replace when he or she makes explicit and thematic claims about the past. Yet it is misleading to speak of replacing it, since this vague background awareness of the past does not, it seems to me, consist even implicitly in a collection of claims. Thus it is not a case of replacing one set of claims with another; and it can be argued that the kind of pre-thematic awareness of the past of which I am speaking is operative even in the historians' view of the world.

All of this suggests that it would contribute to our philosophical understanding of history as a discipline if we were to relate its cognitive approach to the past to the larger context of this pre-thematic "background" awareness.

Edmund Husserl argued[1] that we can fully comprehend *natural* science only if we trace its cognitive accomplishments back to their origin in the world of everyday, prescientific experience. It is obvious that we are in constant contact with the natural world, whether we are scientists or not, and that we misconstrue both the nature of that contact and the accomplishment of science if we suppose that our only awareness of nature is what we have as scientists or through what the scientists tell us. It is in the "life-world" that we actually live, even if we are scientists, and Husserl proposes to "bracket" nature *as* portrayed by the scientists in order to bring back into philosophical view what is actually always there but gets overlooked by reflection because it is so close to us.

I want to do something comparable for history and for our

---

1. Edmund Husserl, *The Crisis of European Sciences and Transcendental Phenomenology*, tr. D. Carr (Evanston: Northwestern University Press, 1970), pp. 103–189.

awareness of the historical past. I want to set aside the historian's cognitive interest and bracket the past as an object of knowledge in order to let the past appear as an element of our experienced world. This movement of thought I share with phenomenology and derive, to some extent, from some of its classical practitioners. Some of these—both Husserl and Martin Heidegger, for example—have used the term "historicity" *(Geschichtlichkeit)* to denote what I have in mind here: the idea expressed by Dilthey when he said that "we are historical beings first, before we are observers [*Betrachter*] of history, and only because we are the former do we become the latter." "The historical world is always there," said Dilthey, "and the individual not only observes it from the outside but is intertwined with it [*in sie verwebt*]."[2] Clearly this means something more interesting than merely that subject and object of historical inquiry are of the same species. Giambattista Vico's idea, also frequently emphasized by Dilthey, that we can understand history in a way we can never understand nature because "he who studies history is the same as he who makes it,"[3] apart from being open to very serious questions, does not go far enough. To say that we are "historical beings" and "intertwined with history" is not merely to say that we are all *in* history as part of the historical process. It means that we are *in* history as we are *in* the world: it serves as the horizon and background for our everyday experience.

This, in any case, is the core of the notion of historicity picked up by the phenomenologists. But Husserl's and Heidegger's treatments of the concept are different from each other, and to my mind neither is very satisfying.[4] I shall try to show why in chapter IV. To the extent that I borrow from Husserl and Heidegger I will draw more on what they say in a general way about *temporality* than on what they tell us about historicity. It might be said that I shall follow more the spirit than the letter of phenomenological approaches to history. Another reason for this is that a second major focus of the following study, apart from time and the experience of time, is narrative—or, more humbly, story and story-telling. The two go together, in that narrative is our primary (though not our only) way of organizing our experi-

2. Wilhelm Dilthey, *Gesammelte Schriften*, vol. VII, 5th edition, ed. B. Groethuysen (Stuttgart: B. Teubner, 1968), pp. 277–78.
3. Ibid., p. 278.
4. Husserl's ideas on historicity are contained primarily in *The Crisis of European Sciences*. . . . See Martin Heidegger's *Being and Time*, tr. J. Macquarrie and E. Robinson (New York: Harper & Row, 1962), division two, ch. 5.

ence of time, and understood in this sense it can elucidate our pre-theoretical past. While the phenomenologists have said a lot about our experience of time, they have said relatively little about narrative. By contrast, narrative has been intensely discussed of late by literary critics (especially structuralists), by historians, and by analytic philosophers of history. I have profited greatly from these discussions even though I shall be discussing narrative and making use of it in a way that differs from most of them.

The focus on narrative is not as such incompatible with a phenomenological approach, but there are deeper problems with that approach, in my view. The phenomenologists' investigations are tied, for important methodological reasons, to *individual* experience. While I think it is necessary to start with individual experience, and shall do so in what follows, I believe that we are unable to understand the necessarily *social* dimensions of historicity until we go beyond individual experience in a way methodologically precluded by phenomenology. As I shall try to show in chapter V, to the extent that we genuinely get beyond the individual's experience, we must also move beyond phenomenology.

While the shift to the social dimension requires this move, it is the discussion of narration that renders it possible. Central to the analysis of stories and story-telling, apart from the temporal unfolding of events, is the relation among the points of view *on* those events belonging to characters in the story, the teller of the story, and the audience to whom the story is told. Further nuances involve distinctions between the real and the implied narrator and the real and the implied audience of a story. While these notions will prove useful in elucidating the historical character of the individual's experience, they will also permit us to detach the crucial notions of *subject of a story*—and *teller of a story*—from the individual, and place both at the social level.

As I have said, this move in the later chapters of our study to the social level, with the help of a theory of narrative, takes the analysis beyond "phenomenology" as I have been using this term so far in this introduction (and as it is usually used in contemporary discussions), that is, to refer roughly to Husserl and his twentieth-century successors such as Heidegger and Maurice Merleau-Ponty. But we shall see that by its means we shall move, by a round-about route, into the domain of that earlier phenomenology—Hegel's—which is at once so near to and so far from what Husserl was doing. Without adopting the central tenets of a Hegelian approach to philosophy in general, or even to history, we shall be able to make use of what Hegel called "the *I* that is *We*, the *We* that is *I*"[5]—in other words, the idea of a social and collective subject of action, experience, and history. This will permit us to move beyond individual subjectivity without leaving behind altogether the idea of subjectivity itself. The combination of phenomenology, narrative theory, and Hegelian phenomenology will permit us to arrive at an indispensable condition for our understanding of history: the idea of a social subject that is flexible, movable, and above all developmental.

I hope in this brief preview to have given readers some idea of what to expect and of what I fervently hope they will *not* expect. I believe that what follows can qualify as a philosophical reflection on history, but it is not "philosophy of history" in any of the usual senses of that term. Nor is it to be identified as a bit of phenomenology in the narrow sense—nor, for that matter, a bit of conceptual analysis, literary theory, "narratology," or whatever. While I draw gratefully on work done in all of these fields and with all these methods, my work seeks to establish its subject matter on its own and to chart its own methodological course. If it thus runs the risk of seeming too diffuse and methodologically eclectic, I would prefer that risk to the one posed by a predetermined methodological strait-jacket. I should add that I am neither a historian (except, in a modest sense, of philosophy) nor a writer of or expert on literary narratives. At best I am a philosophically reflective and admiring reader of both.

These prefatory remarks will also serve as an explanation and excuse for the fact that I seem to take so long to get around to my subject matter, history. I have explained that I am looking as it were behind historical inquiry to its roots in ordinary experience. But even there I find it necessary to speak at some length about our individual experience of the past and of time in general before getting on to that of the historical past and historical time, just as I shall talk a good deal about story-telling and narrative in general, and at the level of individual experience, before coming to narrative in the specifically historical sense. I hope that what I have to say will contribute, along the way, to our understanding of individual experience and existence; but the discussion will have a certain preliminary character until it finds its *raison d'être* in the discussion of history. Thus the present study, though it hardly qualifies as a story,

---

5. G. W. F. Hegel, *Phenomenology of Spirit*, tr. A. V. Miller (Oxford: Clarendon Press, 1977), p. 110.

illustrates one of the most important features of lived time, narrative, and history itself that we shall be discovering along the way: namely, that only from the perspective of the end do the beginning and the middle make sense.

2.

The foregoing remarks have been designed to introduce the following study by stating its basic questions and situating them in relation to other philosophical problems and methods. A word needs to be said now, for the further orientation of the reader, about previous work related to my subject.

I have said that in order to contribute to the philosophical understanding of history I shall be speaking about narrative and its relation to historical time. The connection between narrative and history has been a lively subject of debate among English-speaking philosophers and historians since the mid-1960s, when works by W. B. Gallie, Morton White, and Arthur Danto appeared almost simultaneously.[6] All three emphasized the role of narrative in the historian's work and were subsequently criticized for this emphasis by some philosophers and historians. Placing so much emphasis on narrative was seen as a too "literary" view of a discipline which sought to be objective and scientific.[7] The narrative conception of history was strongly defended against those attacks, notably by the historian J. H. Hexter and the philosopher Louis Mink.[8]

The literary study of narrative has of course had a long history, with significant developments in recent years. The work of Wayne Booth and Kenneth Burke, Robert Scholes and Robert Kellogg, and especially of Frank Kermode are regarded as classics in Anglo-American criticism.[9] The work of the Canadian Northrop Frye concen-

6. Morton White, *Foundations of Historical Knowledge* (New York, Harper & Row, 1965); W. B. Gallie, *Philosophy and Historical Understanding* (London: Chatto and Windus, 1964); Arthur C. Danto, *Analytical Philosophy of History* (Cambridge: Cambridge University Press, 1965).

7. See Maurice Mandelbaum, "A Note on History as Narrative," *History and Theory* 6 (1967): 416–417, and Leon Goldstein, *Historical Knowing* (Austin: University of Texas Press, 1976), especially the introduction.

8. J. H. Hexter, *The History Primer* (New York: Basic Books, 1971); Louis O. Mink, "History and Fiction as Modes of Comprehension," in *New Literary History* I (1970): 541–58.

9. Wayne Booth, *The Rhetoric of Fiction* (Chicago: University of Chicago Press, 1961); Kenneth Burke, *A Grammar of Motives* (New York: Meridian Books, 1962);

trates heavily on narrative structure.[10] And the rise of French
structuralist literary theory in the last twenty years has featured a
strong emphasis on narrative. Building on the earlier work of Eastern
European linguists, such as Vladimir Propp and Roman Jakobson,
the French theorists, principally Roland Barthes, A. J. Greimas, and
Claude Bremond, have produced significant studies of narrative
structure.[11]

These two lines of development, philosophy of history and theory
of literature, ran parallel, without much reciprocal influence, until
the appearance of Hayden White's *Metahistory* in 1973.[12] This extremely influential book, whose author is neither a philosopher nor a
literary critic by training but a historian of ideas, draws on the
analysis of literary narratives, especially those of the structuralists
and of Northrop Frye, and applies them in detail to writings of
classical historians and philosophers of history of the nineteenth
century. As might be expected, White's book too has proved controversial,[13] but on the whole it has provided support for the views of
those philosophers—especially Gallie and Mink—who emphasized
the narrative character of historical writing, by supplying them with
both a theoretical underpinning and a richly detailed illustration.
Something similar has been done quite recently in a book by Paul
Ricoeur.[14] The French philosopher draws on his own theoretical
work on language, especially literary language, and his extensive
knowledge of the analytic philosophy of action and of history to
produce a strong defense for and account of the narrative character of
history. Like White he then applies his theory to the work of historians; but, in a bold stroke, he applies it not to the great classical
historians but to the recent social history of the French *Annales*
school; in other words, to those historians whose work appears to be,

---

Robert Scholes and Robert Kellogg, *The Nature of Narrative* (New York: Oxford
University Press, 1966); Frank Kermode, *The Sense of an Ending* (New York: Oxford
University Press, 1968).

10. Northrop Frye, *The Anatomy of Criticism* (Princeton: Princeton University
Press, 1957).

11. Roland Barthes, "Introduction à l'analyse structurale des récits," *Communications* 8 (1966): 1–27; Claude Bremond, *Logique du récit* (Paris: Seuil, 1973); A. J.
Greimas, *Sémantique structurale* (Paris: Larousse, 1966).

12. Hayden White, *Metahistory* (Baltimore: Johns Hopkins University Press, 1973).

13. See *History and Theory*, vol. XIX no. 4, Beiheft 19: *Metahistory: Six Critiques*
(Middletown: Wesleyan University Press, 1980).

14. Paul Ricoeur, *Temps et récit, Tome I* (Paris: Seuil, 1983). An English translation
has appeared: *Time and Narrative* vol. I, tr. K. McLaughlin and D. Pellauer (Chicago:
University of Chicago Press, 1984). Since this writing two further volumes have
appeared: *Temps et récit II: la configuration dans le récit de fiction* (Paris: Seuil, 1984),
and *Temps et récit III: le temps raconté* (Paris: Seuil, 1985).

and is self-proclaimed to be, non-narrative in character. Ricoeur claims that in hidden form the narrative structure is present even in their work.

Putting this brief survey together with what was said at the beginning of this introduction, it should be easy to see the relation between this previous work and the present project. The focus of these studies of narrative, whether in history or in literature, has been the written work (books, articles, novels, plays) in which a story is told about the past or about fictional events. To be sure, in many cases questions are asked (though this is not considered proper by the structuralists) about how the author constructed the story, so that the examination is shifted from the text to the author's act in creating it. Many of these studies, moreover—though again not the structuralists'—are interested in the relation between the narrative and the events it portrays. But at the center of attention, and the occasion for it, is the narrative as a *text*.

The "narrativist" philosophers of history such as Mink and H. White have been roundly criticized, especially by Maurice Mandelbaum and Leon Goldstein,[15] for missing the essence of history by favoring its literary presentation over the hard work of discovery, explanation, evaluation of sources, etc., which lies behind it. History, say these critics, is not a literary genre but a disciplined inquiry whose goal is knowledge. Narrative is merely the way— indeed only one way—in which its results are "written up" for public consumption.

My own response to the narrative analysis of history is similar, but with an important difference, as might be expected from what I said earlier. I too want to shift the focus "backward" *from* the literary products, but neither *to* the author's creative act nor *to* the historian's scientific procedure. Instead my focus is beyond even the latter to the historical experience that lies behind and precedes both.

The shift of focus I am proposing does not constitute a criticism of the narrativists like that of Mandelbaum and Goldstein. In fact, what I shall do may provide a response to these critics' objections. For if I am right in thinking that narrative structure pervades our very experience of time and social existence, independently of our contemplating the past as historians, then we shall have a way of answering the charge that narrative is nothing but window-dressing or packaging, something incidental to our knowledge of the past.

---

15. See Mandelbum's and Goldstein's works cited above.

But here I run up against a curious resistance on the part of the narrativists themselves, or at least some of the strongest among them, to the view that narrative is anything but a literary structure. This resistance becomes evident when these theorists consider the capacity of narratives to *represent* the events of the past.

Writing of "Narrative Form as a Cognitive Instrument,"[16] Louis Mink speaks of our "implicit presupposition"[17] that historical narratives tell what really happened, in the sense that there is a true but "untold story" in the past waiting to be told.[18] This is, he says, the principal way we distinguish historical from fictional narratives. Yet narrative structure, particularly the closing off of a sequence of events provided by the story's beginning and end, is a structure derived from the telling of the story itself, not from the events it relates. Even the "events," as real occurrences of the past, become cognitively suspect when we realize that "we cannot refer to events as such, but only to events *under a description*"[19] and that the description is a function of the narrative the events make up. But "narrative form in history, as in fiction, is an artifice, the product of individual imagination."[20] So historical narrative presents us with a dilemma: "as historical it claims to represent, through its form, part of the real complexity of the past, but as narrative it is a product of imaginative construction which cannot defend its claim to truth by any accepted procedure of argument or authentication."[21]

As for the past, "there can in fact be no untold stories at all, just as there can be no unknown knowledge. There can be only past facts not yet described in a context of narrative form."[22] As he puts it in another essay: "stories are not lived but told. Life has no beginnings, middles and ends. . . . Narrative qualities are transferred from art to life."[23]

Mink is saying, then, that narrative is constitutionally unable to represent "life" (the real events and actions of the past) because of the narrative form itself. This form is a "product of individual imagination" which arises from the historian's act of telling and has no part

---

16. Louis O. Mink, "Narrative Form as a Cognitive Instrument" in *The Writing of History*, ed. R. H. Canary and H. Kozicki (Madison: University of Wisconsin Press, 1978).

17. Ibid., p. 147.

18. Ibid., p. 143.

19. Ibid., p. 145.

20. Ibid.

21. Ibid.

22. Ibid., p. 147.

23. Mink, "History and Fiction as Modes of Comprehension," pp. 557–58.

in the events narrated. Narrative imposes on the events of the past a form that in themselves they do not have.

There is some irony in Mink's arriving at this view, since he seems at first to be continuing a tradition whose purpose was to defend the cognitive pretensions of traditional, narrative history. The positivist analysis of historical knowledge put forward by Carl Hempel[24] suggested that history could become a respectable body of knowledge if only it would cast off its vague and "literary" form and get down to rigorous causal explanations, thereby assuming the form of natural science. In other words, it was the form of historical discourse (typically narrative) which prevented it from being genuine knowledge of the past. William Dray, drawing on earlier work by R. G. Collingwood (and helped along by the later Wittgenstein's pluralism of language games), argued that history should be seen as employing its own modes of explanation—principally reconstructing the reasons rather than giving the causes of human action.[25] The "narrativists" of the 1960s then further refined the idea of history's autonomy vis-à-vis the natural sciences by emphasizing the activity of constructing a story. By speaking of historical narrative as a "mode of comprehension" and a "cognitive instrument," Mink seems to be pursuing the same line. In the end, however, he seems at least to suggest the same conclusion reached by the positivists. The very form of historical discourse undermines its epistemic pretentions.

If Mink exhibits some reluctance in arriving at such skeptical conclusions, Hayden White embraces them boldly. Like Mink, he raises the question of narrative's capacity to represent: in a recent article he asks after "the Value of Narrativity in the Representation of Reality"[26] and concludes, in essence, that its value is nil. Developing ideas that were implicit but not directly stated in *Metahistory*, he conveys his view in a series of loaded questions: "What wish is enacted, what desire is gratified," he asks, "by the fantasy that *real* events are properly represented when they are shown to display the formal coherency of a story?"[27] "Does the world really present itself to perception in the form of well-made stories . . . ? Or does it pre-

---

24. Carl G. Hempel, "The Function of General Laws in History," *The Journal of Philosophy* (1942) and "Explanation in Science and History" in *Frontiers of Science and Philosophy*, ed. R. Colodny (Pittsburgh: University of Pittsburgh Press, 1962).

25. William Dray, "The Historical Explanation of Actions Reconsidered" in *Philosophy and History*, ed. S. Hook (New York: New York University Press, 1963).

26. Hayden White, "The Value of Narrativity in the Representation of Reality" in *On Narrative*, ed. W. J. T. Mitchell (Chicago: University of Chicago Press, 1981).

27. Ibid., p. 4.

sent itself more in the way that the annals and chronicles suggest, either as a mere sequence without beginning or end or as sequences of beginnings that only terminate and never conclude?"[28] For White the answer is clear: "The notion that sequences of real events possess the formal attributes of the stories we tell about imaginary events could only have its origin in wishes, daydreams, reveries." It is precisely annals and chronicles that offer us the "paradigms of ways that reality offers itself to perception."[29] In a comment on the paper I have been quoting, Louis Mink summarizes White's view in three propositions: "(1) That the world is not given to us in the form of well-made stories; (2) that we make such stories; (3) that we give them referentiality by imagining that in them the world speaks itself" (that is, that they tell the untold story, in Mink's earlier formulation); and Mink says that with these three propositions "I entirely agree."[30] He goes on to disagree with a fourth proposition concerning the motive for constructing such stories; White believes the motive is to establish "moral authority" while Mink still insists on a cognitive motive. But there is a deeper disagreement Mink does not notice. Mink places the origin of narrative explicitly in "the individual imagination" of the author whereas White, as quoted, traces it to "wishes, daydreams, reveries." This may seem a subtle difference, but the shift is away from the sort of conscious "creative" act Mink suggests. This ties in with White's earlier theory, in *Metahistory* and articles written at the same period,[31] that historians draw on the "plot-structures" identified by Northrop Frye as Romance, Comedy, Tragedy, and Satire. But they do not do so consciously, of course, since they think of themselves as telling us simply *wie es eigentlich gewesen*; in fact they would vehemently deny such literary inspiration. These plot-structures are simply "culturally provided rules for story-telling"[32] in Western culture, and writers of narrative seize on them without realizing they are doing so.

Thus when Mink asserts that he and White hold the view that "we make such stories" he may be overlooking a difference of opinion on just who "we" are, and what constitutes "making." We shall have occasion to return to this point. For our present purposes, however, it

---

28. Ibid., p. 23.
29. Ibid.
30. Mink, "Everyman His or Her Own Annalist" in ibid., p. 238.
31. See White, *Metahistory*, pp. 7–8; and "The Structure of Historical Narrative," *Clio* I (1972): 5–19.
32. White, "The Structure of Historical Narrative," p. 17.

is more important to stress what they do agree on: that the narrative, as a literary artifact produced by historians, reads into the reality of the past a narrative structure that the past does not "really" have.

That Mink and White should have taken the analysis of history in this skeptical direction attests to the importance for both of the parallel between historical and fictional narrative. And if we look to some of the most influential studies of literary narrative mentioned above, we shall see evidence of the same view on the relation between narrative and the real world. To be sure, fictional stories do not represent reality because what they portray by definition never happened. But it is often thought that stories can be life-like precisely by virtue of their form. That is, they are capable of representing the way certain events, if they had happened, might have unfolded.

But to attribute narrative coherence to real events is, according to some theorists, wishful thinking at best. As F. Kermode puts it in *The Sense of an Ending:* "In 'making sense' of the world we . . . feel a need to experience that concordance of beginning, middle and end which is the essence of our explanatory fictions . . . ."[33] But such fictions "degenerate," he says, into "myths" whenever we actually believe them or ascribe their narrative properties to the real, "whenever they are not consciously held to be fictive."[34] As for the structuralists, it is generally not done to speak of a relation between text and world, either for methodological reasons or because the real world is thought to be so unstructured as to be incapable of being spoken of at all. It seems that the latter view may motivate the methodological principle, if we consider the few remarks that are let fall on the relation between story and world. Seymour Chatman, in his valuable presentation of structuralist theories of narrative, also speaking of the beginning-middle-end structure, insists that this structure applies "to the narrative, to story-events as imitated, rather than to . . . actions themselves, simply because such terms are meaningless in the real world."[35] In this he echoes his principal mentor Roland Barthes. In his influential "Introduction à l'analyse structurale des récits" Barthes says that "art knows no static"; that is, in a story everything has its place in a structure while the extraneous has been eliminated, and that in this art differs from "life," in which

---

33. Kermode, pp. 35–36.
34. Ibid., p. 39.
35. Seymour Chatman, *Story and Discourse* (Ithaca: Cornell University Press, 1978), p. 47.

everything is "scrambled messages" *(communications brouillées)*.[36] Barthes thus evokes the old question about the relation of art and life with respect to narrative, as does Mink, and arrives at the same conclusion: the one is constitutionally incapable of "representing" the other.

We noted that Paul Ricoeur draws together the study of literary narrative and the analytic philosophy of history, and he presents in his *Temps et récit* a complex theory of narrative which is supposed initially to be neutral with respect to the distinction between history and fiction. And for Ricoeur, too, the problem of representation is of central importance. This is seen in the fact that the key concept in Ricoeur's account is that of *mimesis* derived from Aristotle's *Poetics*.

At first Ricoeur's theory seems to run counter to the emphasis we have found in others on the *discontinuity* between narrative and the "real world." In his studies of language and literature Ricoeur has long resisted the structuralists' denial of all connection between a text and the world beyond. In *Temps et récit* he puts the structural or "configurational" aspect of narrative in a central position but insists on situating it in relation to the world of human action from which it is drawn, and on which it has its effects as it is read and appreciated.

It is for this reason that Ricoeur maintains the term *mimesis*, but he declines to translate the term "representation" (or "imitation"), for he believes the relation between the narrative and its world is much more complicated than that traditional translation suggests. In working out how this is so he reveals himself to be much closer to Mink, White, and the structuralists than he at first appears. He does not go so far as to say with them that the world of action is simply chaotic, maintaining instead that it has a "pre-narrative structure"[37] of elements that lend themselves to narrative configurations. In particular he mentions the "conceptual network" provided by the "semantics of action."[38] Literature, he says, "vient configurer ce qui, dans l'action humaine, fait déjà figure."[39]

Yet this pre-figuration is not itself narrative structure, and it does not save us from what Ricoeur seems to regard as a sort of constitutional disarray attached to the experience of time, which in itself is "confused, unformed and, at the limit, mute."[40] From a study of

---

36. Barthes, "Introduction à l'analyse . . .," p. 7.
37. Ricoeur, p. 113.
38. Ibid., p. 88.
39. Ibid., p. 100.
40. Ibid., p. 13.

Augustine's *Confessions* he concludes that the experience of time is characterized essentially by "discordance." Literature, in narrative form, brings concord to this "aporia" by means of the invention of a plot. Narrative is a "synthesis of the heterogeneous" in which disparate elements of the human world—"agents, goals, means, interactions, circumstances, unexpected results, etc."[41]—are brought together and harmonized. Like metaphor, to which Ricoeur has also devoted an important study, narrative is a "semantic innovation" in which something new is brought into the world by means of language.[42] Instead of describing the world, it re-describes it. Metaphor, he says, is the capacity of "seeing-as."[43] Narrative opens us to "the realm of the 'as if.'"[44]

So in the end for Ricoeur narrative structure is as alien from the "real world" as it is for the other authors we have been discussing. Ricoeur echoes Mink, White, *et al.* when he says: "The ideas of beginning, middle, and end are not taken from experience: They are not traits of real action but effects of poetic ordering."[45] If the role of narrative is to introduce something new into the world, and what it introduces is the synthesis of the heterogeneous, then presumably it attaches to the events of the world a form they do not otherwise have. A story redescribes the world, that is, it describes it *as if* it were what, presumably, in fact it is not.[46]

This brief survey of important recent views of narrative shows not only that narrative structure is being considered strictly as a feature of literary and historical *works*, but also, as we said, that that structure is regarded as one that pertains *only* to such works. The various approaches to the problem of representation reveal that stories or histories are considered alien to, separated from the real world they profess to depict because of the narrative form itself. It follows that fictional narratives cannot, for structural reasons, really be "life-like" and that historical or other non-fictional narratives, such as biography, journalism, etc., must inevitably impose upon their subject-matter a form it does not possess. At best narrativization dresses up reality, reflecting our need for satisfying coherence, and, if we really believe it, derives from wishful thinking. It is an "escape" from

41. Ibid., p. 102.
42. Ibid., p. 11. See Ricoeur, *La Métaphore vive* (Paris: Seuil, 1975).
43. *Temps et récit*, p. 13. See *La Métaphore vive*, pp. 305–21.
44. *Temps et récit*, p. 101.
45. Ibid., p. 67.
46. For a longer critical analysis of *Temps et récit* vol. I, see my review-essay in *History and Theory* XXIII: 3, (1984): 357–70.

reality. At worst (and this is an idea put forward by Barthes and picked up by H. White[47]) narrative seeks to put across a moral view of the world in the interests of power and manipulation.

My view is that while these theorists have contributed much to our understanding of narrative they have misunderstood its relation to the "real world." By stressing the discontinuity between "art" and "life," as regards narrative, they have not only miscast the relation but contributed to the misunderstanding of both terms, especially the latter.

As I said, I shall be stressing the continuity between narrative and everyday life, but my account will not take the form of claims about how literary and historical narratives "represent." Instead I shall begin by uncovering narrative features of everyday experience and action. If I succeed in showing a certain community of form between "life" and written narratives, my account may have some implications for the problem of representation. But that is not my initial concern. To the extent that I discuss narrative at all in its literary guise, I shall be stressing the fact that it arises out of and is prefigured in certain features of life, action, and communication. Historical and fictional narratives will reveal themselves to be not distortions of, denials of, or escapes from reality, but extensions and configurations of its primary features.

In my survey of theories which stress the discontinuity between narrative and reality I have presented the views of some of the strongest and most influential thinkers in recent literary theory and philosophy of history. But while the discontinuity view predominates, there are dissenting voices. One of the most eloquent is the literary critic Barbara Hardy, who holds that "narrative, like lyric or dance, is not to be regarded as an aesthetic invention used by artists to control, manipulate, and order experience, but as a primary act of mind transferred to art from life. The novel merely heightens, isolates and analyses the narrative motions of human consciousness."[48] The historian Peter Munz, in *The Shapes of Time*, has also stressed the continuity between narrative and everyday life.[49] The German philosopher Wilhelm Schapp, a renegade phenomenologist writing in

---

47. See especially Barthes's essay "Historical Discourse" in *Introduction to Structuralism*, ed. Michael Lane (New York: Basic Books, 1970) pp. 145–55.

48. Barbara Hardy, "Towards a Poetics of Fiction: An Approach through Narrative," in *Novel* 2 (1968), p. 5.

49. Peter Munz, *The Shapes of Time* (Middletown: Wesleyan University Press, 1977).

the 1950s, made the idea of being caught up in stories *(In Geschichten Verstrickt)* the key to a whole theory of human existence and much more besides.[50] A chapter of Alasdair MacIntyre's *After Virtue* is devoted to the narrative structure of human existence.[51] One of the most detailed and explicit defenses of the continuity thesis is to be found in Frederick Olafson's *The Dialectic of Action.*[52] I have made grateful use of all these studies, some of which appeared since I began this project. Naturally I hope to improve on them; I find that each puts the emphasis on a different side of what I try to present as the over-all phenomenon. None succeeds, in my view, in doing justice to the social dimension of narrative which is necessary for the full comprehension of history.

One further note: I must admit that my procedure may seem to exhibit one methodologically suspect feature. I aim to show that full-fledged literary story-telling arises out of life. But in order to show this I shall be examining life with constant reference to a pregiven "model" which is precisely full-fledged literary story-telling. The danger with all "models" is that their use will distort the subject-matter it is their purpose to illuminate. I can only leave it to the reader to decide whether I have applied this model judiciously and with all appropriate and necessary qualifications.

---

50. Wilhelm Schapp, *In Geschichten Verstrickt*, 2nd ed. (Wiesbaden: B. Heymann, 1976). A third edition, with a foreword by Hermann Lübbe, has recently been published by Vittorio Klostermann (Frankfurt, 1985).

51. Alasdair MacIntyre, *After Virtue* (Notre Dame: University of Notre Dame Press, 1981).

52. Frederick A. Olafson, *The Dialectic of Action* (Chicago: University of Chicago Press, 1979).

I

The Temporal Structure
of
Experience and Action

1. From Real Time to Real Human Time

We began by announcing our intention to display and explore the pre-theoretical awareness we all have of the historical past. The term "pre-theoretical" suggest an awareness not informed by the cognitive interest of a discipline like history but belonging to "ordinary experience," where "ordinary" refers simply to the lay person who is not a historian. But we are not speaking here merely of the fact that the ordinary person from time to time thinks about the historical past. The awareness we seek to describe is not only pre-theoretical but also "pre-thematic"; that is, it is an awareness in which the historical past is involved in ordinary experience even when we are not explicitly thinking about it. As we said, it has the character of a "background" for present experience.

We have indicated that the place to look for this awareness of the past is our ordinary experience of time and that the key to its nature is the narrative or story-telling character of that experience. But we have just encountered, precisely among some theorists who make the strongest connection between narrative and history, the view that if ordinary experience has an identifiable and describable structure at all, it is certainly not a narrative structure. It will be our purpose in this chapter, then, to display something of the temporal character of everyday experience in order to show its relation to narrative structure. We shall not yet be speaking specifically of the *historical* past. Indeed, insofar as we speak of the past at all, it will be in the context of a discussion of temporality as a whole, the interconnection between past, present, and future.

In discussing the "representational" character of narrative, theorists such as Mink and Hayden White are sometimes unclear on exactly what it is in their view that narrative tries, but is constitutionally unable, to represent. "The world," "real events" are terms they often use. But this way of speaking introduces a very misleading equivocation. Narratives, whether historical or fictional, are typically about, and thus purport to represent, not the world as such, reality as a whole, but specifically *human* reality. But when the term "reality" is left unqualified, we are tempted by the strong naturalist prejudice that what counts as reality must be physical reality. What this suggests is either the random activity and collision of blind forces, devoid of order and significance, or, alternatively, a reality totally ordered along rigorous causal lines without a flaw or gap in its mechanism. These two notions are of course incompatible with each other, but what they have in common is the idea that in either case "reality" is utterly indifferent to human concerns. Things simply happen, one after the other, randomly or according to their own laws. Any significance, meaning, or value ascribed to events is projected onto them by our concerns, prejudices, and interests, and in no way attaches to the events themselves.

Another of the authors we quoted, Frank Kermode, invites us to consider the ticking of a clock. When asked what it says, "we agree that it says *tick-tock*. By this fiction we humanize it . . . . Of course, it is we who provide the fictional difference between the two sounds; *tick* is our word for a physical beginning, *tock* our word for an end."[1] By his use of the word "fiction" here, Kermode is suggesting that the *reality* of the clock's sound is a "mere sequence" without structure or configuration, and that the organization we assign to it in calling it "tick-tock" is mere appearance, something in our minds with no basis in reality. In context, it is clear that the "fictional" narrative structure Kermode has in mind is that associated with our literary tradition.

All this confuses the issue because, as these theorists very well

---

1. Kermode, *The Sense of an Ending,* pp. 44–45.

know, what stories and histories represent or depict is not purely physical events but human experiences, actions, and sufferings, including the human activity of projecting meaning onto or finding meaning in physical and other events. Thus the physical world does find its way into stories, but always as back-drop or sphere of operations for human activity. But it seems that human reality, in order to make good on the sharp contrast between "art" and "life," is being construed according to the model of the ticking clock. Hayden White, we recall, speaks of "the world" as presenting itself as "a mere sequence without beginning or end" where it is clear that he is speaking not of physical events but of human events of the sort set down in historical chronicles.[2]

But how plausible is the idea of human events as a "mere sequence"? Is this an accurate way to describe the temporal character of the experiences and actions that make up our lives? Philosophers in the phenomenological tradition, beginning with Husserl, have come up with very different results and have developed some sophisticated conceptual means for describing the temporal features of our experience.

Husserl asks what it is to experience a "temporal object," that is, something that endures, like a steady tone, or something that changes, like a succession of tones that make up a melody and thus constitute an event. By considering purely auditory phenomena he seeks to simplify his analysis, excluding the spatial aspects of events involving objects we see. Let us recall some of the salient features of Husserl's analysis, limiting ourselves for the moment to the sort of example he uses. Like him we shall adopt the first-person perspective, describing the experience from the inside, as it appears to the person who has it.[3]

---

2. H. White, "The Value of Narrativity in the Representation of Reality," p. 23.

3. What follows is a free rendering of what I take to be the essentials of Husserl's theory. Occasionally I refer the reader to the primary source, Edmund Husserl, *Zur Phänomenologie des inneren Zeitbewussteins (1893–1917)*, ed. Rudolf Boehm, volume X of Husserliana, Husserl's collected works (The Hague: Martinus Nijhoff, 1966). A small part of this material has been translated (Edmund Husserl, *The Phenomenology of Internal Time-Consciousness*, tr. James S. Churchill [Bloomington: Indiana University Press, 1964]), and where possible I include a page reference in parentheses to the translation. For commentaries that are much closer to the text, readers are referred to the best work in English: Robert Sokolowski, *Husserlian Meditations* (Evanston: Northwestern University Press, 1974), ch. 6; and John Brough, "The Emergence of an Absolute Consciousness in Husserl's Early Writings on Time-Consciousness," *Man and World* V (1972).

nomenological critique by Merleau-Ponty in the *Phenomenology of Perception* of the concept of sensation (or sense-datum) in classical empiricism.[12] The sensation is supposed to be the basic unit or building block of experience. But if we consult our experience and attempt to describe it, the simplest thing we can discover is the figure–background scheme; a "patch" of color, for example, standing out from a field which seems to extend behind it. The supposedly punctual, distinct, and in themselves "meaningless" units of sensation, far from being elements of experience, are in fact the products of a highly abstract analysis which forms part of a causal explanation (not a description) of our experience. Sensations, then, are theoretical entities or constructs. On the basis of Husserl's description of time-experience, one would have to say the same of the idea of a mere or "pure" sequence of isolated events; it may be thinkable or conceivable, but it is not experienceable. The idea of an "event" is already that of something that *takes* time, has temporal thickness, beginning and end; and events are experienced as the phases and elements of other, larger-scale events and processes. These make up the temporal configurations, like melodies and other extended occurrences and happenings, that are the stuff of our daily experience. Even though as temporal they unfold bit by bit, we experience them *as* configurations thanks to our protentional and retentional "gaze" which spans future and past. Like the spatial horizon, the horizons of the future and the past recede indefinitely, and it would surely be a mistake to identify retention and protention with "short-term" memory and expectation. As we have seen, what distinguishes retention from recollection, and protention from "secondary expectation," is not the length of their term but their functioning as horizons for ongoing, present experience. As with the horizon of space, *how much* (in objective terms) is "taken in" by these horizons will vary according to the character of the foreground and may, in fact, be quite extensive.

The horizons of time, like those of space, are not undifferentiated plena but are "inhabited" by, articulated into more or less distinct events. As Merleau-Ponty has correctly pointed out, a pure Heraclitean flux or Bergsonian *durée pure* is as much an abstract version of time as is its atomization into timeless points. Just as we have no

---

12. Maurice Merleau-Ponty, *Phenomenology of Perception*, tr. Colin Smith (New York: The Humanities Press, 1962), pp. 3–4.

2. *The Temporality of Experience*

The simple perception (or sensation)–plus-memory account is a fairly standard one in dealing with our consciousness of ongoing events, like melodies, and Husserl credits his teacher Franz Brentano with having seen that memory cannot be treated, in Humean fashion, as giving us merely the weakened presence of the object; for weakened presence is still presence and does not equal pastness.[4] But Brentano does not go nearly far enough, for the notion of memory does not give us all we need. As I hear the present note sound, I could remember notes from different points in my past experience—yesterday or ten years ago—that have no connection with the note I am hearing now. What is unaccounted for is the just-pastness, the very previousness of the previous note, in virtue of which I hear two notes as a succession—or, more precisely, in virtue of which I hear one note *as* succeeding the other. If consciousness of the past is memory, then we must recognize here, says Husserl, a special sort of memory, whose object is the just-past which attaches itself immediately to the present. Thanks to this sort of memory, I have consciousness not only of the succession of notes which make up the melody, but of the very presentness of the present; to hear the present note sound is to be conscious of its occurring or *taking place*; but its taking place is precisely its taking the place *of* its predecessor. To be conscious of its occurrence is to be conscious also of the "comet tail" that trails behind it.[5] Husserl's great contribution here lies in his recognition of this peculiar form of memory which he calls primary memory or retention, and in the sharp distinction he makes between it and memory in the usual sense, secondary memory or recollection. It is true that they are both consciousness of the past, but their functions in the life of consciousness are entirely different.

The best way to understand retention is to turn, as Husserl does, to the comparison between the experience of space and the experience of time.[6] Present and past function together in the perception of time somewhat as do foreground and background or focus and horizon in spatial perception. To see a thing is to see it against a spatial background which extends behind it and away from it and from which it stands out. Seeing always "takes in" this background as well as the particular object seen; that is, corresponding to the horizon is a

---

4. Husserl, *Zur Phänomenologie*, pp. 10–19 (29–40).

5. Ibid., p. 30 (52).

6. Ibid., pp. 5 (23), 31 (52).

horizon-consciousness that belongs to every perception. Just as there is no object without background (and no background without object; the two notions are correlative), so there is no perceptual consciousness of space which does not include horizon-consciousness. Now Husserl says that the temporal is experienced by us as a kind of "field" like the visual field: the present is its focus and the just-past forms the background against which it stands out.[7] Consciousness of the present always involves retention as the horizon-consciousness of this background.

This combination of foreground and background, and their correlates, consciousness of present note (Husserl calls it "impressional") and retentional consciousness of the past horizon, go to make up our experience of the melody's sounding, its actual occurrence or happening. By contrast, to "remember" a note in the usual sense of that word (Husserl speaks of "recollection" or "secondary memory") is to be conscious of an event that is *not* happening, but that did happen.[8] It is, according to Husserl, to reproduce the melody's sounding, including all its temporal features.

Retention and recollection are thus two radically different ways of being conscious of the past. Recollections come and go, whereas retention belongs to all experience. Returning to the parallel with spatial perception once again: the past which I retain, like the spatial background, is constitutive of the presence (note that the word has both a spatial and a temporal sense) of my object; whereas recollection is like my *imagining* an object somewhere else in space but not within my visual field. In the latter case, I "call to mind" or render present something that *is* not present.[9]

Husserl adds a significant dimension to his account of how we experience events by recognizing that an expectation of the *future* is as much a part of the experience as a retention of the past. In fact, on the side of the future, there is something parallel to the distinction between retention and recollection. He speaks of "primary" (as opposed to secondary) expectation which corresponds to primary memory, and calls it "protention" to correspond to retention.[10] It is one thing to "call to mind" some future event (plan it, dread it, look forward to it, just think about it) and quite another to anticipate the immediate future as the horizon of the present. Again this horizon is

7. Ibid., p. 31 (52).
8. Ibid., p. 35 (57).
9. Ibid., p. 158.
10. Ibid., p. 39 (62).

constitutive of the present: the note's sound *takes place* only to be replaced by its successor.

Taking past and future horizons together, then, one may speak of the temporal as a "field of occurrence," in which the present stands out from its surroundings, and of our consciousness as a kind of gaze which "takes in" or spans the field in which the focal object stands out. A Bergsonian may object to this use of spatial concepts, which we are admittedly emphasizing here even more than Husserl does. In our defense, and Husserl's, we can point out that it is not the conceptualized or objective space of geometry that we are using as an analogy, but precisely lived or experienced space, just as we are speaking here of lived or experienced time and not time "in itself" or "as such." It is just as well, however, to heed the warning and to remind ourselves constantly of the limits of the analogy even as we continue to profit by its use.

The analogy can be pushed one step farther. We started with the problem of "hearing the melody," and pointed out that we do not at any time hear all the notes in the melody. Still, we do speak of hearing the melody, and this conveys the fact that it is the melody as a whole, and not the individual notes, that is the *object* of my awareness. Now just as a spatial thing reveals itself to me only one side at a time, but such that the side is seen *as a side* of the thing which is my object, and not as an object in its own right, so the melody reveals itself one note at a time, and each note is heard as "presenting" the melody, not as standing on its own.[11] In spite of all the obvious differences between the temporal and the spatial object (the order of presentation cannot be reversed, the object does not outlive its presentations, it is not differently presented to different observers, etc.) this analogy is useful. It enables us to invoke the Husserlian difference between internal and external horizons: those that belong to the object, such as its hidden sides, and those from which it stands out *as* an object. In the case of the melody, our use of the foreground-background analogy must be subtly differentiated. Within the melody, notes that are given in any moment as past, present, and future are like salient and hidden features of the object. But the melody as a whole also stands out against the background of the "silences" before it begins and after it ends.

What Husserl offers us is the counterpart of the well-known ph

11. Ibid., pp. 26–27 (47).

experience of space except by experiencing objects *in space,* so we experience time as events, things that take or take up time.

Kermode is quite right, then, to say that "we can perceive duration only when it is organized."[13] We need not even go so far as to organize the clock's ticking into groups of two, as suggested by our expression "tick-tock." Even without such grouping, such a sound will be heard as a function of its place in a temporal configuration. The individual sounds will clearly be experienced very differently depending on whether they are the first or second in a just-begun series, or come after a long sequence of sounds. Equally, their occurrence will have a different character depending on whether we expect them to continue monotonously or whether, say, we are worried they might lead up to an explosion. These, too, are ways of organizing the series. Kermode's mistake lies in calling the organization "fictional" and opposing it to the "reality" of the "mere" sequence. Where is reality here, and where fiction? The reality of our temporal experience is that it is organized and structured; it is the "mere sequence" that has turned out to be fictional, in the sense that we speak of a "theoretical fiction."[14]

If temporal consciousness can be compared, according to Husserl, to a gaze which spans or takes in the temporal horizons of future and past, against which the temporal object presents itself, this is not to say that such consciousness rises above or stands outside time. In his lectures on time-consciousness Husserl nowhere has recourse to a substantial, underlying, or persisting ego which exists outside the multiplicity of temporal phases and views them all on an equal basis, "spread out" as in a simultaneous array. Time-consciousness is rooted in the inalienable perspective of the *now* just as space-consciousness is rooted in the *here.* But in both cases this "location" is not a limitation of or its separation from the multiplicty of time or space, but precisely the opening onto it, the experienced access to its reality.

This leads to one more thing which must be noted before we part company with our version of the Husserlian approach to time-consciousness. Husserl, by limiting himself to the auditory example, seems at times to believe that he has bracketed not merely the spatial aspects of the sound but all external reference altogether, as if he had

---

13. Kermode, p. 45.
14. See Olafson's similar critique of Kermode in *The Dialectic of Action,* pp. 49–52.

to do merely with non-intentional or "hyletic" contents of consciousness. But it seems clear that the hearing of a melody, or even of
just a tone, is still intentional in the strict sense that we must
distinguish between the object heard and the hearing of it. So far we
have paid attention, with Husserl, to the temporality of the object
(the melody) and our manner of experiencing that temporality of our
experiences themselves, the flow of our consciousness. But a perception of succession does presuppose, even if it does not equal, a
succession of perceptions. Another way to put it is this: when I
experience something such as a melody that *is* happening, my experience is itself something that happens: it is an event. Now, strictly,
we would have to say that it is a full-fledged event not for me but only
for a possible external observer, or for a later recollection of mine.
That is, I do not experience my own experience; I just *have* it.

Still, its temporality is not something hidden from me. This can be
best seen in cases of genuinely non-intentional experiences, such as
a throbbing tooth-ache or a wave of sadness.[15] These are experiences
that I have, not objects that I encounter. But they do begin and end,
and thus endure, even develop and change. To say simply that I *have*
these feelings suggests something too punctual; it could better be
said that I *live through* them.[16] In the same manner, I live through the
experience of an objective event like a melody. Again, the parallel
with spatial perception holds: the temporality of my experience of a
temporal object (event) is like the *spatiality* of my perception of a
spatial object. My perception is not an object (or configuration of
objects) *in* space for me, as it could be for an external observer, but it
does comprise a vantage point (my body) which is its own "lived
through" spatiality. Like the vantage point in spatial perception, the
temporality of an experience of a temporal object is not itself an
object but a structural feature of the experience.

Thus the life of consciousness is no more an undifferentiated
Bergsonian continuum than are the experienced events happening
around us. It is articulated into experiences: acts of awareness, feelings, episodes which begin and end, experiences which are composed of other experiences and combine to make up larger ones.
According to Husserl's theory, *intentional* experiences are at least
partly differentiated by what they are of. Thus when I hear the
melody, the melody is not only distinguished from other events; my

---

15. See Husserl's discussion of non-intentional feelings, *Logical Investigations*, tr.
J. N. Findlay (New York: The Humanities Press, 1970), vol. II, pp. 572–76.
16. This is Husserl's concept of *erleben* as opposed to *erfahren*. See ibid., p. 540.

hearing of the melody is distinguished as such from other experiences. And just as the melody is composed of the successively sounding notes, so my hearing of the melody is a complex experience composed of my hearings of the notes. As we said before, I do not experience as events the experiences I am living through. Nevertheless, their articulated structure belongs to the "background" of what I am experiencing, which is melodies, concerts, trees falling, persons talking, and other events in the world.

The life of consciousness *is* composed, then, in the phenomenological view, of a sequence of more or less distinguishable experiences. But clearly they constitute more than *just* a sequence of events in time, at least for the person who has them. Nor is their interrelation the causal relation of natural sequences of events though they may be construed this way by an external observer. It must be remembered that in order to have experiences I must have them one at a time; or rather, I am always "located" in the now with respect to past and future experiences. If we ask: In what way do past experiences relate to the one I am now having? we should not, I think, follow F. Olafson's suggestion that the proper way to view this relation is as an "intentional linkage" giving rise to a "cumulative" progression.[17] He is saying that the relation of my past experience to the one I am now having is not that the former causes the latter, but that the former has meaning for me now. Its function is not to cause present consciousness but to be *for* present consciousness. An effect is not aware of its various causes, but a consciousness is aware of and thus accumulates its past experiences and proceeds in light of them.

This suggestion does not, I believe, do justice to the conception opened up by Husserl's lectures on time-consciousness. It is appropriate, perhaps, for the level of *recollection* or secondary memory, in which I often remember not the objects of my experiences but my experiences themselves. These do then become intentional objects for me. But Husserl's account of retention and protention suggest a more indirect yet at the same time more intimate relation. What is remarkable about hearing the melody is the manner in which consciousness spans past and future to encompass the melody as a whole and construes the note sounding as a part within this whole. When I experience a melody, I do not experience my hearing as an object; but the temporal phases of my hearing stand in the same part-whole relation to each other as do the notes of the melody I hear. Just

---

17. Olafson, pp. 49, 101–102.

as each note is experienced *as* part of the melody as a whole, so the experience of it is lived through *as* part of the complex experience of the melody.

We shall be returning to this notion that the flow of conscious life, like the temporal objects (events) we encounter around us, is lived as a complex of configurations whose phases figure as parts within larger wholes. Let us now conclude our account of the phenomenological approach to the temporality of experience by reflecting on what it has accomplished.

The phenomenologists' strategy, as can be seen in the investigations for which Husserl and Merleau-Ponty are best known, is to consider the most passive of experiences, such as the seeing of things in space or the hearing of tones and simple melodic lines, and to exhibit the richness of their structure. By contrast to the empiricists' who attempt to begin with a *tabula rasa* and account for experience as a causally additive process, they discover instead a complex interplay between consciousness and world. Too elementary to be called "activity," since it is not the purposeful, goal-directed, and self-conscious operation of practical reason, it is nevertheless no blind or automatic process. Whereas the empiricists conceive experience as a reactive and usually internal mental process, the phenomenologists stress the openness of experience toward the world. The terms "field" and "horizon," used in connection with both time and space, express this conception.

Nowhere is it more in evidence and more crucially important than in the notion of protention, the openness toward the future. If we think of ourselves as passive receivers of impressions which then leave their "trace" in "memory," the future seems to play no role at all. We must simply wait for things to happen to us. At most, certain expectations are "awakened" in us by past experience, simply as additional, causally induced items of experience. It is impossible with these conceptual means to do justice to the protentional horizon which is an extension of the present, opens onto the future, and is at once limited and open. As we saw in the case of the melody, the character of the protentional future is a function of the nature of the objects or events we are attending to. In our most routine and habitual experiences the protentional future can be almost completely determinate—and we are all the more vulnerable to surprise. But even in the midst of the most novel and disconcertingly confusing experiences, the protentional future is still determined to some extent. At the very least we expect our bodily equilibrium and coordination to maintain themselves, that is, our very capacity to continue experiencing. Merleau-Ponty is quite right to stress the role of the lived body in the temporal continuity of experience. If bodily coherence and coordination themselves fail us we are edging toward the nightmarish or toward unconsciousness, as on the margins of sleep or under the influence of drugs. The horizons of future and past are not empty forms. We can no more conceive of an experience empty of future than one empty of past—speaking here, of course, not of the recollected past or the expected future, but of those of retention and protention. As these notions are understood by Husserl, without past and future there can be no present and thus no experience at all.

We have made the point that *intentionally*, that is, *as* envisaged in protention, the future has varying degrees of openness. But it is also factually open in the sense that it can surprise and frustrate even our most undetermined protentions; probably the most unpleasant instance, in keeping with what we said about the body, is that of momentarily losing our equilibrium or our coordination. This factual openness has important consequences for our understanding of time-experience. If, as we have said, what we experience temporally are not isolated instants, but configurations which extend protentionally into the future, and if present and past are a function of the whole which includes that future, when what actually happens surprises us, then in an important sense the past is changed. That is, earlier, now-retained phases have become parts of a different whole and thus change their significance for us altogether.

This is best seen, again, in the example of hearing a melody. Tunes can take surprising turns; that is, we have protentions that are not fulfilled. When this happens, it has turned out that, in effect, we are not hearing the melody we thought we were. The notes, even the past ones, are now parts of a different whole: what they are "heard as" is revised retroactively. Thus many of the temporal wholes whose parts we experience are configurations destined never to be realized and indeed, in a certain sense, configurations which never existed "except in our minds."

This, however, does not free the parts from their status as parts, as far as our experience is concerned. The fact is that both before and after the surprising turn, it is as parts of a temporal whole that they were experienced.

Thus the configurational character of our passive temporal experiences has as a crucial component this protentional forward reference in virtue of which present and past are experienced as a function of what will be. It is important to stress that this is true *even* of the passive experiences described by Husserl and Merleau-Ponty since it is clearly *all the more* true of our active, practical lives. It is possible to criticize Husserl and to some extent even Merleau-Ponty for putting too much emphasis on the passive. Husserl's thought, especially, contains significant remnants of the empiricism he absorbed from his study of the British philosophers under the tutelage of Franz Brentano. His use of the term "impression" in his analysis of time-consciousness is but one indication of this. To some extent the subsequent development of phenomenology, especially in Heidegger's *Being and Time*, involves an implicit criticism of this. It can be argued that human existence is properly characterized as an active and practical existence, and that even its supposedly passive aspects, like perception, are ultimately determined by activity. To some extent Merleau-Ponty's phenomenology of perception, with its emphasis on bodily movement and orientation, admits this, though he is more inclined to view perception as "pre-practical" and "anonymous." That is, the process of perception establishes us in a world which becomes the field of practice, the condition of the possibility of a more explicitly goal-oriented and reflective activity. In any case it can always be argued that some aspects of experience are passive in the simple sense that we are open and receptive to what is happening around us. And our point has been that even here, the temporality of this experience must be characterized in configurational terms with a strong emphasis on the future or protentional dimension. It is true that Husserl's empiricist bias, especially in his early work, leads him to a relative neglect of the phenomenon of protention. But there is no question that he recognizes not only its importance but its necessity as part of our consciousness of time. As he says in one of the manuscripts, "we have . . . *determinate* expectations. We are not and can never be completely without a forwardly directed grasp. *The temporal background also has a future [der Zeithof hat auch eine Zukunft].*"[18]

3. The Temporality of Action

In the last section we tried to show, with Husserl's help, the degree to which and the manner in which experienced time is a structured and configured time. Our experience is directed towards, and itself

18. Husserl, *Zur Phänomenologie*, p. 167.

assumes, temporally extended forms in which future, present, and past mutually determine one another as parts of a whole.

We have noted that Husserl and other phenomenologists concern themselves with relatively passive experiences and we must not forget that a large part, if not the larger part, of our everyday lives, the "reality" of human experience whose temporality we are trying to describe, is active rather than passive. It is to this that we must now address ourselves.

As we said, if our passive experience is characterized by a complex temporal structure, our active experience is all the more so. The key to this structure is the purposive or means-end character of action, usually regarded as its basic feature.

Philosophers have devoted much attention to action and to its purposive structure. Their attention has been drawn there not so much, it seems, by their desire to clarify or understand the phenomenon of action itself as by the cluster of other problems, especially in epistemology and metaphysics, to which this phenomenon is related. Action has been considered one of the paradigm cases of mind-body interaction, and its analysis has been undertaken with a view to solving or dissolving that traditional problem. Classically action has been analysed into a thought or act of will, which is mental, and a bodily movement, the one causing the other. Some recent philosophers have hoped that if they could undercut the dualistic analysis of action and find it in a unitary phenomenon, they could thereby find a means to a more general assault on the broader metaphysical problem itself.[19] A difficulty with this approach is that some things that have no overt bodily components can be regarded as actions (rather than passive experiences), such as mathematical reasonings and other purely mental activities. A slightly different perspective on the phenomenon of action has been provided by a concern with what counts as explanation of human (as opposed to non-human) behavior. We often explain someone's action by citing its "reasons," and the question is whether and how such an explanation differs from one which assigns causes. A long tradition affirms that there are fundamental differences between the two, and prefers the term "understanding" over "explanation" when dealing with human action. To understand an action is to know not what caused it but rather what justified it, either in general or in the eyes of the agent.[20]

---

19. See Arthur Danto, "Action, Knowledge and Representation," in *Action Theory*, ed. M. Brand and D. Walton (Dordrecht: Reidel, 1976), p. 11.

20. This tradition goes back to Dilthey and the neo-Kantians. Recent discussions include Dray, "The Historical Explanation of Actions Reconsidered"; Donald David-

The distinction between explanation and understanding has also brought with it two different approaches to the logic of action. If the action is conceived in terms of explanation and causation, philosophers think of sufficient conditions, general laws, and a deductive relation between descriptions of the causing and of the caused states of affairs. The context of justification or the "reasonableness" of actions has led to logical relations governing not what is or will be the case, but what ought to be the case, that is, the deontic domain of practical reasoning.[21] Here one approaches the natural affinity of the phenomenon of action to problems associated with ethics and the theory of value. Needless to say, issues of freedom and determinism are also relevant.

It is remarkable, given this wealth of analysis from so many perspectives, that very little attention has been paid to the temporality of action. Yet it is clear that the various aspects of action brought out by these analyses (means and end, intention and execution, thought and movement) are deployed in time and instantiated in temporal relations. It is to these that we need to direct our attention.

Let us consider an example which is in some ways comparable to the example used by Husserl of hearing a simple melodic line. Our example will be serving at tennis, a relatively small-scale, unified, and simple action. It is true that there are some small-scale, purely mental actions, such as doing quick mental calculations, which would be even simpler because they do not seem to require any overt bodily movements. But it is more valuable for our purposes to choose an example not just for its simplicity but because it involves elements included in the standard discussions of action. And one of those is bodily movement.

Let us note first that the action unfolds in temporal phases, like the melody. The purpose of the action is to hit the ball in a certain way, which is thus the temporal as well as the teleological end of the action—though it could be argued, interestingly, that the "follow-through," which occurs after the ball is hit, is part of the means to the end which precedes it. In general one is inclined to think it standard that means temporally precedes the end of the action, just as it is

son, "Action, Reasons and Causes," in *Essays on Action and Events* (Oxford: Oxford University Press, 1980); and G. H. von Wright, *Explanation and Understanding* (London: Routledge & Kegan Paul, 1971).

21. For the causal approach see Hempel, "The Function of General Laws in History"; for that of practical reasoning see G. H. von Wright, *An Essay in Deontic Logic and the General Theory of Action, Acta Philosophica Fennica* 21 (Amsterdam: North Holland Publishing Company, 1968).

thought standard that cause precedes effect. In both cases, of course, there are important exceptions involving contemporaneity: for example, a heavy object causing a hollow in a pillow on which it rests. In the practical sphere, one can act not to *attain* but to *maintain* some end, such as physical fitness, or a particular skill, or a friendship or a marriage. Aristotle's notion of happiness as virtue seems also to have been conceived in this way. Here the end is simultaneous with all the phases of an action whose end it is. Such examples are very different from the one we have in mind, not only because they involve relatively long-term projects, but because they are clearly divided into many sub-actions, a division we are trying to avoid for the moment by choosing a simple and seemingly unified action.

Our example may not be thought simple enough, however, to qualify as what Danto calls a "basic action," that is, one which is not performed by performing some other action.[22] Here it may seem that I serve the tennis ball *by* drawing back my right arm, tossing the ball into the air with my left, etc., each of which is a distinct action describable in its own right. Such is the interrelation of the elements of a tennis serve, however, that an accurate description would have to sound like this: the *sort* of arm movement required to hit the ball at a certain height, the *kind* of toss designed to place the ball in the path of the racquet, etc. In short, each of the phases must be described precisely *as* a phase of this action and cannot be described independently in terms applicable to other contexts. If it be thought that the same sort of inseparability from context applies to the tennis serve itself, that is, as an element in the game of tennis, it can be countered that the action can be performed in repetitive practice, aimless volleys, etc., without having the function it has, and without falling under the rules applying to it, within the game. To the conceptual inseparability of the elements of the serve corresponds, we might add a kind of psychological and even physiological inseparability. We do not think of the elements of the action as separate actions performed in sequence, nor could we easily perform one of the elements, even in a mimed demonstration, without combining it with the other movements that make up the action as a whole.

Granted that this action unfolds in time, not in a series of sub-actions but rather in what we choose to call interdependent phases, we must note further, and still in parallel with the experience of the

---

22. Arthur Danto, *Analytical Philosophy of Action* (Cambridge: Cambridge University Press, 1973), chapter 1.

melody, that the agent, at whichever stage of the action he or she is "located," has a kind of prospective and retrospective "grasp" of the other successive phases of the action, past and future. Are the Husserlian concepts of protention and retention applicable here? After all, by bringing in the agent's point of view on the action, as indeed we must, are we not in effect reverting to a phenomenological treatment?

Those concepts can indeed be useful provided one frees oneself sufficiently from the unstated paradigm of passive experience, perception in particular, that is always operative in Husserl's investigations. In particular, one should avoid the suggestion that my action is a process like a melody whose unfolding I am simply observing. If anything, my action is comparable not to the temporal object or event (the melody) which I experience, but rather to my temporal experience of it. That is, in keeping with our earlier terminology, my action is not an event I encounter but one I "live through." But this expression also has too passive a connotation, especially as regards the future. In the midst of an action the future is not something expected or prefigured in the present, not something which is simply to come; it is something *to be brought about by* the action in which I am engaged. If we are to use the term protention in connection with action then we must avoid the idea, clearly present in Husserl's account, that protention is a species of the genus expectation. In action the content of my protention is not a state of the world that I *expect*, it is something I *effect*. As I serve a tennis ball, simultaneously throwing the ball into the air and drawing back my arm, the future state in which my racquet connects with the ball and sends it on its way is not merely something I expect to happen. It is the outcome or completion of what I am doing. In an important sense it *is* what I am doing.

The same caution must be made about using the notion of retention, which for Husserl is a species of memory. In the sense of the tennis serve, the movements which precede my present position are not simply successive states of my body which I remember; they lead up to and prepare the way for present and future.

If one takes these cautions into account one can usefully appeal to the concepts of protention and retention when describing the temporality of action, for they offer certain important advantages. The intimate and complementary interrelation of present, future, and past, which we followed Husserl in rendering metaphorically as a kind of foreground-background or front-back relation, is an important part of action, or at least of a relatively short-term action such as that of hitting a tennis ball. If we combine a strong appreciation for this intimacy with our caveats about expectation, we can avoid the pitfall of portraying the agent as entertaining a "representation" of a future state. It is psychologically implausible to attribute to a tennis player, in mid-swing, a series of mental pictures depicting the ball being struck and then sailing on its way to the far court. And if the mental picture proves to be dispensable in this case, perhaps it is just as much out of place in discussions of longer-term, more reflective and complicated actions.

But is it really dispensable? It might be countered that the mental representation is brought into the discussion not because it is introspectively observable, but simply because it is conceptually required. How else characterize the prospective "grasp" the agent has on the future? Perhaps one can avoid the suggestion of a mental picture by speaking of a "conception" or an "idea" of the future rather than a "representation." But one way or another, is it not necessary to say that the agent envisages, somehow, a state of things which is different from the present one, and then arranges things to fit it, and that that is what action is?

But this suggestion seems to intellectualize beyond recognition the simple action of hitting a tennis ball. The fact is that we are short of philosophical terminology for dealing with action and we are forced to fall back on the dominant epistemological repertoire of concepts and terms: conception, idea, representation, mental picture, etc.

This same terminological embarrassment, with its obvious conceptual implications, affects our use of the concept of causality in the present context.[23] In some obvious sense, when I hit the tennis ball I cause it to move. There is also, though less obviously, something like a causal connection among all of movements that make up the action. Yet since Hume we are led to think of cause in terms of observations, memories, and expectations of what will happen. Hume explicitly rejected the inner, "felt" sense of causality put forward by Locke as the key to our understanding of the concept, in favor of what amounts to an external observer's point of view, suggesting, implausibly, that we come habitually to expect our own movements in the same way that we expect external objects to move.[24] At other moments, for example in connection with the

---

23. See ibid., chapter 3.
24. David Hume, *An Inquiry concerning Human Nature*, ed. C. W. Hendel (New York: The Liberal Arts Press, 1957), pp. 78–79.

problem of freedom, he admits that there is a peculiar first-person perspective on our own actions, but he rejects it as misleading and illusory compared to the external point of view.[25] Most discussions of causality, including many which try to repudiate other aspects of Hume's analysis (such as its assumption of discrete events instead of continuous process) maintain this observer's perspective.[26] But this is neither surprising nor illegitimate since in most cases the issue is raised in connection with our knowledge of physical events and even of human actions in our capacity as external observers. The mistake is only in applying the results of such a treatment, as Hume did, to the performing of one's own action.

If we wish to understand and describe correctly this performance, and its temporality in particular, we need to put aside altogether the terminology of causation, memory and expectation, and representation. Especially at the level of a simple action such as the one under discussion, when I am in the midst of it the future completion of my action is not something I predict on the basis of available evidence, nor is it a mere expectation that springs to mind by habitual association. But even less is it a mere representation, the entertaining of a possibility. Terms like prediction and expectation at least convey the fact that we are "ontologically committed" to the occurrence of the future state. But they do not capture the obvious fact that this future occurrence is something I *effect*.

It is what I *am doing*: the English durative captures many of the features of the temporality of action. It conveys the temporal span of the action and at the same time stresses its unity. Retention and protention, properly qualified in the senses we have been suggesting, may be the best terms to use in capturing and preserving this peculiar sort of unity-in-multiplicity. Future and past "horizons" as encompassed by protention and retention are of a piece with the present and constitute its completion or wholeness. I no more represent the future than I represent the present phase of my action. They are simply different aspects of what I am doing. And the same is true of the past. Because they are parts or phases of a temporal whole, my engagement in them or grasp of them is of a piece even though (still the presupposition of our temporal analysis) part of the action is over and part is yet to come.

25. Ibid., p. 103, n. 7.
26. See Maurice Mandelbaum, *The Anatomy of Historical Knowledge* (Baltimore: The Johns Hopkins University Press, 1977), pp. 49–57.

The need for exercising extreme care in applying the phenomenological approach to action can be seen in the work of Alfred
Schutz. This well-known and influential theorist is one of the few
who have attempted to apply Husserlian concepts to an analysis of
action. Furthermore, unlike the analytic theories we mentioned, his
analysis does attempt explicitly to take account of the temporality of
action. Unfortunately, Schutz begins by trying to combine Husserl's
and Bergson's analysis of the experience of duration, and the retention-protention scheme is hardly differentiated from the Bergsonian
durée pure.[27] All is so fused and interpenetrated that only a reflective glance, in which the agent disengages himself from his experience, succeeds in finding structure or even distinguishing one experience from another. Retention and protention somehow blindly take
place but "I know nothing of this while I am simply living in the flow
of duration." Only an "act of reflective attention" assures that experiences are "distinguished, brought into relief, marked out from one
another."[28] It is this reflective act that bestows meaning on the
experience and this act is always retrospective. This brings Schutz to
the remarkable conclusion that "only the already experienced is
meaningful, not that which is being experienced."[29]

Turning more explicitly to action, Schutz realizes that it must be
concerned with the future. But he portrays the agent as executing a
"projected act" which is a "phantasy" or "mental picture" of the
action as already completed.[30] "We are *conscious* of an action only if
we contemplate it as already over and done with."[31] He suggests that
without this quasi-retrospective "contemplation" we are really only
engaged in "unconscious behavior."

Schutz seems to me to overlook here what is genuinely valuable in
Husserl's analysis and to adopt its least appropriate features. The
merit of Husserl's concept of retention-protention is precisely that it
recognizes the structured and organized character of pre-reflective
experience. This is its great advantage over the Bergsonian *durée
pure*. On the other hand, the Husserlian notion of meaning-bestow-
ing as an objectivating act is geared to contemplative or theoretical
understanding and seems least appropriate to the sphere of action, at

---

27. Alfred Schutz, *The Phenomenology of the Social World*, tr. George Walsh and
Frederick Lehnert (Evanston: Northwestern University Press, 1967), pp. 45–96.
28. Ibid., p. 51.
29. Ibid., p. 52.
30. Ibid., p. 59.
31. Ibid., p. 64.

least as performed by the agent. Schutz over-intellectualizes action, perhaps because his ultimate aim, like that of Dilthey, G. H. von Wright, and many others, is an epistemology of the human sciences and thus an understanding of action viewed from the outside. Schutz's agent seems to relate to his own action as if he were an external observer trying to understand it. As we shall see, such an attitude does sometimes arise in relation to one's own action, but only at rather complex levels and as a privation of the sort of conscious engagement we have in the case of an action like hitting a tennis ball. To suggest for such a "basic action" that it is blind and unconscious unless reflectively observed in a detached way seems to miss the phenomenon altogether. It is clearly anything but blind: it is directed, structured, articulated. If anyone is *conscious* of what he is doing, it is the tennis player serving the ball. If he tries to observe himself as if from the outside, however, he is sure to miss the ball. Such simple, straightforwardly-carried-out bodily actions are important not only in their own right but because they are the central element in more complex, long-range actions where reflection, contemplation, and detachment are genuinely involved. This is why it is so important not to distort them in our analysis by describing them in terms appropriate to other levels of action.

One useful insight of Schutz, however, must be retained. Though his whole description is couched in the language of picturing, he admits that "once the action begins," the goal is not just pictured but also *"wished for* and *protended."* This means that for the agent it is in the future while at the same time, on his analysis, it is pictured as past. The compromise is that it is "thought of in the future perfect tense [*modo futuri exacti*]."[32] If we detach this notion from Schutz's representationalism and his over-intellectualization of action we can see its value. Since in acting we protend or intend the future goal, rather than just picturing it, there is a sense in which it occupies the center of our concern in action and reflects back upon and determines the present and past. There is indeed something quasi-retrospective about action, as if we were located *at* the end and from its point of view arranged and organized the present.

A somewhat better sense of what Schutz has in mind here is conveyed by a felicitous expression of Heidegger's from his analysis of everydayness in *Being and Time*. In everyday concerns and preoccupations the agent, says Heidegger, is always *sich vorweg*, ahead of

---

32. Ibid., p. 61.

himself.[33] As we have noted, Heidegger, while still calling his analysis "phenomenological," shifts his emphasis toward action and away from contemplation, eschewing the language of representation, perception, and even consciousness in favor of a new vocabulary. So here instead of speaking of mental pictures and the like, he says the agent is simply ahead of himself. Human existence, he says, is characterized by its *Entwurfcharakter*: its projective character. What is projected or thrown into the future is not some picture of what might be but the very being of the agent.

We can connect this Heideggerian point with the Husserlian analysis, and appreciate the radical *temporal* difference between passivity and activity, if we recall the figure-background scheme and the manner in which it was used as an analogy by Husserl. According to this analogy, the present "stands out" from its past and future horizons, which make it what it is: present. In the attitude of passive reception the present seems the focus of our concern, while past and future, taken in by our horizon-consciousness, make this focus possible.

Considering now the temporality of action we are forced, I think, to revise this analogy. In a significant sense, when we are absorbed in an action the *focus* or direction of our attention, the center of our concern, lies not in the present but in the future; not on the tools, as Heidegger says, but on the work to be done.[34] Though it may be stretching the analogy beyond usefulness, it seems more appropriate to say that the future is salient while the present and past constitute its background. This is one way, at least, of rendering account of the difference between activity and passivity. Activity is future-centered or focused. And it is not simply *attention* but *intention* that is focused there, to take up the point we made earlier. It is the striking of the tennis ball, something I effect, toward which I bend my concern just as I bend my whole body toward its realization. It is that goal which organizes not only my bodily disposition and my implement but my whole environment (the ground beneath my feet, the net before me, the boundaries of the court, etc.) into a kind of predicament or problem my action has to solve. And the arrangement that results, it is clear, is a temporal arrangement as well as a spatial one: the phases of the action must be deployed and must unfold, not merely in time but in a certain order.

This emphasis on the future-orientation of action, and on the role

---

33. Heidegger, *Being and Time*, pp. 191–92. As the English translation contains the German pagination in its margins, I refer to the German pages only.
34. Ibid., p. 69.

of the end in organizing "backward" in time the various phases of the action which are the means to its realization, must not obscure the fact that the agent is still rooted in the present. Though his concern is in the future *he* is still in the present. Any retrospective element in action (looking back on it as completed) can only be a *quasi*-retrospection, as Schutz acknowledges by speaking of the future perfect. As was the case with passive experience, protention encloses the envisaged future and unites it with present and past, but the whole action, thus unified, stands vulnerable to the real future which can intrude on the action in the rudest way. In this respect it is perhaps not different from the passive experience, but the nature of the disappointment or surprise is different in the case of action, simply because, as we have emphasized, it is an intention or purpose rather than a mere expectation that is disappointed. It is a matter of the way in which present and future are related. What I expect, in passive experience, is the continuation and outcome of what I am now experiencing. But in action, the future is the completed execution of what I am doing. The outcome depends on me.

In this sense the future, and thus the success of the whole action, may be more vulnerable and fragile in the case of action. But at the same time, for the agent it is more determined, less open to variation than the passively protended future. Also, it exercises more retroactive control, so to speak, on the present, since it governs not just my view of things but what I am doing. Both experience and action are to a large extent in the thrall of the future, but of the two action is the more so.

4. The Melodic Element of Time

In the foregoing discussion of the temporality of action (practical time) we have been at pains to show how it differs from the temporality of experience (experienced time). Let us sum up this discussion now by reminding ourselves of the many features the two temporalities have in common.

Like experienced time, as we have seen, practical time involves at bottom a sequence of distinguishable events or event-phases that we live through or act out one at a time, one after the other, such that we are always "located" at one such point at a time. In both action and experience, however, this ever-changing point is a vantage point from which the other phases of the sequence, future and past, are grasped.

What is thus grasped, moreover, is not two undifferentiated continua or sequences simply receding into the infinite distance. Rather, the temporal span is structured or configured into *events*, in the one case, and *actions*, in the other. For experience and for action, then, in order to qualify as a *present* phase, a given point in time must not only be a member of a sequence but must be an integral, functioning *part* of a temporal configuration constituting an event or an action.

To repeat the point we borrowed from Merleau-Ponty: it may be possible to conceive of space as an empty expanse or a mosaic of points, but it is only as an arrangement of things and places, shapes and spaces between them, that space can figure in our experience and action. And by the same token, time may be conceivable as a Bergsonian *durée pure* or as a sequence of now-points, but it is lived as events and actions. The same retentional-protentional grasp which reaches forward and back in time also effects or constitutes a *closure* which articulates time by separating the given temporal configuration (action or event) from what goes before and after.

This global closure, which separates the event or action from its "surroundings," also yields the whole which is internally articulated into its constitutive parts: the notes that make up the melody, the movements that make up the action, etc. As we have seen, the part-whole relation here is a specifically temporal one, and distinguishable as such from other instances of this relation: spatial, for example, or conceptual. The movements that effect the tennis serve, like the notes in a melody, must relate to each other in a temporal way, and not, for example, in a purely spatial way. Both the notes and the movements *could* have merely spatial values, such as the arrangement of the notes on a music staff or the spatial relations among different body positions captured in a group of still photographs. But these exist simultaneously in space—literally side by side. Nor do we achieve the melody or the action by realizing them one after the other, unless the proper order is followed. Action and events are thus temporal *Gestalten* of whose parts, in their temporal arrangement, the subject has a protentional-retentional grasp; a changing and flowing grasp, to be sure, since the whole is grasped successively from each of its parts, each time (metaphorically speaking) from a different "perspective."

It is important to stress this last point in order to avoid the tendency to place the subject in some position above or outside the flow of events in order to account for his grasp of the whole. In trying to describe the role or function of future and past in present experience we must avoid saying, as Augustine does, that they are "present" to us. To use this expression would be to deny precisely what we are trying to affirm here, namely the genuinely temporal character of experience and action. The past *is* past, gone, no longer actual. The future *is* not yet and may turn out other than I expect it. To have an experience or to carry out an action is always to be engaged in one of its phases "at a time." If I were engaged in its phases "all at once" it would not be the same thing: a temporally extended experienced event, a temporally deployed and unfolding action.

Thus descriptively we must strike a balance between two extremes: over-stressing our inherence in the present by treating it as an isolating *from* past and future, and over-stressing our openness to past and future by treating it as a supra-temporal perspective. It may be that these two extremes derive from certain metaphysical prejudices. As regards the former, we have already made reference to the empiricist tendency to conceive of ourselves as passive receivers waiting for stimuli to come along and hit us. The latter may derive from an intellectualist or idealist inclination to absolutize the unity and synthetic power of the "ego" to the point where an almost God-like perspective is attributed to it.

It may be as well that the two extremes rest on a tendency to favor certain kinds of examples: If we think of our passive experiences as being exemplified by the intrusion of the unexpected, then we may be inclined to think of the present as being cut off from the past (it does not fit in with what has gone before) and the future (it shatters our expectations of what will come next). The response to this sort of paradigm is that it confirms rather than denies the role of retention and protention. Without a temporal *Gestalt* including past and future there would be no past pattern to disturb, no expectation to shatter. And as we pointed out in the last section, while such intrusion may rob us of and leave us searching for certain concrete expectations (a very uneasy situation), we are still left "counting on" the continued coordination of our bodies and the further general coherence of the world around us.

The intellectualist extreme, by contrast, may favor as examples the sort of routine activities that are characteristic of so much of our lives in which we deal capably with our surroundings and things go pretty much as expected. Here we may seem to be in possession of some timeless "laws" governing the behavior of things and persons, so that the past and future course of events lies spread out unproblematically (and thus apparently timelessly) before us. The

dominance of such a paradigm is undermined by reminding ourselves not only of the annoying orneriness of things, and of our own
fallibility as agents, but also of the fact that in action we always make
allowance for these contingencies and keep a certain modicum of our
calculative rationality in reserve to deal with the unforeseen.

Our account of experienced time and practical time was undertaken as a response to the claim that human events exhibit in themselves no structure apart from constituting a "mere sequence." We
have attempted to bring out something of the richness and complexity of the structure of passive experience and action at their most
basic level.

It is true that we have not gone very far toward making good on our
claim that this structure can be understood as a narrative structure.
The structures we have uncovered so far do have some kinships with
narrative structure, but this is not easily discernible on so small a
scale. To make this point properly we must get beyond the simple
actions and experiences we have used as examples and move to more
complex and long-range phenomena. We must also bring in reflection, planning, and deliberation, which are genuinely and importantly involved in the more complex temporality of extended actions
and experiences. We reserve all this for the next chapter.

It was necessary however to begin in the present chapter with the
simplest actions and experiences because they constitute the basis of
everything that comes after. We could call them building blocks or
basic elements if this did not give the misleading impression that
their relation to each other is merely cumulative or aggregative. In
fact, we shall find that this relation is not unlike the one obtaining
among the parts of the experiences and actions already discussed.
The phenomena we have described are basic in a sense other than
being building blocks, and the importance of beginning with such
small-scale phenomena, when our ultimate purpose is to get to the
large-scale historical temporality which extends beyond even the
individuals, is two-fold.

First, it permits us to correct the view that structure in general and
narrative structure in particular is imposed upon a human experience intrinsically devoid of it so that such structure is an artifice,
something not "natural" but forced, something which distorts or
does violence to the true nature of human reality. Our procedure is
strategically not unlike that of Danto's attempt to arrive at "basic
actions." He was attempting among other things to undo the mind-
body distinction, and his argument was that some simple bodily

actions cannot be further analyzed into a movment and a further action called "volition" or "act of will." Thought and movement are logically interconnected and in fact inseparable, and the analysis does not work, even if we accept the threat it entails of infinite regress. As long as we are speaking of action there is nothing more basic than actions which have both mental and physical aspects.[35] Our own strategy concerns temporality, and argues that where we are speaking of experience and action, what is basic or irreducible is more complex than a mere sequence. While there is necessarily a sequential order underlying experience and actions, this is not an order that can figure in our experience by itself, apart from the configurational organization represented by events and actions. The bedrock of human events, then, is not sequence but configured sequence.

Our second reason for beginning with and devoting so much description to these small-scale actions and experiences is one that cannot be fully appreciated until later, but we can mention it now in a preliminary way. Essential to the ensuing discussion is the idea that these basic experiences and actions enter into combinations and larger configurations which differ in some important respects from those discussed so far. In particular, as we have already noted, a reflective element, what we might call a certain loss of immediacy, will figure prominently in our discussion. With it will come an account of how the coherence of temporal configurations can be broken and fragmented. In spite of all this, something like the original temporal coherence of the most basic phenomena, what we might call the "melodic" element in honor of our first example, will retain an important place in our account, not really as a description of what goes on but as an ideal or standard of measurment. Because this melodic element will remain a basic presence in everything that follows, it is necessary to have found it and described it where it has its home—in the most basic and rudimentary of our actions and experiences.

35. It should be noted that this strategy, undertaken in *Analytical Philosophy of Action*, was judged to have failed by Danto in his later essay, "Action, Knowledge and Representation."

II

Temporality and Narrative Structure

In the previous chapter we dealt with the temporal structure of passive experience and of action. In the interest of discovering how the past (the historical past in particular) figures in our experience, we need to look at the over-all temporal structure of experience. We have indicated that the key to this structure is its narrative character.

We began by countering the view we found prevalent among many theorists of narrative that human experience is in itself devoid of structure, or at any rate of narrative structure. We tried to show the configurational character of the most elementary and basic experiences, thereby demonstrating the inaccuracy of the claim that at some fundamental level human events are "merely" sequential in their temporality.

What we have done so far goes some distance, but not far enough, toward establishing our point. It is true that temporal configuration has been seen by some (Ricoeur and Mink, for example) as essential to narrative structure. And if we have shown that configuration inheres in experience itself, then what we have said counts against their view that such structure is overlaid or imposed upon experience by a retrospective and "literary" effort extrinisic to experience itself. But the narrative character of experience is a much more complex affair than the notion of configuration alone indicates, and can be demonstrated only if three critical hurdles are negotiated.

1. Surely narrative structure is not merely configuration, but configuration of a particular kind. Is there anything peculiarly narrative about the configuration we have so far exhibited?

2. Narrative structure is in any case not associated with the short-term elementary experiences and actions which have served us as examples, but pertains to longer-term or larger-scale sequences of actions, experiences, and human events. Do the specific configurational characteristics associated with the phenomena we have examined extend beyond them to the kinds of actions and events we normally associate with narratives?

3. Even if we are able to answer these first two questions in the affirmative, it can be argued that narrative involves more than just a certain temporal organization of events. To our concept of a narrative belongs not only a progression of events but also a story-teller and an audience to whom the story is told. And it may be thought that this imparts to the events related in a story a character that is in principle denied to the occurrences of "real life." Unless we are able to find some semblance of this complex relationship in the ordinary experience of time, it may be thought that the concept of narrative is badly miscast as a key to understanding the experience of time in general and of historical time in particular. At most it would find its place only where most theorists have in fact situated it, namely at the level of historiography, the retrospective literary reconstruction of the past, where its relation to real events may be considered adventitious at best. We wish to show, on the contrary, that the events addressed by historiography are already narrative in character; and this indeed means that they display not only the character of events narrated, but also the element of narration itself.

It is to these three points in turn that we shall now address ourselves.

1. Configuration and Narrative Structure

We have had occasion to designate as temporal configurations not just two but three sorts of phenomena. The melody, Husserl's example of a temporal experienced object, was seen to exist as a multiplicity of distinguishable phases arranged internally in a certain temporal order and set off externally from its "surroundings," that is, what goes before and after. Similar features are attributable, we recall, to the correlate of the melody as experienced, that is, to the experience of the melody. It takes its configurational character from its object, including its inner articulation, its external demarcation, and its principle of unity. As we shall see, experiences can also have such features even if their object is not a temporal object. Finally, our example of an action was analyzed as a temporal configuration in much the same terms, with account taken of the differences between an experience and an action.

The kinship between these structures and narrative configuration should be obvious: each constitutes a temporal closure, which can only be expressed by speaking of a beginning, a middle, and an end. This is of course the set of concepts that is associated by Aristotle with the wholeness or unity of the action of a tragedy[1] and that is most often invoked by the theorists we mentioned as a mark of narrative structure. A sequence, a series, or a process can theoretically be endless, but an event, an experience, or an action is something that begins and ends.

To be sure, even this notion must be further specified. A purely physical event, remote from human concern, can also be said to begin and end, and thus to have a middle in between. But from the start we have limited ourselves to human experience, so it is events *as* experienced that have concerned us. What counts about the melody as an example of an event is that it is heard *as* beginning, and each of its phases is heard in anticipation (whether correct or not) of an ending. True, a melody has perhaps more internal structure and unity than other sorts of experienced events: a tree sways in the wind, a dog barks, a friend passes in the street. But each of these can be noticed, observed for its own sake, and distinguished from other events around it. To the extent that this happens it is grasped in protention-retention by the person who experiences it. Even the most unarticulated or instantaneous of occurrences, like a loud bang or a sudden extinguishing of all the lights, is experienced as an event with a certain temporal thickness which assures it the status it deserves alongside other events that develop in more leisurely fashion. Such an event is more than the mere *difference* between two states, at least for experience, for it must be experienced along with the two states it separates. The sudden black-out, itself perhaps without discernible thickness, is the middle of an event that begins in light and ends in darkness.

Other events can be seen to contain more complex temporal structure, even if they are of very short term. A movement can be a departure from A and arrival at B, or can go from rest to motion and back to rest. In the latter case, beginning and end in some sense

1. Aristotle, *Poetics*, 1450b27, 1459a20.

coincide, giving a quasi-circular closure to the event. Many melodies involve not only departure and arrival, but arrival *back* at the beginning note or chord. In all these cases it is the experiencer, whether in protention, retention, or direct experience, who makes the connection (identity of state or place or note or chord) between beginning and end, and experiences it as separated by the intervening "departure." Insofar as the event consists of unfolding and distinguishable phases, each of these is experienced either as a beginning, or as an end, or as an intervening phase which gets its sense and its place by its reference backward and forward to beginning and end.

Experiences, as we saw, may borrow their structure from their temporal objects, but they may also have their own temporal structure when their objects are not temporal at all in the sense in which we have been using that term. I can explore with my eyes or hands an object (say a statue) which we would designate not an event but a thing. But my visual or tactile observation of it is itself an event with its own duration, its own beginning, middle, and end. As we saw in the previous chapter, this experience is not an event that I encounter, unless I reflect, but one I live through. Yet its temporal configuration is one of which I have a protentional-retentional awareness, in virtue of which it has for me its unity, its inner articulation, and its distinctness from other experiences and actions. It must be recognized too that when we speak of observation or exploration we are on the borderline between passive experiences and actions.

Actions, finally, as we saw, are also not events that I encounter, nor are they experiences that I live through. I perform them, and in doing so I protentionally and retentionally hold together the various phases that make them up. The "principle" by which they are held together and organized articulates the action even more clearly into beginning, middle, and end. Though teleological and temporal end are different concepts and can diverge, as we saw they most often coincide; and the same is true of the closely related though not identical concepts of middle and means. The beginning of an action is its initiation, which bears within it, thanks to the protentional orientation of action, both means or middle and end. Or rather, as we saw, it points first or primarily to the end which then organizes quasi-retrospectively the intervening steps and stages toward its realization.

Closely associated with the means-end structure of action, and likewise intimately related to its beginning-middle-end structure, are certain features action shares with phenomena discussed so far and finally with narrative structure. To perform or carry out an action is to achieve its end. This achievement is the *resolution* of a certain suspense engendered by the contingency of the action. The notion of suspension and resolution, of course, is often associated with music and reminds us of our example of the melody. Action begins with a divergence between what is the case and what is to be done, a divergence that has to be overcome and which, but for my action, would remain. If the action took care of itself, I would not need to act. Nor can I be sure I will succeed. *Effort* is required to get the thing done. Completion of the act is thus not only a *temporal* closure, which brings a certain sequence (of movements, for example) to a close, but the *practical* closure of a gap between envisaged or pro-tended result and reality. Another way of describing this feature of action, to which we have already had recourse, is to speak of the action as solving a *problem* or predicament presented by the situa-tion obtaining beforehand. Lest it be thought that the notion of problem-solving over-intellectualizes some actions, recall that we used it in a quasi-metaphorical way to describe the action of serving a tennis ball, where deliberation, calculation, or other rationcination seem not explicitly involved.

Let us now take stock: though we have not yet departed from the sort of simple, short-term actions and experiences that have so far served us as examples, we have found that the notion of "temporal configuration" can be elaborated in a number of ways: first as closure or beginning, middle, and end, the most general designation of the phenomenon; then as departure and arrival, departure and return, means and end, suspension and resolution, problem and solution.

Now these are some of the very structures most often cited as features of narrative, in the sense that they represent the manner in which the events of stories are arranged into coherent wholes. Yet these structures are often spoken of by some theorists, as we have seen, as if they were imposed on meaningless data by the act of narration itself, as if the events of life, experiences and actions, had no such structure in themselves and achieved it only at the hand of a literary invention. If we have succeeded in showing that these struc-tures inhere in the phenomena from their inception, at the very lowest level, then it cannot be maintained that they are imported from outside.

One way in which the separation is often made between the lived reality and the literary artifice is to say that the narrative arrangement of events departs altogether from the *temporal* order to install itself in the *logical* domain. Louis Mink speaks of the configurational aspect of narrative as if it were atemporal ("time is not of the essence of narratives," he writes[2]) in the sense that the multiplicity of events is seized all at once by an authorial overview. This idea of transcending the temporal is especially favored by the structuralists, though they, unlike Mink, want to avoid altogether the appeal to an author or act of creation. Barthes speaks of *l'illusion chronologique* of narrative and quotes favorably a sentence of Claude Lévi-Strauss: "L'ordre de succession chronologique se résorbe dans une structure matricielle atemporelle."[3] Greimas, Bremond, and others tend to dechronologize narrative, taking its temporal features as a mere surface aspect, mere sequence, and analyzing anything beyond pure sequentiality as atemporal, quasi-logical structures and relations. After characterizing a narrative as a "message" being transferred from a "sender" to a "receiver," structuralist analysis typically draws up an inventory of the "existents" (persons, gods, nations) portrayed in the text, then a similar inventory of "occurrents" (events, actions, transactions). The latter are then treated, following Propp's original mathematical metaphor, as "functions" into which the former enter in various combinations. The abundance of terminology borrowed from mathematics and artificial intelligence often permits us to overlook the fact that the events portrayed unfold in time and that the order of their unfolding is important to their significance.

Many of the structural features we have been speaking of here can indeed be seen to have a "logical" air; we have already spoken of the deductive and the deontic logical analyses of the means-end relation. The idea of problem and solution reminds us of mathematics. Even the notion of departure and return makes us think of—indeed presupposes—the relation of identity and difference. And it is certainly true that there is a distinction between purely logical and purely temporal relations. But it must be noted that even if the above-mentioned structures do "partake of the logical," these structures are to be found here, where we have located them, namely in the midst of experience and action, not in some higher-level linguistic construction or reconstruction of the experiences and actions involved. They are structures and relations that exist for the experiencer or the agent in the process of experiencing or acting; they constitute the

---

2. Mink, "History and Fiction as Modes of Comprehension," p. 555. Schapp's *In Geschichten Verstrickt* has similar things to say about time, p. 144.
3. Barthes, "Introduction à l'analyse structurale des récits," p. 12.

meaningfulness or direction of the experience or action; it is in virtue of them that these things "make sense" prior to and independently of our reflecting on them and explicitly recounting them to ourselves or to others.

Furthermore, it should be clear that however "logical" these structures and relations may be, they do not in this instance constitute a transcendence of time. Deductive relations, relation of identity and difference, etc., may hold among propositions or objects in a quite timeless way, but here they obtain among events, both mental and physical, or they are reflected in the thoughts and experiences of persons as they live through events and perform actions. That is, they are temporally embodied.

What is more, the most fundamental configurational relation we have pointed to, that of beginning, middle, and end, is a strictly temporal ordering principle, and it is a serious confusion to describe it as if it resided in a non-temporal domain. Other ordering principles may resemble it superficially and are indeed timeless: an argument has its premises (including a "middle term") and its conclusion; the alphabet has its first and last letters; a hierarchy may have a highest and lowest instance of authority; and a design may have a middle point between its top and bottom. But none of these features become beginnings, middles, and ends unless the order in question is deployed in time, run through in sequence, whether in thought or action.

The same is true, incidentally, of a narrative in written form. A double error is committed by those who associate beginning, middle, and end only with the narration (rather than the events narrated) and then go on to consider this relation atemporal because the written text, as a collection of marks or sentences, is all there at once. A text is no different from anything else: without time it can have no beginning, middle, and end. Its sentences are *spatially* arranged and some may be *logically* interconnected, and its pages are *numerically* ordered, but unless it is gone through temporally it neither begins nor ends. It just sits there on the shelf. And its only middle is a spatial point equidistant from its edges.

But the more serious mistake is the one which identifies the beginning-middle-end structure exclusively with the narration in the first place. As we have seen, this structure belongs just as surely to the human events—experiences and actions—about which stories are told, and, more important, it belongs to them whether or not a story, in the sense of a literary text, is told about them at all. What is more, if we are right, this structure belongs essentially to such events; they could not exist without it. Just as the beginning-middle-end structure requires a temporal sequence in order genuinely to be what it is, so the temporal sequence requires this sort of closure; insofar, that is, as it is a human sequence, one whose phases and elements are the stuff of human experience and action.

2. Complex and Extended Experience and Action

We must next take up the question of whether the structural features of experience and action that we have discussed so far have any application beyond the relatively simple examples we have used. If not, it makes little sense to seek a fruitful comparison between the temporality of human events and the narrative structure. Stories, after all, are told not about single actions but about complicated sequences of events and actions. And if these sequences diverge in important ways from the narrative structures we have been examining, it may turn out that those theorists whose view we have opposed are right. Those who claim that ordinary experience, unnarrated, consists of a "mere sequence," and that beginning, middle, and end are concepts having no application to it, may be willing to concede what we have said about the temporal structure of the "basic" events and actions we have so far examined. But it is the actions and experiences of everyday life taken together, over a longer period of time, that fail in their view to add up to anything like a coherent narrative. The "mere sequence" spoken of is not that of the miniscule phases of events like melodies and tennis strokes, but that of events and actions themselves added together.

The best way to respond to this view is to point out that it is not in the nature of events or actions, insofar as they figure in our experience, to combine in a merely additive way. Rather, they combine according to the very same principle by which their elements combine to make them up. That is to say, events combine to make up larger-scale events of which they become structural, not merely sequential, elements. A melody may serve as a theme in a movement constructed according to sonata form, where it is presented in contrast to a second theme, then subjected to development, and finally repeated, perhaps with harmonic variation. Or, to choose a simpler and less "contrived" example, a book falling from a shelf may be the first phase of a general collapse of the whole row. In our experience, events foreshadow, augment, and repeat other events so that the complex events they make up, while constituting a sequence at base, are criss-crossed with lines of resemblance (to quote Hume), contiguity, and causality.

In the case of actions, again the structural features are carried over to a larger scale. Actions which have their own means-end structure become means toward the performance of other actions. In tennis, the serve and each of the other strokes in a particular volley are actions in their own right, each with its way of responding to a given situation and achieving its end; but all together contribute to the action of winning (or trying to win) the point, which is in turn a part of the action of playing the game, the set, the match, etc. Most of what we said before will apply here: the goal is usually the temporal as well as the teleological end of the action. The end in prospect or protention organizes retrospectively the elements of the action (some of them actions themselves now) that are its means, requiring not only that they be done but in many cases determining the order in which they are done. To complete my stamp collection there are many stamps I need to acquire but I need not acquire them in any particular order. But to build a bookcase, or to reach my home by public transportation, I must follow certain steps in their proper turn.

In stressing this interlocking aspect of these phenomena beyond the simple level, we are not denying, of course, that some of them can be isolated: there are events, experiences, actions that seem to belong to no larger context, which lead nowhere or have no "point" beyond themselves. But such cases seem to stand out by their very intrusiveness and prove themselves thereby to be exceptions to the rule. In any case, the point is that when an experience or an action enters into a larger context it is not usually by being a mere member of a series, but by having a function or a value in a larger structure. It is as such larger contexts that we experience them; in fact, it is in virtue of our tendency to expect such larger contexts that the isolated and intrusive stands out by contrast.[4]

Complex events, experiences, actions thus "shape" the sequences of sub-actions and other components that make them up and provide them, at this level too, with the closure constituted by their beginnings, middles, and ends.

As for events, the term itself, as designating some change and some

---

4. See chapter III, pp. 90–91 for a further development of this point.

identifiable and distinguishable temporal content, seems indefinitely expandable. We count as events everything from the smallest
scientifically measurable change to the Renaissance, the Ice Age, and
the astronomic events measured in light-years. Since we have been
speaking here of human events, or more particularly of events that
are humanly experienceable (as opposed to thinkable or conceivable)
we obviously cannot proceed so far in either direction of magnitude.

As for experiences considered as events, one can hear a melody or
see a bird's flight, one can hear a concert or see the World Series, one
can experience a mid-life crisis or experience (live through) the
Second World War.

And finally, we designate as "actions" such long-term and complicated undertakings as writing a book, getting an education, raising a
child. Each of these can be said to begin at some more or less easily
identifiable point and to proceed to its end through various intermediate steps.

We shall have to raise later the question of the "outer limits" of
these temporal configurations. Obviously, when we turn to historical
time proper we shall have to concern ourselves with phenomena
whose dimensions exceed the experience and the lifetime of individuals, and before that we shall have to ask what kind of temporal
configuration the "lifetime" itself is. For the present we restrict
ourselves to what might be called the medium-range phenomena
which clearly lie within the experience of the individual, phenomena whose beginnings, middles, and ends can be taken in or
encompassed by the individual's experience.

We need to do this because it is clear that a difference in the
"dimension" of the phenomena considered brings with it a difference in the manner in which these phenomena are dealt with in
our experience. As long as we remain at the level of the melody and
the tennis serve we can speak of a more or less immediate protentional-retentional span which temporally holds together the event or
action and unites its beginning, middle, and end. We are absorbed in
the melody, we simply serve the tennis ball, as we saw, without any
reflective distance between ourselves and what we are doing, and yet
in such a way that we are not blind or unaware, but in fact perfectly
conscious of what we are doing. When the events and actions are
longer-term and more complex, it is clear that something more and
different is required. It is not merely that a longer attention-span is
required, and that more and more disparate elements must be held
together and related. Nor is it merely that the longer-term leaves open

more opportunity for changing circumstances to intrude and to require revision of plans. Even more important is the fact that events
and actions maintain their identity and integrity for us even though
they are interrupted and criss-cross one another. Our ability to experience events is at this level the ability to follow them through these
interruptions, and our ability to act is that of pursuing and maintaining a course of action while intermittently carrying out other actions
which may be unrelated.

What is indicated here is something like the reflective stance
suggested by Schutz. If the structure of complex experiences and
actions can be considered a replica at a larger scale of the part-whole,
beginning-middle-end structure of the simple phenomenon, it nevertheless requires a different subjective role on the part of the experiencer or agent. The subject is no longer immersed in the larger-scale
phenomenon through a retentive-protentive awareness. Retention
and protention are always at work, of course, in the immediacy of
whatever I am doing. But when the larger-scale activity spans a
multiplicity of actions or experiences, these must be held together by
a grasp which attends not only to the object, or objective, but also to
the disparate and temporally discrete parts of my experience or
activity that render the object present or constitute my engagement
in the action.

If we are to call this grasp "reflective" or "reflexive," however, we
must not suppose that it is detached and contemplative. In fact it
involves a great deal of "mental activity" even in the case of those
experiences we have called passive. Following a ballet performance
in progress is protentional-retentional as it goes along, but if it is
interrupted by an intermission, during which I converse, buy a
drink, and visit the washroom, I need to "pick up the thread" of the
story and re-establish myself in the retentive-protentive frame of
mind. To do this, I may need to consult my memory, reawaken
certain scenes from the first act, etc.

Likewise, returning to my workbench after a pause, I need to
remind myself of what I have done and what needs still to be done.
The sense of "where I stand" in the project, which was so clear to me
while I was immersed in it, now needs to be restored by an act of
recollection and reflection.

In Husserlian language we are speaking here of the transition from
retention and protention to recollection and expectation—except
that in the case of action, as we have seen, the notion of expectation
is inappropriate and one would have to speak instead, perhaps, of

deliberation or planning. Deliberation, of course, is something required not only in the midst of action but also, and perhaps more typically, before it begins. In any case, what distinguishes these "reflective" components of action and experience from the pre-reflective "immersion" we have spoken of so far is that here the temporal object, experience, or action is taken apart, broken down into its elements, such that each can be attended to separately. This means of course that it no longer occupies the position of "background" or "horizon" that it has when my pre-reflective attention is focused on present or future. Instead it becomes thematic. This is not to say, however, that any such elements or sub-actions are viewed in isolation. The recollection, expectation, and deliberation of which we are speaking here are *practical* concerns whose purpose is to organize or reorganize these elements into a unified whole. Thus the elements are taken together and considered in their interrelation. It is the whole as an interrelation of parts which becomes thematic.

The kind of reflective stance we have in mind here is what the Germans call *Besinnung. Sich besinnen* means to take stock, to remind oneself where one stands. Its relation to the term *Sinn* suggests "making sense" of what we are doing, experiencing, or living through. The term is used by Husserl in a very different sense from the term *Reflexion*, which indicates the self-directed but contemplative and epistemic conscious intention.[5] The term *Besinnung* is even more important, and more characteristic, in the work of Wilhelm Dilthey. Both Husserl and Dilthey take as the basic units of conscious life what they call *Erlebnisse*, lived experiences, which they both view as temporal wholes or configurations unified from within. Such *Erlebnisse*, furthermore, are themselves dependent parts of larger wholes which make up the configuration of conscious life.

As for Husserl, so for Dilthey, the experience of music is often used to illustrate the temporality of conscious life. Dilthey describes our following a melody, hearing the notes one by one, but in such a way that past and future determine the present and each note is experienced as belonging to the temporal whole whose part it is.[6] But Dilthey goes one step further than Husserl. He uses the melody not

---

5. On Husserl's use of *Reflexion* and *Besinnung*, compare section 15 of *Cartesianische Meditationen*, ed. S. Strasser (The Hague: Martinus Nijhoff, 1963), pp. 72–75, with the late manuscript appended to *Die Krisis der europäischen Wissenschaften*, ed. W. Biemel (The Hague: Martinus Nijhoff, 1962) pp. 508–13.

6. Dilthey, *Gesammelte Schriften*, vol. VII, pp. 220–21.

only as an example of a temporal object we experience, but as a metaphor for the whole which experiences go to make up. Life itself, he says, is like a melody, whose parts, experiences, are related to each other as are individual notes.[7] The larger-scale "melodic" character of life, however, is not guaranteed by simply living through it. What he calls the *Zusammenhang des Lebens*—the coherence of life—must be found or constituted by *Besinnung*.[8] We shall return to the *Zusammenhang des Lebens*, a term Dilthey uses primarily to refer to the whole of a person's life, and a term taken up by Heidegger in that sense as well. For the moment it is sufficient to have shown, first, that the configurational character of the events of "real life" is maintained at the level of longer-term, larger-scale, and more complex phenomena than those we considered initially; second, that the nature of such configurations is substantially the same at this level as before, comprising such features as temporal closure, beginning-middle-end, means-end, suspension-resolution, etc.; and, third, that those configurations are constituted (to use a Husserlian word) by a temporal "grasp" which is like the protentional-retentional structure at least insofar as it spans past, present, and future to unify the various aspects, elements, or phases of the temporal configuration in question. The only important difference that arises at this level, apart from the differences of complexity or scale themselves, is that of the nature of this conscious stance. Instead of being protentional-retentional it has the reflective, deliberative character of a *Besinnung* in which the larger-scale action or event becomes thematic as a whole.

3. Narrative, Narrator, and Audience

This last consideration provides us with the means for answering the third objection to associating experience and narrative structure. This objection derives, we recall, from the claim that narrative structure requires not only a temporal configuration of events but also a narrator and a possible audience. This objection can be better understood if we consider three features of narrative in its ordinary "literary" embodiment. First, in a good story, to use Barthes's image, all the extraneous noise or static is cut out. That is, we the audience are told by the story-teller just what is necessary to "further the plot." A

7. Ibid., p. 234.
8. Ibid., pp. 196–98.

selection is made of all the events and actions the characters may engage in, and only a small minority finds its way into the story. In life, by contrast, everything is left in; all the static is there.

This first point leads to a second. The selection is possible because the story-teller knows the plot in a way both audience and characters do not (or may not). This knowledge provides the principle for excluding the extraneous. The narrative voice, as Scholes and Kellogg point out, is the voice of authority, especially in relation to the reader or listener.[9] The latter is in a position of voluntary servitude regarding what will be revealed and when. Equally important, the narrative voice is an *ironic* voice, at least potentially, since the story-teller knows the real as well as the intended consequences of the characters' actions. This irony is thus embodied primarily in the relation between story-teller and character; but it is related to the audience as well, since their expectations, no less than those of the characters, can be rudely disappointed.

The ironic stance of the story-teller can be seen as a function (and this is the third point) of his or her temporal position in relation to the events of the story. Conventionally this is the ex *post* position, the advantage of hindsight shared by the historian and (usually) the teller of fictional stories. As Danto points out, this position permits descriptions of events derived from their relation to later events and thus often inaccessible to participants in the events themselves.[10] But this standpoint after the story-events can just as well be seen in the fashion preferred by Mink, as a standpoint *outside* or *above* the events which takes them all in at a glance and sees their interrelation. This apparent freedom from the constraints of time, or at least of following the events, sometimes manifests itself in the disparity between the order of events and the order of their telling. Flashbacks and flashforwards bring home in no uncertain terms the authority of the narrative voice over both characters and audience.

In sum, the concept of story seems to involve not just a sequence of unfolding events but, as Scholes and Kellogg put it, the existence of three distinguishable points of view of those events: those of story-teller, audience, and characters. To be sure, these three may seem to coincide in some cases: a story may be told from the viewpoint of a character or in a character's voice. Here even the audience knows no

---

9. Scholes and Kellogg, *The Nature of Narrative*, pp. 240–43. See also H. White, "The Structure of Historical Narrative," pp. 12–18.

10. Danto, *Analytical Philosophy of History*, p. 151.

more or less than the character and all points of view seem identical. But even a first-person account is usually narrated after the fact, and the selection process is witness to the difference in point of view between participant and teller. In any case the very possibility of the disparity among the three points of view seems enough to establish this point, which is that the events, experiences, and actions of a story may have a sense and thus a principle of organization which is exlcuded from the purview of the characters in the story.

As participants and agents in our own lives, according to this view, we are forced to swim with events and take things as they come. We are constrained by the present and denied the authoritative, retrospective point of view of the story-teller. Thus the real difference between "art" and "life" is not organization versus chaos, but rather the absence in life of that point of view which transforms events into a story by *telling* them. Narrative requires narration; and this activity is not just a recounting of events but a recounting informed by a certain kind of superior knowledge.

This point is related to the distinction, long standard in the philosophy of history, between narrative and chronicle: the chronicler simply describes what happens in the order in which it happens. The narrator, by contrast, in virtue of his retrospective view, picks out the most important events, traces the causal and motivational connections among them, and gives us an organized, coherent account. The counterpart of the chronicler at the level of small-scale events would be the radio announcer giving us a live description of a baseball game: "There's the pitch . . . the batter swings . . . line drive to center field!" etc. The *story* of the game, by contrast, is told afterwards and in full knowledge of who won. It will mention only the most important events, especially those that contributed to scoring points and thus to the outcome. All else will be eliminated, except perhaps for touches of human interest or comic relief.[11]

It is in this sense, perhaps, that Hayden White can compare the events of "real life," "reality as it presents itself to perception," to chronicle rather than narrative.[12] Whatever shape or configuration the events may have, the best we can do is register them as they happen, describe them as in a chronicle. The reason for this lies not in the nature of the events but in our own "position," temporally

---

11. On telling the story of a baseball game, see Hexter, *The History Primer*, pp. 175–87.

12. See Introduction, p. 12.

speaking. Nor is it a question of identity, since we can narrate events of our own lives after the fact. But while they are going on these events make up a mere sequence *for us* because that is all we are in a position to see.

There is no doubt much truth to the foregoing analysis. But it neglects many of the features of experience and action which have turned up in our investigation so far. Even at the level of passive, short-term experiences the present is not something to which we are confined in isolation from future and past. As we have seen with Husserl, it is more like a vantage point which opens into future and past. The present is only possible for us if it is framed and set off against a retained past and a protentionally envisaged future.

If this is true of the actions and experiences in which we are pre-reflectively absorbed, it is all the more true of those longer-term and more complex configurations which require our reflective and deliberative attention. The essence of the reflective and deliberative stance or activity is to anticipate the future and lay out the whole action as a unified sequence of steps and stages, as required by the envisaged end. This prospective-retrospective principle of organization, though it does not literally eliminate the noise or "static," does permit us to distinguish the relevant and useful from the intrusive, and allows us to push the extraneous into the background. This capacity to attend to what counts is like the author's principle of selection.

The obvious rejoinder here, of course, is that the future involved in all such cases is *only* the envisaged or projected future, and the agent has only a quasi-hindsight, an as-if retrospection at his or her disposal. What is essential to the story-teller's position is the advantage of *real* hindsight, a real freedom from the constraint of the present assured by occupying a position after, above, or outside the events narrated. The story-teller is situated in that enviable position beyond all the unforeseen circumstances that intrude, all the unintended consequences of our actions that so plague us in everyday life.

Of course this is true; the agent does not occupy a real future with respect to current action. Our point is simply that action does involve, indeed quite essentially, the adoption of an anticipated future-retrospective point of view on the present. We know we are in the present and that the unforeseen can happen; but the very essence of action is to strive to overcome that limitation by foreseeing as much as possible. Action is thus a kind of manoeuver between two points of view on the events we are living through and the things we are doing. Not only do we not simply sit back and let things happen to us; for the most part, our negotiation with the future is successful. We are, after all, able to act.

What we are saying, then, is that we are constantly striving, with more or less success, to occupy the story-teller's position with respect to our own actions. Lest this be thought merely a farfetched metaphor, consider how important, in the reflective and deliberative process, is the activity of literally telling, to others and to ourselves, what we are doing. When asked, what are you doing? we may be expected to come up with a story, complete with beginning, middle, and end, an accounting or recounting which is description and justification all at once.

The fact that we often need to tell such a story even to ourselves, in order to become clear on what we are about, brings to light two important things: the first is that such narrative activity, even apart from its social role, has a practical function in life, that is, it is often a constitutive part of action, and not just an embellishment, commentary, or other incidental accompaniment. The second is that we sometimes assume, in a sense, the point of view of audience to whom the story is told, with regard to our own action, as well as the two points of view already mentioned, those of agent or character and of story-teller.

Louis Mink was thus operating with a totally false distinction when he said that stories are not lived but told.[13] They are told in being lived and lived in being told. The actions and sufferings of life can be viewed as a process of telling ourselves stories, listening to those stories, and acting them out or living them through. And here I am thinking only of living one's own life, quite apart from the social dimension, both cooperative and antagonistic, of our action, which is even more obviously intertwined with narration. Sometimes we must change the story to accommodate the events, sometimes we change the events, by acting, to accommodate the story. It is not the case, as Mink seems to suggest, that we first live and act and then afterward, seated around the fire as it were, tell about what we have done, thereby creating something entirely new thanks to a new perspective. The retrospective view of the narrator, with its capacity for seeing the whole in all its irony, is not in irreconcilable opposition to the agent's view but is an extension and refinement of a viewpoint inherent in action itself.

To be an agent or subject of experience is to make the constant

---

13. See Introduction, p. 10.

attempt to surmount time in exactly the way the story-teller does. It is the attempt to dominate the flow of events by gathering them together in the forward-backward grasp of the narrative act. Mink and the other theorists are right to believe that narration constitutes something, creates meaning rather than just reflecting or imitating something that exists independently of it. But narration, intertwined as it is with action, does this in the course of life itself, not merely after the fact, at the hands of authors, in the pages of books.

When we speak of narration being intertwined with the course of life, it should be noted that we are not referring to the simple fact that a great deal of everyday conversation is devoted to telling stories. It is certainly true that narratives, especially in the form of anecdotes about acquaintances or about oneself, make up a large part of our conversational exchanges, and the role of these narratives in social communication can be a fascinating subject of study. But our interest in narrative to this point is limited to its role in constituting the sense of the action we are engaged in and the events we are living through, its role in organizing temporally and giving shape and coherence to the sequence of experiences we are having *as* we are having them. Some of the above-mentioned anecdotal narratives may play such a role: as Schapp points out,[14] when we tell the story of an accident to a doctor or lawyer, we seek his or her intervention so as to affect the subsequent course of the story, or perhaps its sequel or next chapter. Telling the story to others may be part of the story itself; but it need not be.

This may help clarify why it is that in a discussion of the narrative character of everyday experience it is only now, relatively late, that we have begun to speak of language. We already pointed out that what is essential to narration is not that it is a verbal act of telling, as such, but that it embodies a certain point (or points) of view on a sequence of events. Furthermore, narrative structure refers not only to such a play of points of view but also to the organizational features of the events themselves in such terms as beginning-middle-end, suspension-resolution, departure-return, repetition, and the like. We maintain that all these structures and organizational features pertain to everyday experience and action whether or not the narrative structure or the act of narrative structuring takes the form of explicit verbalization.

This is true even of the relation of story-teller to audience we

---

14. Schapp, *In Geschichten Verstrickt*, pp. 107–109.

mentioned earlier. While story-telling in its usual social and literary forms is an intersubjective activity which assumes a hearer's or reader's point of view on the events narrated, as we have seen this point of view is at times assumed even by the agent regarding his or her own action, and by the experiencer on his or her own passive experiences. Sometimes I do have the sense of observing myself act or experience as if I were observing another person, and as if I did not understand what that person was doing and thus needed to be told. This calls for the kind of *Besinnung* which "makes sense" of the action or experience, and in which I (the narrator) tell or remind or explain to myself (the hearer) what I (the character) am doing. None of this requires that I literally talk, even silently, to myself.

This interior narration, even if it is not explicitly linguistic, could nevertheless be taken as evidence that the kind of narrative structure and structuring we are examining here is essentially intersubjective and thus social. In the activity of self-explication or self-clarification, the "self as audience" to whom I address myself is perhaps really a stand-in for the genuine other: the peers, friends, and authorities of my social milieu to whom I so often give an accounting of myself by recounting what I am doing and what I am about. Thus if the self as agent and as experiencer has, in our theory, fragmented itself into different roles or functions, this is simply an interiorization of the real social situation in which I find myself.

Yet it could also be said that when I do give an account of myself to others, my ultimate purpose is to remind myself, convince myself, justify myself to myself, rather than to the others. Perhaps it is the others who are the stand-ins and who simply play the role of sounding-board for what is essentially a self-reflective operation.

Which is, in fact, "essential" here, the intrasubjective or the intersubjective? Or is this a valid question? What seems clear is that the narrative accounting and recounting does take place, that it is sometimes directed at oneself and sometimes at others, and occasionally the one addressee stands in for the other. It is also clear that the individual cannot be treated as if he did not exist in a social situation; it is clear that the social milieu is somehow constitutive of what the individual is. Part of this is no doubt the fact that others are called upon to hear and to accept the narrative accounting that the individual gives of his or her actions and experiences in making sense of or constituting them temporally. Self-reflection and other-reflection seem to go hand in hand. But it may be a false question to ask whether one is more important or original than the other, whether one precedes the other in the sense that it is the original of which the other is only a secondary manifestation.

None of this, however, affects our current concern. The social dimension of narrative has several aspects to which we shall have to turn when we consider historical time and the manner in which it is shaped and structured. For the moment we are still speaking of the individual, however, and the narrative character of everyday action and experience. Let us sum up what constitutes such narrative character as revealed in our treatment so far.

1. The events we experience, the experiences themselves, and the actions we perform consist not of "mere" sequences but of structured and contoured sequences of temporal phases. These sequences begin and end, and are thus separated from their temporal "surroundings"; and they are internally articulated in relations of suspension-resolution, departure-return, means-end, problem-solution, etc.

2. These temporal phenomena have such a structure for us in virtue of a temporal grasp which can be described as protentional-retentional at the pre-reflective level of short-term or simple experiences and actions, and as reflective and explicitly narrational at the level of more complex experiences and actions. In both cases temporal multiplicity is spanned, gathered, or held together; in the latter case this takes on the character of assuming a story-teller's point of view on the action performed or the experience had. The result is that in the complex actions and experiences of everyday life we are subjects or agents, narrators, and even spectators to the events we live through and the actions we undertake.

With this we have cleared the three hurdles mentioned at the beginning of this chapter and have thereby substantially justified our use of the term "narrative" to characterize the structure of everyday life.

We can give this point further support by appealing briefly to the work of Paul Ricoeur. Speaking of the temporal character of narrative, Ricoeur characterizes "emplotment" (*mise en intrigue*) as mediating between events and story, unifying the chronological with the non-chronological. The events constitute the episodic dimension, succeeding one another in linear fashion. Emplotment is a "configurational act" (a term he borrows from Mink) which transforms the events into a story by "grasping them together," and directing them toward a conclusion or an ending. This gives to the sequence of events its wholeness and its "point" or "theme." In the end it is as if the natural order of time were reversed: "reading the end in the beginning and the beginning in the end, we also learn to read time itself backward, as the recapitulation of the initial conditions of a course of action in its final consequences."[15]

The difference between Ricoeur's account and ours, of course, is that he is speaking of what is accomplished by *literary* narrative (both historical and fictional). Our contention is that this same accomplishment occurs every time we experience and act. If Ricoeur has correctly characterized what literary narratives do, then it seems that their accomplishment is but a recapitulation of the structure of everyday experience and action.

4. Some Concurring Views and Some Clarifications

In the present chapter we have tried to show that narrative is what Barbara Hardy calls a "primary act of mind." It is our primary way of organizing and giving coherence to our experience. Yet it is not as if "our experience" existed somehow independently of it and that our capacity for story-telling then intervened to impose a narrative structure upon it. To say this would come close to that view of narrative we have been resisting and criticizing from the start, according to which the literary imagination super-imposes on real events, or ascribes to an invented or fictional world, a structure alien to real life. This was the view which declared narrative constitutionally incapable of representing the world, even the human world.[16] A variant of this view, transposed from its original reference to literary and historical texts, would perhaps claim that in our conversations with others or with ourselves we "dress up" our experiences in narrative form, but in doing so invariably falsify them.

What we have been arguing, by contrast, is that narrative form is not a dress which covers something else but the structure inherent in human experience and action. We started in chapter I by exhibiting the rudiments of this form in the simplest experiences and actions. In the present chapter we have specified further characteristics of this form, exhibited its presence in more complex experience and action, and examined the pre-reflective and then the reflective grasp which holds together and relates the various temporal phases of experience or action in a quasi "story-telling" fashion. In our view

---

15. Ricoeur, *Temps et récit*, vol. I p. 105.
16. See Introduction, pp. 10–17.

there is nothing below this narrative structure, at least nothing that is experienceable by us or comprehensible in experiential terms. As with the sense-data theory, as we said before, we may analytically dismember our experience and treat its distinguishable temporal phases as if they were distinct. But we experience them as parts of temporal wholes which get their sense from the configurations to which they belong.

Should we say, then, further citing Hardy, that it is "nature, not art, which makes us all story tellers"?[17] It depends on how the notoriously ambiguous term "nature" is used. Hardy clearly wishes to deny to the literary artist the sole rights to narrative, and in this we agree with her. But is nature being contrasted with culture, or to society in the broader sense as well? Presumably not. We have already seen that there is something inherently intersubjective, and thus social in a sense, in even the solitary story-telling we have attributed to the individual. It would be a mistake to think that narrative is "natural" in the sense that it is unrelated to and unaffected by our social existence.

Nor does narrative seem "natural" in the sense that it is related to what we know about ourselves through the natural sciences. Better to follow Frederick Olafson in this regard: he invokes Wilfred Sellars's distinction between the "manifest image" and the "scientific image" of man.[18] Implicit in Sellars's distinction, of course, is the idea that thanks to science we are penetrating the appearances to find the realities behind them. Olafson in effect reminds us that both are, after all, images, and as a philosopher he opts, along with the rest of what we call the humanities, for the descriptive elaboration of the manifest image. We have done as much from the start by insisting here that we are speaking not simply of time or events *tout court* but of time and events *as* we experience them, as they enter our experience. And likewise, in speaking of actions, we are not concerned with the sort of causal explanation that would go beyond our understanding of our action as we perform it. Our approach, like Olafson's, is to this extent phenomenological: we bracket the "in itself" in order to bring into view and describe the "for us."

But who are "we"? Another sense of "natural" is "universal" in the

---

17. Barbara Hardy, *Tellers and Listeners: The Narrative Imagination* (London: The Athlone Press, 1975), p. vii.

18. Olafson, *The Dialectic of Action*, p. 6. Wilfred Sellars, "Philosophy and the Scientific Image of Man," in *Science, Perception and Reality* (London: Routledge and Kegan Paul, 1963), pp. 1–40.

sense of what is common to all cultures. Is the narrative organization of time through actions and experiences, as we have portrayed it, a transcultural—or rather omni-cultureal—phenomenon? Some theorists clearly think so. This is true of Olafson, for example,[19] and of Ricoeur, who speaks explicitly of a *necessité transculturelle* linking the activity of telling a story and the temporality of human experience.[20] And this would seem to be the import of our discussion so far. After all, we think of all persons, not just some, as the subjects of experiences and the performers of actions. Our analysis of temporality began with Husserl's account of time-experience, an analysis clearly designed to capture the universal "essence" of consciousness in all its possible instantiations. And it is in just this sense that it is so convincing: it is hard for us to think of a person *not* experiencing in the manner Husserl describes; and likewise, it is hard to think of action in any other way than as a teleologically ordered, "narrative" construction.

Yet it is precisely *for us* that it is "hard" to think any other way. And again, who are we? Thus I do not think we should be so hasty in adopting this conclusion about the transcultural nature of narrative structure. We have said with Hardy that narrative is a "primary act of mind," but it is not the only possible one. Even in our own culture we have different ways of organizing our experience, and even of dealing with its temporality. Events that unfold in time can exemplify timeless relations or even themselves approximate timelessness by endless repetitions. Bodily events (waking-sleeping, digestion, menstruation) are cyclical, as are many natural events around us, notably the change of seasons and the observable motions of the sun and moon. And even if "events," "actions," and "experiences," the three sorts of human phenomena we have examined, are internally structured in narrative form, and constitute distinguishable themes within our experience, it may be that they are externally related to one another in more ways that just those we have discussed.

The whole question of the cultural relativity versus the universality of narrative structure will have to await our discussion of history for a fuller treatment, and that for two reasons. The first is that that discussion will be attended by a consideration of the social

---

19. Olafson, pp. 112–14, is speaking specifically of "historicity," but for him this is equivalent to narrative structure.

20. Ricoeur, p. 85.

dimension of narrative, and this will permit us to view the manner in which the individual organization of time is embedded in a social situation. The second is that historical relativity is itself a variant of cultural relativity, and a discussion of history will provide us with better means of approaching the latter problem.

For now, leaving this question open does not prevent us from claiming that the narrative organization of time, even if it is not "natural" in any of the more questionable senses we have just reviewed, is certainly, for us (whoever *we* are) not "artificial," as if it were imposed on our experience from without. Nor does it require a special creative or reflective act separate from the elements it orders and organizes. It is simply the *way* we experience and the *way* we act. This is clearly what Hardy must have meant by calling it "natural."

It might be objected that if we use the language of organizing or ordering certain "elements," and especially if we now admit that there are ways other than narrative of organizing the same elements, it must follow that those elements are "there" prior to and independently of the principle of their organization. But this does not follow at all. We can even admit, without leaving the sphere of narrative structure, that the same elements can be differently construed. Nothing is more common than the retrospective revision whereby the elements of one story become the elements of another: the movements and strokes of my tennis game were supposed to be part of my victory in the tennis match; instead, they are part of the sad story of my developing back problems which forced me out of the match. Similarly, the "same" elements can be viewed by different persons, at the same time, as parts of very different stories.

It does not follow that such elements have any status in our experience apart from their involvement in stories, at least until we reach a very abstract level of analysis. In a revision of the sort mentioned above, they can maintain their identity across different stories. It may further happen, as we shall see, that some isolated elements intrude or stand out as if in search of a story to belong to. But no elements enter our experience, we maintain, unstoried or unnarrativized. They can emerge as such only under a special analytical view. It is this latter, not the narrativization, which is "artificial" and runs so counter to the normal current of our experience that it requires a special effort.

The case is comparable to the *Gestalt* spatial phenomena so often used in discussions of perception. The figure is seen *either* as a duck or as a rabbit; a special effort is required to see a figure which is both or neither, or contains certain "objective" features that lead themselves to alternative interpretation. The mistake is to transpose the result of such an analytic effort back into the original experience itself, as if we first *saw* the objective figure and *then* imposed one or the other interpretation on it. This is a confusion of what we see with what we take (or decide on reflection) to be really there.

Before we dismember them analytically, and even before we revise them retrospectively, our experiences and our actions constitute narratives for us. Their elements and phases are lived through *as* organized by a grasp which spans time, is retrospective and prospective, and which thus seeks to escape from the very temporal perspective of the now which makes it possible.

The foregoing is offered as an elaboration and confirmation of Barbara Hardy's remarks that narrative is a "primary act of mind" that derives from nature rather than art. What Hardy says about literary narratives, Olafson extends to historical narratives and in general to the way the "humanities" go about understanding human behavior; the narrative structure they employ is not original to them but is borrowed from the very phenomena to which they turn their attention. In discussing this structure, Olafson stresses primarily the intentional character of an agent's relation to past events and experiences. Human events are not lined up in sequence, with at best causal relations obtaining among them. In the course of an action, an agent has "intentional access to past events and a capability for logically cumulative description of subsequent events in the light of such past events."[21]

We have already remarked that Olafson's account can be improved upon, especially in light of some of the concepts we have borrowed from Husserl and Merleau-Ponty. Olafson deals almost exclusively with our relation to the past, and when he does mention the future, while acknowledging its importance, he discusses primarily its logical status as "envisaged possibility."[22] His treatment of both future and past seems to overlook that configurational character, which we first discovered in Husserl's analysis of time-consciousness, according to which past, present, and future are fused into the unity of an event, experience, or action, thanks to the retentional-protentional grasp. Especially in the case of action, which is the focus of Olafson's

21. Olafson, p. 102.
22. Ibid., p. 103.

attention (as the title of his book indicates), we have seen that the future has a status considerably more important for the agent than something merely envisaged as a possibility. And if there is an intentional "backward reference" in action (to use another of Olafson's terms), then this reference extends backward not so much from the present as from the protended future, corresponding to the prospective-retrospective intention which constitutes the action as a whole. This configurational intention seems no less involved, furthermore, in larger-term and more complex actions than in the simple phenomena in which we first encountered it, in spite of the shift from protention-retention to a more reflective, recollective frame of mind.

It is these features which impart to human events the "story"-like character and even a "story-telling" aspect, as we have seen. While Olafson's insight into the relationship between the conceptual approach of the humanities and the basic structure of action is a valid and important one, his theory needs these refinements if we are fully to appreciate the genuinely "narrative" character of that structure.

These features are better recognized by two other philosophers, Schapp and MacIntyre, who, along with Olafson, share our views on both the naturalness and the pervasiveness of narrative structure in human affairs. For both, to give an account of some human event or action is ultimately to tell a story about it.

But "stories are lived before they are told," says MacIntyre, echoing Hardy's views.[23] That is, to act is to live out the account which is part of the action itself. For Schapp, it is to be involved or caught up (*verstrickt*) in the story of that particular action as both teller and actor (or agent or character).[24] In both theories one can see an anticipation of the idea of an interplay among points of view which we began to outline in the last section, and which we shall be developing in greater detail.

One notion that is shared by all these concurring views, whatever their differences, their advantages, and their shortcomings, is that of the preeminently *practical* character of narrative structure. When narrative is associated primarily with its embodiment in fiction and in historiography, its function may be counted either "aesthetic" (in a very loose sense of that term) or "cognitive," respectively. That is, in fiction it is used to produce a work of art, or perhaps simply one of

23. MacIntyre, *After Virtue*, p. 197.
24. Schapp, *passim*.

entertainment or diversion, but in any case not something directly practical. In history it is thought of as an expression of or means towards knowing the past; a "cognitive instrument," in Mink's words, even though he and others have grave doubts about its success in that role.

We have tried to show that before it has either of these functions narrative is practical, and that in two senses: first, practice or action unfolds in a sequence shaped by beginning, middle, and end, suspension-resolution, means and end. Second, the reflective, narrating grasp of these elements, the story-telling aspect of actions, has the practical function of holding the action together, organizing its parts, and doing so, if need be, in the face of changed circumstances. Narration has this practical function, as we saw, even with our passive experience, insofar as we need it to keep track of what is going on around us. This is not to mention the social dimension of both individual and collective action, in which narrative discourse plays an even more obviously practical role. But even if we abstract from that and limit ourselves to the individual's organization of his or her own experience and action, this practical role is central.

To be sure, having introduced this distinction between the "practical," the "aesthetic," and the "cognitive," we may have to qualify it somewhat. If we think of narrative as "organizing," "making sense of," and rendering "coherent" our action and experience, we can recognize elements of all three of these categories: coherence versus incoherence may be regarded as an aesthetic property, and narrative organization of action may be considered cognitive in the sense that the action's implicit "story" is nothing but our knowledge of what we are about or what we are doing.

While action and experience may thus fall under aesthetic and cognitive as well as practical categories, fictional and historical narratives may themselves be practical. That is, such narratives may serve to organize and make sense of the experience and action of their authors and their readers, focusing their attention in certain directions and orienting their actions toward certain goals. If novels play this practical role primarily in the lives of individuals, histories do it primarily for groups, as we shall see later on. It would doubtless be a mistake to say, as some theorists do, that fictions and histories have *only* this practical role, and deny them any purely aesthetic or purely cognitive interest. Nevertheless, their capacity for a practical function may attest to the manner of their relation to the social context of action and experience from which they spring.

We should rephrase our point then, perhaps, by saying that narrative has its first role in the pre-literary structuring and shaping of real life, before it is employed in its literary embodiments for purposes which may be purely aesthetic or purely cognitive.

And our use of "before" here is logical, not really temporal. That is, while literary narratives may have a practical role, the narrative structure of experience exists even in their absence; they, on the other hand, exist within and arise out of a real world already organized in narrative fashion, as we have been at pains to point out. They may at times, in particular contexts, have an effect on the social and personal world by suggesting particular narratives, stories, or courses of action. But the structure itself is something they do not create and impose on the world on their own. On the contrary, in our view, they get their narrative structure from the human world in which they have their origin. It is to this origin that they owe not only their capacity to represent the real world (a capacity we would maintain, they have, *contra* Hayden White *et al.*) but also the very idea of undertaking such a representation.

But this is not the place to argue for the capacities and purposes of fictional or historical narratives. Our present preoccupation is still the world of action and experience as it exists apart from its representation in these literary genres. It is this world we can designate as practical in a very broad sense: broad enough to include elements of both the aesthetic and the cognitive; too broad to permit either of those interests to be pursued exclusively. It is in this broadly practical sphere, as we have tried to show, that narrative has its first and continuing role, that of organizing and structuring our experiences and our actions.

III

The Self and the Coherence of Life

In the previous chapter we have attempted to develop to the fullest extent our view that narrative structure pervades everyday life as the form of our experiences and actions. The complex structure of narrative that we have outlined represents the manner in which our experiences and actions are organized over time.

In the present chapter we shall take the conception of narrative structure a step further by attempting to show that it is the organizing principle not only of experiences and actions but of the self who experiences and acts. The broad sense of the "practical" which emerged at the end of the previous chapter is broad enough finally to merge with the moral and ethical, provided that these terms too are taken in the broadest of their many possible senses. This broadest sense is concerned not with the right and wrong of particular actions or even rules for action, but with the question how to live one's life as a whole, and with questions about the nature of individual human existence, character, and personal identity. Though it is possible to distinguish a "metaphysical," an "epistemological," and a "moral" sense of the notion of personal identity, we shall see that in some measure all of these are involved. Here too we shall find that narrative provides the key.

1. Coherence and Narrative Structure

Some theorists we have already encountered, notably Schapp and MacIntyre, have also developed the notion of narrative along these lines. "Die Geschichte steht fur den Mann," says Schapp, meaning that we get to know another person by learning his life-story—what he's done and where he's been.[1] One's own identity for oneself is no less a question of such a story. Schapp's views are often presented as if they were a radical departure from his teacher Husserl,[2] who is sometimes believed to have postulated a substantial self ("transcendental ego") underlying the flow of experience. Yet Husserl himself wrote that the ego "constitutes itself for itself, so to speak, in the unity of a *Geschichte*"; or, as one could say, in one possible translation of *Geschichte*, the unity of a *story*.[3]

For MacIntyre, similarly, the question of personal identity is resolvable into that of the "unity of life," which is really that of the coherence of a life-story.[4] MacIntyre's ultimate purpose, of course, is to steer the attention of moral philosophy away from its modern preoccupation with justifying actions and to reinstate the Greek concept of virtue, which for Aristotle was explicitly linked with the whole of a life and its coherence and unity.[5] For MacIntyre one's own life can be viewed as a story in which one functions as both author and principle character or protagonist.[6]

Thus Schapp and MacIntyre take up in their own way the question we have already encountered in connection with Dilthey's conception of *Besinnung*, namely, the question of what the latter calls *Zusammenhang des Lebens*. Up to now we have spoken of narrative structure in connection with individual, distinguishable *events*, *experiences*, and *actions*. We have described the configurational character of each of these, including their outer boundaries (beginning and end) and their internal structure. We noted in the last chapter that as larger-scale, complex phenomena these maintain their integrity and structure even though they are interrupted and criss-crossed in our experience by other like phenomena. Natural and social events, such as the movements and actions of others around us, are configurations we follow through time in spite of their discontinuities. Some of our more complex actions are performed

---

1. Schapp, *In Geschichten Verstrickt*, p. 103.
2. See Hermann Lübbe, *Bewusstsein in Geschichten* (Freiburg: Verlag Rombach, 1972), pp. 103–14.
3. Husserl, *Cartesianische Meditationen*, p. 109. The English translator (*Cartesian Meditations*, tr. Dorion Cairns, [The Hague: Martinus Nijhoff, 1960]) renders *Geschichte*, of course, as "history."
4. MacIntyre, *After Virtue*, p. 201.
5. Aristotle, *Nicomachean Ethics*, 1100a5.
6. MacIntyre, p. 198.

discontinuously as well, and in the intervals we are occupied with other actions which serve other ends. Each of these is like a distinguishable "story-line" constituted by our protentions, retentions, and intentions.

If each of these stories requires a narrative grasp, a quasi-narration which holds the story together, my *life*-story requires yet a further, more comprehensive grasp which takes them all as mine and establishes the connections among them. My "life," in the sense in which Dilthey and MacIntyre use the term, is of course composed of all the experiences I have and the actions, small-scale and large, short-term and long, in which I engage. But like each of them singly, it is itself something temporal which unfolds in time and whose phases I survey prospectively and retrospectively from within an ever-changing present. As such it seems to call for the same sort of description we have so far used, in connection with events, experiences, and actions, and to invite us to look in it for similar principles of unity, coherence, and structure. Can my life be regarded as an event I experience, an experience I have (or live through), or perhaps an action I perform? Is it thus the sort of "story" in which I am character, story-teller, and audience all at once?

For Dilthey the question of the *Zusammenhang des Lebens* is the occasion for a discussion of the art of autobiography, and he devotes a brief discussion to three of his favorite works of the genre: Augustine's and Rousseau's *Confessions*, and Goethe's *Dichtung and Wahrheit.*[7] He recounts how each envisages the coherence of his life in his selection, organization, and presentation of its component parts. But for Dilthey it is clear that autobiography is only the literary expression of the kind of reflection on life as a whole that we all engage in from time to time, whether we ever write it down or not.

On the model of literary autobiographies we may think of autobiographical reflection as being conducted in the present and being directed entirely toward the past. More often, however, it is concerned with the past in order to render it coherent with or comprehensible in terms of a present and a future. The larger biographical past figures as a sediment or horizon, of course, in everything we do. But a multiplicity of activities and projects, spread out over time and even existing simultaneously in the present, calls for an active reflection that attempts to put the whole together. The most striking occasions for such reflections are those radical con-

---

7. Dilthey, *Gesammelte Schriften,* vol. VII, pp. 198–99.

versions, usually religious or political, in which a new view of life, of oneself, and of one's future projects and prospects requires a break with and reinterpretation of one's past. Psychoanalysis and other forms of psychotherapy often involve a similar sort of radical revision.

In keeping with what we have said, it is not as if a story was being imposed on or invented for events that originally had none; rather, events that were lived in terms of one story are now seen as part of another. For example, what was lived as the innocent, self-interested pursuit of life's pleasures is now seen as a life of sin; or a life of service to world revolution and the salvation of mankind is now seen as a youthful combination of enthusiasm, idealism, and gullibility. Early family life is radically recast as an Oedipal drama tinged with sex and violence.

Most of us do not experience these radical breaks and revisions, but most engage in some form of autobiographical revision, often occasioned by the transitions and stages of life. We are composing and constantly revising our autobiographies as we go along.

Dilthey attempts to penetrate further into the nature of the understanding that is sought in this sort of reflection on one's own life, and his approach can be instructive. Coherence (*Zusammenhang*) is the aim. For Dilthey, understanding as a cognitive endeavor is always correlated with coherence.[8] But how do we go about achieving it? Here Dilthey calls to mind three "categories of thought" that are relevant to the understanding of life: value, purpose, and meaning or significance (*Bedeutung*).[9] These come into play according to the temporal standpoint one takes. Significance emerges primarily through memory, as in retrospect elements of the course of life stand out and make up a pattern. Value corresponds to the present, and attaches positively and negatively to the realities of the world around us. And purpose belongs to the future as the projected realization of our values.

Dilthey at first says that the three categories cannot be distinguished in importance because they represent different and incommensurable points of view on the whole of life. On second thought he recognizes a certain order of priority among them. Values in the present, he says, are in themselves merely ranged alongside one another and neither they nor the purposes devised for their

---

8. Ibid., p. 257.
9. Ibid., p. 201.

realization make up a pattern. Music is invoked once again: "It is like a chaos of chords and discords. Each is a structure of notes which fills a present but has no musical relation to the others."[10] Only the category of meaning overcomes the chaos of this array and brings order. Under this category belongs the notion of the development of a life *(Entwicklung)*, its unfolding according to a pattern not imposed on it from above or outside but arising out of its own internal shaping *(Gestaltung)* of itself.[11] The category of meaning is thus central for the understanding of the course of life because it encompasses and orders the things we value and the purposes we pursue. Meaning in this sense is precisely the *Zusammenhang* or coherence sought by all understanding.

But this priority of the category of meaning involves some paradoxes, as Dilthey is aware. He thinks of meaning primarily, as we saw, as the category of memory and of restrospect, and indeed associates it with the kind of understanding the historian can achieve of the past. But here he is speaking of it as a category through which the individual reflects on life as it is going on. And this is precisely why the relationship between the parts and the whole of a life is "never quite completed." "One would have to wait for the end of a life, for only at the hour of death could one survey the whole from which the relationship between the parts could be ascertained."[12] We cannot wait, of course. For us the meaning of the whole is discernible, if at all, only from the perspective of one of its parts; and yet its part is understandable, if at all, only as belonging to the whole. "Understanding always hovers between these two points of view. Our view of the meaning of life changes constantly. Every plan for your life expresses a view of the meaning of life."[13]

In these passages Dilthey is touching on issues that have far-reaching consequences. Obviously the concept of the hermeneutical circle, inherited from his own work on Schleiermacher, is being expressed here. And there is no doubt that Dilthey has his eye on the sort of understanding that is proper to the historian's work and which is found in other *Geisteswissenschaften* as well. He is not speaking here *only* of the kind of understanding a person has of his or her own life. At one point he suggests that a second person (a biographer, as Dilthey was of Schleiermacher) has a distinct advan-

---

10. Ibid.
11. Ibid., p. 232.
12. Ibid., p. 233.
13. Ibid.

tage over his subject precisely because he does come along after the death of the first and can assess the whole.[14] At the same time no biographer's or historian's hindsight can be definitive, since "one would have to wait for the end of history to have all the material necessary to determine its meaning."[15] Thus the problematic interrelation between meaning and retrospection is a quite general one, as other authors (especially Danto) have seen,[16] and is not limited to the individual's autobiographical reflection.

Still, Dilthey does begin at the autobiographical level, and his remarks are applicable there first of all. In what he has to say about *Besinnung* we find three features of narrative structure that we have already encountered in our discussion of events, experiences, and actions. 1) It is characterized by the backward reference, whereby the unfolding phases of a series receive their description and their significance from the end-point. Like Danto, Dilthey connects this with the historian's perspective and sees it more generally as a narrative structure. 2) The idea of the special temporal relation between wholes and parts, which we found earlier instantiated in the particular events and activities of life, is here treated as a feature of life as a whole. 3) In the notion of the search for self-understanding, and in that of the reflective composition and re-composition of our implicit autobiographies, we find again the idea that we are at once the spectators of, agents in, and tellers of a story which, in this case, is a life-story.

These features which "life," as a phenomenon, shares with experiences, events, and actions, should not, however, obscure for us the differences. In several very important senses life, for the person who lives it, is *not* like an experience he lives through, an event he experiences, or an action he performs. In spite of the term "life-story," furthermore, it differs in some important ways from most other sorts of stories. My birth is not a beginning that I myself can experience, or even remember (unless we extend those terms beyond their usual meanings, as some psychological theories wish to do.) Nor can I experience my death. The impossibility of witnessing the beginning and of *actually* retrospectively viewing the whole, after its end, does not prevent, as we have seen, that quasi-retrospective view

14. Ibid., p. 237.
15. Ibid., p. 233.
16. Danto, *Analytical Philosophy of History*, p. 151.

of the whole of which Dilthey speaks, *as if* we could view the whole, or *as if* we were someone else looking back. Such a quasi- or prospectively retrospective view is indeed part of any action or experience, as we have also pointed out. But clearly the character of this prospective view is affected by the fact that in the case of one's life the retrospection can never become real, that I can never literally live *through* (survive) my own life. Even the most literal believer in an after-life must deal somehow with this paradox, which would lend to the putative heavenly retrospection a character which is odd at best, and in any case very different from our normal way of looking back on things we really experienced or did. In this sense one's life as a "whole" is very different from those other temporal wholes we have examined so far.

The same can be said of the interrelation of its parts. Events are unified by being parts of larger events. Actions subserve larger-scale actions. But the events of someone's life may make up a larger event only in the trivial sense that they all happened to that person. As for life as an action, it is true that the "greats," about whom biographies are written, are often treated as if their whole life were a combination of means leading up to the end of becoming president, writing symphonies, etc. It is perhaps by analogy to such persons that some hold the view that one's life has or ought to have some single purpose or end, the performance of some particular action or the production of some product. Few of us, however, lead such single-minded lives. Even for those whose lives are centered in some "profession" or "vocation," such a conception fails to do justice to the complex relation between such an activity and the other spheres of life in which all of us are inevitably involved: the private, the public or civic, the family, the emotional and sexual, etc. To view these spheres and the relation among them as a means-end relation is surely simplistic from several points of view. An individual's life is taken up in a multiplicity of larger-scale practical endeavors, such as raising a family and pursuing a career, or gardening and enjoying music, which simply run parallel rather than serving each other as means or serving some larger end beyond them.

Again it may seem that those activities are unified only because they are the activities of one person. Aristotle remarked that, in effect, such a unity is not narrative unity: "An infinity of things befall . . . one man, some of which it is impossible to reduce to unity; and in like manner there are many actions of one man which cannot be made to form one action."[17] A detailed biography, Aristotle seems to be saying, does not necessarily make a good story.

These considerations make it clear, then, that when we move to the scale of "life" and "life-story" we should not expect the *kind* of internal unity and interconnection that we find in the elements which make up such a life—events, experiences, and actions. It would be wrong to conclude, however, that questions of unity and wholeness do not arise at all or that the concept of narrative structure finds no applicability. We shall find other clues to this applicability if we consider one way in which Dilthey's concept of *Zusammenhang* has been further pursued.

2. Self-Authorship and Authenticity: A Dispute

Dilthey's conception has been deepened in the early work of Martin Heidegger. Near the end of *Being and Time* Heidegger explicitly invokes Dilthey's expression *der Zusammenhang des Lebens*,[18] and says that his own work should be considered an "appropriation" of Dilthey's.[19] Though Heidegger makes this gesture toward Dilthey in the context of his chapter on "historicity," and links it to Dilthey's attempt to provide a foundation for the *Geisteswissenschaften*, it can easily be seen, I think, that Dilthey's influence pervades Heidegger's analysis of human existence. It is in discussing the individual's life, after all, and not in direct connection with history proper, that the latter introduces the concept of *Zusammenhang*.

We have already remarked that Heidegger in this early work shifts the emphasis of phenomenology from the passive to the active and analyzes human existence primarily in terms of the project *(Entwurf)*. His justly influential conception of the "worldhood of the world" is that of a field of operations for the various interlocking projects of human concern. The structure of concern or care *(Sorge)* is a temporal structure: To be human is 1) to be *already* situated in the world (the "already" indicates pastness or having been), thrown into it without my having chosen to be so; 2) to be *present (gegenwär-*

---

17. *Poetics*, 1451a20.
18. Heidegger, *Being and Time*, p. 373 (references are to the German pagination given in the margins).
19. Ibid., p. 377.

tig) to my surroundings which are organized into complexes of equipment; and 3) to be "ahead of myself," as we saw earlier, in the projects which determine the organized usefulness of equipment.[20] Thus we encounter here again the prospective-retrospective structure of temporality.

But for Heidegger my projects are not merely projections of the world and my surroundings but are ultimately projections of my own being. The temporal structure of care is really the structure of the being of *Dasein*. But as such it is a question of the possibility of the wholeness or entirety *(Ganzseinkönnen)* of my existence, a question of the integrity or coherence of the whole complex of projects in which I engage.[21]

As already suggested by Dilthey, it is in the face of death that the question of wholeness arises for the individual, not as an interesting intellectual problem but as an existential issue. We have spoken of human time as configured time in virtue of the structure of the events, experiences, and actions of human existence. As we have seen, this means that the temporal sequence is shaped by beginnings and ends. In terminations, conclusions, achievements, time is provided with a *closure* by the very activities in which we are involved.

By calling attention to death, Dilthey and Heidegger (and MacIntyre makes a similar point)[22] are not referring to the simple fact that we all die, but are pointing to the significance death has for life. For the individual life, death is the ultimate and irrevocable closure. As Heidegger says, the extreme possibility of my being is that of non-being.[23] It is the closure of all my projects. Yet neither the fact of its coming nor the time of its coming is determined, except in the extreme case of suicide, by me. It thus looms as the inevitable closure whose relation to my ongoing projects is forever problematic.

While we all know that death has this sense, according to Heidegger, the character of this knowledge is peculiar. Death is not exactly a possibility we can envisage. In one sense we know of it through the death of another, an event within our world. But my own death is not something I could ever experience as an event *in* the world, for it constitutes the limit of my world. Thus resistant to being thought or experienced, the reality of my own death is more likely to be brought

---

20. Ibid., pp. 191–96.
21. Ibid., p. 309.
22. MacIntyre, p. 197.
23. Heidegger, p. 250.

home to me in a "disposition" such as anxiety. Unlike fear, anxiety has no particular object; what it reveals is the facticity of my being at all, my very being in the world, my engagement in projects in general. My being stands out against the backdrop of my non-being. It thus appears peculiarly groundless. The bottom drops out of my world, as it were. Deprived of a ground it seems bereft of sense.

Though this backdrop of non-being always looms at the edge of our consciousness, according to Heidegger, we resist what it reveals about ourselves. Immersed in our everyday concerns we go from project to project, bored if we stay with anything too long, ever on the look-out for the new and exciting, consumed with idle chatter and too busy to afford the sort of *Besinnung* which would address itself to the over-all sense of what we are doing. We assume that time will go on, and that each project will find its ground and justification in another project.

All this is equivalent, according to Heidegger, to seeking refuge in *das Man*, the impersonal and anonymous everyone-and-no-one in which each individual is interchangeable with every other. What the confrontation with death reveals, by contrast, if we only face it, is the radical my-own-ness *(Jemeinigkeit)* of human existence. Death is that which utterly individualizes or isolates *(schlechthin vereinzelt)*, says Heidegger.[24] Just as no one can die it for me, so no one can live my life for me either. "Resoluteness which anticipates my own death" *(vorlaufende Entschlosseneit)* is Heidegger's expression for taking over responsibility for my own life, wresting it from the anonymity of *das Man*.[25] It is what he calls *Eigentlichkeit*, a term which links genuineness to my-own-ness *(je meines, mir eigenes)* and is usually translated "authenticity." For Heidegger it constitutes genuine self-hood *(Selbstheit)*.[26]

This is, of course, Heidegger at his most "existentialist," the aspect of his early work most influenced by Kierkegaard, most akin to his contemporary Karl Jaspers, and most important for the French existentialists, especially J. P. Sartre. In the terms of our own discussion, linking what Heidegger says to our conception of the narrative features of human existence or "life" as a whole, what seems decisive to Heidegger in the concept of authenticity is really the problem of *authorship*. He takes up Dilthey's notion of autobiographical *Besin-*

24. Ibid., pp. 266, 240.
25. Ibid., p. 329.
26. Ibid., p. 316.

nung on the whole of one's life, though in more dramatic terms: it is occasioned by anxiety and the contemplation of one's own death, and constitutes a "call of conscience."[27] If the closure of birth and death make problematic the integrity of my life-story, what counts for Heidegger, it seems, is whether I am composing it myself or drifting along according to a script of indeterminate or anonymous authorship. This drift is the evasion of responsibility: I am, it seems, responsible for my own life only if I am its author. Or, more precisely, I *am* responsible whether I realize this or not; the question is whether I accept or evade this responsibility.

Both Schapp and MacIntyre object to this emphasis on authorship. Though Schapp does not say so, he seems to be reacting to Heidegger when he affirms that the interlocking stories of which life consists are not authored, not "made" at all. Rather, "one finds them" (*man findet sie vor*) (that is, they are already there and are ongoing) "and one is either caught up in them (*in sie verstrickt*), as one is caught up in one's own story, together with the others who are likewise caught up (*die anderen mitverstrickten*), or one takes a distance from them" as an outside observer.[28] Schapp's graphic and striking term *Verstricktsein*, to be caught up or entangled in, expresses the most intimate possible relation between the self and the various stories of which human reality is made up, including even one's own life story.[29]

MacIntyre, having himself introduced the notion of the human agent as both actor in and author of his own story, immediately retreats from the notion of self-authorship. "We are never more (and sometimes less) than the co-authors of our own narratives," he writes.[30] MacIntyre's remarks are explicitly directed against the existentialist ideal (or idol, he would say) of authenticity, though in Sartre's rather than Heidegger's version. As MacIntyre reads Sartre, the emphasis is slightly different: for Sartre, to be involved in any narrative is to be playing a pre-established social role and thus to be in bad faith. My role is always other than "I" am. But the link with Heidegger is this: the pre-established character of the role suggests that I am not its author. If I could coincide with my narrative (the coincidence of the in-itself and the for-itself) I would be its author

---

27. Ibid., pp. 270–301.
28. Schapp, p. 204.
29. Ibid., p. 86.
30. MacIntyre, p. 199.

and its hero. Heidegger and Sartre share the same ideal of authenticity as self-authorship: it is simply that Sartre, with tragic pathos, believes the ideal unattainable.

Schapp apparently believes, and MacIntyre affirms in no uncertain terms, that the idea of authenticity is an illusion of modern individualism and self-centeredness. Of course the social world consists of pre-established social roles and ongoing stories not of my making, they say. Human existence is to be understood as a matter of assuming and acting out the parts determined by the already existing repertoire of roles, finding oneself caught up in already ongoing stories—including one's own life story. And this is nothing one should apologize for or perceive as alienation from one's true self. There *is* no self apart from the intersection of these stories. My own story was underway in the minds and bodies of my parents even before my birth, and included decisive elements in my early childhood even before I became aware of myself as a distinct individual. As I mature, my life story is then an amalgam of roles and stories: the many social roles I play, the various stories in which I become involved. I affect them all, of course, as what MacIntyre would call a co-author. But to suppose that I could ever take complete charge, or to regret tragically that I cannot, is to succumb to the illusion of being or desiring to be God.

Thus the two authors who have heretofore done the most with the idea of narrative as the key to understanding the structure of the individual's life are alike in rejecting the idea of self-authorship.

What are we to make of this dispute and what effect does it have on our conception of the connection between narrative and personal identity?

It might be thought that by denying to the agent the concurrent role of author, Schapp and MacIntyre are really robbing their theories of what makes the term "narrative" appropriate in the first place. As we saw in the last chapter, the concept of narrative involves not only a series of (human) events unfolding in time, according to a structure, but also a prospective-retrospective grasp which holds together that unfolding and constitutes its structure. It is this grasp which lends to the various phases of action and experience their status of beginning, middle, or end, and thus constitutes a whole from which the parts receive their significance. Put in the simplest terms of the metaphor, narration requires not only a story but also a story-teller. Schapp and MacIntyre seem to be giving us a story without a story-teller, and thus without an organizing principle.

Alternatively, if the authorial role is granted but not accorded to the individual in his or her own life, perhaps it is vested in God, in fate, in History, or indeed in the anonymous *Man* of Heidegger. The first two are popular and recurring literary and religious themes, of course: the idea that one is acting out or carrying out a divine (or perhaps Satanic) plan, that the real Author of Our Being has already composed the script according to which we act. Kafka's *Prozess* gives expression to something close to Heidegger's *das Man*, where the unfolding "plot" is unsettling not because it is straightforwardly evil but because it is anonymous and its authorship and guiding principles are hidden.

Such conceptions of external authorship may thus be either disquieting or consoling but they share the idea that the individual behaves blindly, functioning in ignorance of the true principles behind his or her actions. This may seem an exaggeration, but is it not ultimately the sense of Schapp's notion of *Verstricktsein*, and MacIntyre's of being at most a co-author, sharing authorship with others and with an anonymous tradition? Is this not the result of separating narrative from authorship?

This conclusion, however, overlooks an important distinction. It will be noticed that when we introduced the idea of the different "points of view" on our action and experience in the last chapter, we spoke of the point of view of the *story-teller* or *narrator*, not of the *author*. The distinction between these two has always been important in literary theory, of course, since in a story the narrator often turns up as a quasi-character who is as much a projection of the author (and as distinguishable from him or her) as any of the characters. And even in everyday conversation, one can tell or relate a story without being its author.

This distinction is relevant to the present context because the story-teller or narrator shares part of the author's relation to the events he or she narrates, without being their source. What we picked out as the primary trait of the story-teller remains true, even if he is only the narrator, namely that he *knows the story*. He has command, and embodies the voice of authority vis-à-vis his audience and the voice of irony vis-à-vis his characters, just as if he were the author. What counts in the complex interrelationship of story-telling, accordingly, is not authorship at all, but just narratorship.

This serves Schapp's and MacIntyre's narrative strategies very well. Denied the kind of authorship envisaged by Heidegger, the individual is not left, as the latter seems to think, a blind automaton. Just as I can perform an action competently, knowingly, and successfully by carrying out someone else's plan rather than my own, so I can live my life in a perfectly coherent fashion without claiming authorship of the story of my life.

Though this response to Heidegger is attractive and in many respects convincing, it does not, to my mind, deal adequately with all the problems raised by that philosopher, or with the full range of phenomena brought to the fore by Dilthey's conception of the *Zusammenhang des Lebens*. It is tempting to try to relativize or trivialize the Existentialists' concern with authenticity by viewing it as the expression of the *malaise* of modern industrial society and the breakdown of traditional roles. Cast adrift in a chaotically changing society, the individual is faced with a plurality of social roles as standardized as the objects of mass production, and if he rejects these roles he is ultimately thrown back upon himself. The call for authenticity or self-authorship, whether one believes it capable of realization or not, is really the belief that the individual ultimately has nowhere else to turn but to himself. Critics such as MacIntyre are suggesting that the alternative is a false one, but it is unclear how it can be avoided short of a return to "traditional" society. Whether such a thing ever existed, and if it did, how its return could be effected, are great enough problems. But even if these were solved, it is unclear whether the individual in such a society would be any less subject to the features of existence which Heidegger brings into the open.

3. Settling the Dispute over Authenticity.

The dispute over authorship and authenticity can be resolved only if we recognize that some insights and some oversights lie on both sides.

Heidegger, to begin with, seems to me to have raised two distinct issues without recognizing their distinctness. One is the problem of coherence versus incoherence, which is separate from the problem of authorship; and the second is the legitimate problem of authorship, which his opponents overlook. Let us examine each of these issues in turn.

We have already seen that *narrative coherence* can become a problem at the level of particular experiences and actions. Criss-crossed and interrupted by other events, extended and complex experiences and actions can lose their coherence for us, their *Zusammenhang* in the literal sense of their hanging together or connectedness. Stocktaking, reflection in the sense of *Besinnung*, deliberation: these are all expressions for the act of restoring our temporal grasp on an experience or action when that grasp seems to be slipping. In the case of action, changing circumstances can bring it about that plans have to be altered to varying degrees, or even completely abandoned. We all know what it is to "lose track" of what we are doing while we are doing it. In some cases it may be perfectly clear *what* we are doing in the immediate sense (hammering a nail, writing a memo) but not *why* we are doing it, that is, *how* it fits into or hangs together with a larger project and the other actions that belong to it. It becomes detached from its original purpose and stands isolated in time from its "surroundings," that is, from what precedes and follows it. The larger project, of which it and other sub-actions are parts, has disintegrated for us, has lost its wholeness, completeness, or coherence.

What Heidegger's concept of *Angst* calls to mind is that such disintegration can at times be radicalized and generalized in a person's life, and can apply not to some particular project but to the whole complex of projects in which the individual is involved and their interrelation. Nothing "makes sense" any more, we tend to say, where "making sense" is just that idea that each item stands in a means-end or similar relation to the others, that the whole is going somewhere and hangs together.

Heidegger's portrait of inauthentic existence contains two distinct features: the concept of anonymous authorship and interchangeability expressed in *das Man* is one; the other is that of idle chatter, the frantic pursuit of novelty for its own sake, the "ambiguity" in which every project loses its distinctness.[31] This second feature emphasizes the degree to which human existence can be full of activity and talk, yet empty of "meaning"—that is, again, of coherence and interconnection. Whether this form of existence is a (false) response to the groundlessness revealed by anxiety, or is itself the very incoherence revealed by anxiety (and for Heidegger it seems to be both), it is clear that it exhibits the radical incoherence whereby the elements of life become detached from each other and fail to add

---

31. Heidegger, pp. 167–75.

up to a whole. *Dasein* is, in Heidegger's well-chosen word, *zerstreut:* fragmented, distracted, dispersed, disconnected.[32]

We should note parenthetically here that this aspect of the notion of inauthenticity permits us to recognize the kernel of truth in the views of the narrativists we criticized in chapter one. Louis Mink, Hayden White, and others, it will be recalled, suggest that human reality "in itself" is nothing but "mere sequence without beginning or end" and that narrative coherence is something essentially alien to it, imposed from without by the literary or historical imagination. We have argued, in opposition to this view, that narrative coherence belongs to even the most elementary experience or action, that it is an essential structural feature of the very fact of *having* an experience or *performing* an action.

In admitting now the importance of Heidegger's notion of *Angst* and of *Zerstreutsein* we are in fact allowing for something we have tacitly recognized from the start: namely that at higher levels of complexity something special is required, in the way of a reflexive temporal grasp, to hold together the phases of these larger-scale phenomena and to preserve their coherence. This is in turn to admit that they have a tendency, or at least a capacity, to fly apart or to fragment, thus losing their narrative coherence.

It is at such times, moments of "distraction" and disconnection, that the events, experiences, and actions of real life do indeed assume the character of a "mere sequence," the senseless progression of "one thing after another" so often mentioned in these theories. This formlessness is a feature not only of moments of frantic confusion but also of experiences of extreme boredom and tedium.

Are we being inconsistent in admitting the possibility of such a "mere sequence" when we have linked narrative coherence so closely with the very essence of human experience? Yet the incoherence of the mere sequence is not so much a possible type of experience as it is the dark and looming outer limit of experience, the chaos which stands opposed to order. It is the threat that experience will pass over into its opposite. This is a threat which is, admittedly, in varying degrees, permanently present at the periphery of our consciousness, the very threat and possibility of madness.

It may seem paradoxical to identify temporal chaos with mere sequence. What is more ordered and reliable than the ticking of the

---

32. Ibid., p. 129.

metronome or the beating of the heart? Yet this steady beat is traditionally associated with disintegration, dissolution and death, with the lack of form, while form is existence and life. Succeeding moments are the sands of time flowing away; they are like an insidious erosion or an unravelling of fabric. "Time like an ever-rolling stream bears all its sons away." Sequence undermines existence itself.

Does this mean that the "struggle" of existence is to overcome time itself? Certainly it is often thought that only refuge in eternity triumphs over the ravages of time. But all this supposes that time is identified with mere sequence. Human existence and action as *we* have described them consist not in overcoming time, not in escaping it or arresting its flow, but in shaping and forming it. Human time in our sense is configured time. The narrative grasp of the story-teller is not a leap beyond time but a way of being in time. It is no more alien to time than the curving banks are alien to the river, or the potter's hands to the clay. Mere sequence is like the "prime matter" of the philosophers and theologians. It is not something we could ever experience. It is a limiting concept: the thought of what lies beyond our experience, yet has a force of its own which runs counter to it, like a gravitational pull. The experience of the pull of chaos is our only experience of mere temporal sequence.

The problem with theorists such as White and Mink is not that they postulate the possibility of such a meaningless sequence, but that they turn things upside down: they place it at the heart of human experience, giving us as sad and depressing (and inaccurate) a picture of human reality as we can imagine. Then they propose narrative coherence as a fanciful but distorting and alien superimposition, a dream of coherence where in fact there is none. For them, the madness is to suppose that the real world has narrative coherence, while the hard-nosed realist supposedly recognizes it has none.

While it is often an arresting intellectual manoeuver to turn things on their heads, can we not say that those views merely express the frustration that comes of too high expectations? It is true that some literary narratives have something definitive about them that life never has. They do not just end; they give us what Kermode calls "the sense of an ending" in which, happily or sadly, all the threads of the plot are neatly tied up and everything is explained. Life, to be sure, is not like that. But are we justified in concluding that, since the events of our lives do not fit together as neatly as those of a good story, they occur randomly, simply one after the other? Or that our lives are scrambled messages, a hubbub of static and noise? Because we experience no neat, absolute beginnings, and no ultimately satisfying and all-explanatory endings, is it correct to say that we have none at all?

When we stress the role of narrative structure and narrative coherence in everyday experience we are far from claiming that the latter exhibits the well-roundedness of a satisfying story. What we are asserting is that narrative coherence is the "norm" or the "rule," and that in two senses of these terms: first, in the rather colloquial sense that it is normal, it obtains for the most part. This is simply to admit the banal truth that for most of us, most of the time, things do, after all, make sense, hang together. Despite all the impediments thrown up by our own incapacities and the infuriating obstructions of outside circumstances and other people, we manage. Our lives may not be works of art or things of beauty, but we muddle through nevertheless and actually get things done. What is dreamlike or fanciful is not, as Hayden White claims, to think that our lives have coherence but, on the contrary, to imagine (perhaps because we read too many good stories) that they have none.

But narrative coherence is the norm or rule in the second sense that it is the *standard* which determines even that which deviates from it. When plans go awry, when things fall apart, it is by reference to or by contrast with story-like projections, "scenarios," that they do so. What occurs "randomly" in "mere sequence," "one thing after another," etc., is, in terms of human reality, the *privation* precisely of narrative coherence. In the last chapter we referred to the radio announcer describing a baseball game to his audience as it happens, and compared his activity to that of the mere chronicler of historical events. He simply describes what happens, in the order in which it happens. But the point often made against the idea of a historical chronicle applies here too, namely, that such a person cannot possibly describe *everything* that happens. Rather he anticipates possible stories (different outcomes of the game, for example) and tries to include in his account everything that may be needed by someone who eventually tells the *story* of the game.

So it is with the events and actions of our lives; either they are already embedded in the stories provided by our plans and expectations or, if they are not, we look for and anticipate the stories to which they do, will, or may belong. Narrative coherence is what we find or effect in much of our experience and action, and to the extent that we do not, we aim for it, try to produce it, and try to restore it when it goes missing for whatever reason. It is in this broad sense that we insist that everyday reality is permeated with narrative. In this sense it is anything but an artifact of the *literary* imagination. That the *imagination* is involved there is no doubt, where we are dealing with the future or otherwise with a reality that does not always match our desires and expectations. But, as we have pointed out, this is a practical and not an aesthetic affair, a matter of coping *with* reality, not of providing alternatives to it. It is our *practical* imagination that is involved.

From these considerations it should be clear that the narrative character or structure of our experience and action is not something that simply *va de soi*. Life can be regarded as a constant *effort*, even a struggle, to maintain or restore narrative coherence in the face of an ever-threatening, impending chaos at all levels, from the smallest project to the overall "coherence of life" spoken of by Dilthey.

It should be noted, furthermore, that this struggle takes two distinct forms. One is the more narrowly practical effort of fitting the "pieces," so to speak, into an already determined story we have at our disposal, such as an accepted account of another person's actions or a firm plan or project of our own. Like the observed data in relation to an established scientific theory, individual events and actions may appear anomalous and some effort may be required to see how they fit into the story. In one's own ongoing projects such a problem is repeatedly posed by unexpected circumstances. But, again like a scientific theory, it may be the story itself which is called into question, whether because of the anomalous or for other reasons, and a different and more general "practical" problem is posed. The question then is not: "How does this or that event or action fit into the story?" but rather: "What is the story?"

In the terms of our earlier description, what comes into play here is that reflective, stock-taking temporal grasp by which we call to mind the narrative whole, at whatever level—whether a whole action or a whole life. But it is this whole which may on occasion disintegrate and leave us searching for an alternative. The distinction between these two levels, or registers, at which the problem of narrative coherence presents itself, is something that is not fully appreciated by Schapp, nor perhaps by MacIntyre either. Both use the notion of "story" as a way of accounting for particular actions and events; we know what some human event is, or we understand a person's action, by placing it in the context of a larger story; and this is the way we account for our own action as well, even to ourselves. That is, we account for the parts by appealing to the whole. As we have seen, their theory is thus parallel to the narrativist philosophers of history, who likewise use "story" as an *explanans*. The difference is that Schapp and MacIntyre use it at the level of everyday action and self-awareness, rather than merely to describe the historian's backward look at past events. MacIntyre goes on to see a moral dimension here as well: "I can only answer the question 'What am I to do?' if I can answer the prior question 'Of what story or stories do I find myself a part?' "[33] To be sure, he admits it is not always possible to come up with an answer: "When someone complains—as do some of those who attempt or commit suicide—that his or her life is meaningless, he or she is often and perhaps characteristically complaining that the narrative of their life has become unintelligible to them, that it lacks any point. . . ."[34]

But notice MacIntyre's wording: "*the* narrative has become unintelligible," as if there simply *were* such a narrative, clearly established, and the individual's problem is merely a lack of comprehension. And when he says that the individual must ask "of what story do I *find myself* a part?" (his terms recall Schapp's *ich finde sie vor*) again he suggests that the story is already written, as by some invisible hand, and his problem as a moral agent is simply making out the text.

Would it were so. It is true, of course, that the chaos and confusion of everyday reality can often be countered by adopting a pre-given role. To do simply what others, or society in general, expect of me *in* my role as father, worker, citizen, or whatever, may indeed provide an answer to specific problems of acting in and comprehending my situation. Provided no conflict presents itself among these various possible roles, and that what is expected is immediately clear, such a solution can be a consoling and comforting one in a difficult situation.

What Heidegger and the other existentialists perceive, however, is that there is no necessity for my taking on any such role, no matter how clearly or unproblematically it presents itself to me, and that my taking it on constitutes a choice or possible choice of my own. When I say "possible choice" I am trying to account for the well-known existentialist paradox that not choosing is also a way of choosing. To fall blindly or gradually and unthinkingly into a role or course of action is *de facto* to choose among possible alternatives, even if the

---

33. MacIntyre, p. 201.
34. Ibid., p. 202.

latter do not occur to us consciously. The non-necessity of any given course of action or life is in any case, according to the existentialists, brought home to us not as a conscious awareness of a multiplicity of alternatives, but rather in the occasional bout of *Angst*, vertigo, or nausea. The language of the emotions and even literally of the "guts" is used to indicate that the phenomenon in question is not an intellectual cognition, but it reveals something to us nevertheless. Heidegger compounds the paradox by linking *Angst* to the term "call of conscience" *(Ruf des Gewissens)*, thus combining the immediacy and directness of the feelings with the lofty appeal and force of a moral obligation. Yet the obligation has no particular moral content, and what *Angst* reveals is not any specific mode of life or course of action. It reveals merely the inevitability of self-choice, and the only obligation is to recognize or acknowledge it.

This is to say that the problem of self-authorship cannot be so easily disposed of as MacIntyre may think. But to see this point one must recognize that authenticity for Heidegger is not a question of the content of the narrative or story of one's life, and certainly not a question of its "originality," though this is a common misconstruction. The fault may lie with Sartre's appropriation of the notion which is, admittedly, MacIntyre's real target. But the fault may be partly Heidegger's as well. In *Being and Time*, inauthenticity is presented primarily in terms of idle chatter, "curiosity," "ambiguity," and fragmentation or distraction *(zerstreutsein)*. The notion of authenticy, by contrast, links coherence *(Zusammenhang* or *Zusammenholen)*, wholeness *(Ganzsein)*, and selfhood *(Selbstsein)*, as if these always went together. But, as we have pointed out, the fragmentation of existence can be overcome by the assumption of a rigidly-laid-out social role which is still at the level of *das Man*. That is, inauthenticity can be a matter of either too little or too much coherence. Authenticity is not a matter of this or that social role, or of the fact that it *is* a social and thus traditionally prescribed role; it consists rather in the recognition that, whatever the role, it is I who choose it in the end, one way or another.

The moral aspect of this is that the question of responsibility is not entirely disposed of by reference to the relation between a given conduct and the story which renders it intelligible. For I am responsible not only for the particular action itself but also for the story or stories in which I "find myself" involved.

In the terms of our narrative metaphor, this means that while I may not *write* the story, I *choose* the story in which I am cast as a character, even if the story has already been written and the part I play has been played before.

That this is the more appropriate interpretation of the notion of authenticity becomes clear near the end of *Being and Time* where Heidegger treats the concept of historicity.[35] He takes up such topics as the historical past, the relation between the individual and his generation, and (briefly) the concept of communal existence. But his primary concern is to relate these topics to the individual caught up in the drama of existing authentically. Heidegger wants to show that *Dasein* can inherit and continue a tradition, emulate heroes from the past and be loyal and true to them, even defer to their "authority," even act out a "fate" indicated by one's historical position, and do all this authentically, provided one realizes that all these are chosen, freely taken over in a resolute manner. The difference, in other words, is between the blind and unreflecting follower and the proud and conscious bearer of a tradition.

When one reads *Being and Time* backward through the Sartrean theory it helped influence, one is struck by a sharp contrast when one arrives at this chapter: the authentic self, which had seemed a figure of iconoclastic rebellion from the mass, all erratic originality in rejecting humdrum conformity, now emerges as a stern and proud traditionalist paying homage by obedience to the authority of the past. This is a figure with which MacIntyre should feel comfortable.

Yet the element of authenticity as self-choice remains, and it is hard to see how MacIntyre and others can avoid this aspect. The story which knits together and renders coherent and whole the loose strands of my life, whether it is new and original or has been told and lived many times before me, is ultimately my responsibility, whether I consciously choose it or assume it by default or inadvertence.

4. Being in Time

Let us now try to draw together the loose strands of our own account.

As many other authors have noted (and we have drawn primarily on Husserl, Heidegger, and Dilthey), to be a human individual is to instantiate a special sort of relationship to time. At bottom it is, to be sure, to be always "located" in an ever-changing now and thus to be

---

35. Heidegger, pp. 372–404.

subjected, like everything else, to temporal sequence. But it is much more than this. It is not merely to undergo or endure or suffer this sequence as it comes, one thing at a time. (The view we have criticized of Hayden White, Louis Mink, and others seems to be that since human existence has this sequential character at some level, it is in reality nothing but this). Nor is the individual merely a temporally persisting, underlying substance which supports the changing effects of time as subject to its predicates or properties, like a thing. Nor yet does it merely accumulate "traces" of what goes by, as does a path which bears the footprints of those who have passed. Each of these metaphors for human temporality has been tried, and each contains some truth, but all are inadequate.

Like the Here in relation to the space we perceive, the Now is a vantage point from which we survey the past and the future. To exist humanly is not merely to be in time but to encompass it or "take it in" as our gaze takes in our surroundings. It is not that I exist in the present and then happen to have the capacity to envisage the future and remember the past: rather, human reality *is* a kind of temporal "reach" or "stretch"; what Heidegger calls an *Erstreckung*.[36]

Whatever else it is, to exist as a person is to experience and to act. We have tried in the previous two chapters to show how our temporal "reach" applies itself to and is manifested in the events we experience, in our experiences themselves, and in the acts we perform. It is these that fill in the three-dimensional temporal field and make up its contours and articulations. In Husserlian language, to be conscious temporally is to "constitute" these phenomena from an ever-changing now-perspective through our protentional-retentional grasp. It is by virtue of this grasp that the phenomena have for us the beginnings and endings which make them wholes and set them off from their surroundings, as well as the internal articulation which orders and arranges their parts.

We have seen how this temporal grasp, in varying degrees of complexity and explicitness, makes us both participants in and surveyors of the temporal flow, both characters in and tellers of the stories constituted by it.

This is also true of the story which encompasses all the particular stories in which the individual is involved, that is, the individual's life-story, bounded by birth and death. As with all the particular narratives (experiences and actions) in which we consciously par-

36. Ibid., p. 374.

ticipate, to live this story is to tell it, to ourselves and possibly to others; and in this case to retell it again and again, revising it as we go along. This does not mean that we are *always* telling it; we are actively concerned at any moment now with this, now with that project or experience, large-scale or small. But the whole of life is always there, and concern with its wholeness is an underlying and recurring concern. Birth, childhood, youth, and all the intervening stages up to now (wherever "now" is) are always with each of us, unchanging and familiar, yet always subject to discovery and reinterpretation. And complementing this ever-growing and ever-changing retrospect is the prospect of death, as certain in its inevitability as it is uncertain in its manner and moment of arrival.

The whole question of authorship or authenticity has turned on the fact that at no level, and certainly not at the scale of the life-story itself, is the narrative coherence of events and actions simply a "given" for us. Rather it is a constant task, sometimes a struggle, and when it succeeds it is an achievement. As a struggle it has an adversary, which is, described in the most general way, temporal disorder, confusion, incoherence, chaos. It is the chaos and dissolution represented, paradoxically, by the steady running-off of mere sequence. To experience, to act, to live in the most general sense, is to maintain and if necessary to restore the narrative coherence of time itself, to preserve it against this internal dissolution into its component parts.

What is at stake at the level of events and experiences is the temporal coherence of my surroundings, their "making sense"; at the level of my actions and projects, their completion and success. What is at stake on the plane of "life" is my own coherence as a self, the unity and integrity of my personal identity.

MacIntyre may be right that at this level the self does not author itself, that is, create itself *ex nihilo* out of the chaotic night of temporal incoherence. But the narrative coherence of a life-story is a struggle nonetheless, and a responsibility which no one else can finally lift entirely from the shoulders of the one who lives that life. It is a struggle with two aspects, furthermore, as we have already seen: one to live out or live up to a plan or narrative, large or small, particular or general; the other to contruct or choose that narrative. The first is constrained by the choice of the second. But the second is also faced with constraints. At issue is a whole which comprises future, present, and past. The past (what the existentialists call situation or facticity), while subject to reinterpretation, nevertheless is to some extent fixed: I am provided with certain talents and capacities (or lack of them); I have made certain choices and had certain experiences which make me the person I am, for good or ill.

Seen in this light the problem of the unity of self can be seen as that of bringing together the roles of narrator, character, and audience of which we spoke before. It may be thought that modern philosophy teaches us that there is no "problem" of unity. Hume showed that the self is not to be found *in* experience; Kant agreed and concluded that it must be recognized instead as a condition of the possibility *of* experience. If the unity of consciousness is assured at such a rudimentary level, why should it become an issue, a matter of concern and even anxiety? After all, experiences and actions must already be *mine* if I am to worry how they hang together or make up a coherent life-story.

It is true that such unity exists but it is no more than a necessary condition, never a sufficient one, for selfhood in the broad moral sense of which we have spoken. The question is, what is the arrangement of the multiplicity of experiences and actions that belong to this pregiven self? Mere sequence would be the fragmentation or dissolution of self; it is one of our ways of representing madness. Our lives admit of sometimes more, sometimes less coherence; they hang together reasonably well, but they occasionally tend to fall apart. Coherence seems to be a need imposed on us whether we seek it or not. Things need to make sense. We feel the lack of sense when it goes missing. The unity of self, not as an underlying identity but as a life that hangs together, is not a pregiven condition but an achievement. Some of us succeed, it seems, better than others. None of us succeeds totally. We keep at it. What we are doing is telling and retelling, to ourselves and to others, the story of what we are about and what we are.

We proposed this discussion of temporality as a way of beginning to answer the question: how are we aware of the past, prior to or independently of its becoming thematic in a disciplined inquiry like history? The answer that has emerged is that the past *figures* for us in a temporal configuration (or, better, configurations) that includes present and future. To continue the analogy we have used before, time surrounds us like space, and like space it is inhabited by shapes and forms. The shapes of time are determined by our ongoing experiences and actions in which we project or protend the future and retain the past. But it is not simply *the* past; one feature of this temporal structure is that it is always a *particular* past, the past that forms part of the progress of this particular event I am following (a movement, a game, the illness of a beloved) or of this particular action or project in which I am engaged (serving the tennis ball, doing the shopping, preparing a class, finishing this book). These story-lines may combine to make up larger stories; or, unrelated, they may criss-cross and interrupt one another, sometimes hindering and sometimes contributing to one another's progress. Elements of one may be elements in another (suppose I meet a woman I have admired, or a business client, on the tennis court) by accident or design.

The events I experience have one or another kind of coherence (depending, say, on whether they are natural or human events); the actions in which I engage have another sort of coherence, determined primarily by the means-end relation; my life-story, as the multiplicity of these experiences and actions, has yet another kind of coherence—has, or, as in the other cases as well, *should* have and may fail to have.

The point is that in all these cases we are aware of the past elements of any temporal sequence *as* part of the temporal whole in which they figure. It is true that we may focus with varying degrees of explicitness on particular elements of the past (or present and future, for that matter): reflective stock-taking or deliberation may require precisely that I take apart the sequence and examine its elements in detail. (Where am I? did I add the salt and then stir in the eggs? Can I put it in the oven now?) At such moments we move toward a thematic attention to the past for its own sake. But such attention is still part of the practical narration that constitutes an action as a whole, and the past is still viewed in light of its connection to present and future in an ongoing project. Before the past can become an object of concern in its own right, it is of interest and importance to us because of its relation to present and future.

Reminding ourselves in this way of the practical character of narrative permits us to touch on another issue which will arise when we move on to consider history: what of the *truth* or *truthfulness* of our awareness of the past? We have spoken so much about the *coherence* of a story, particularly of a life story, it may appear to take precedence over truth, or to suggest a suspicious-sounding "coherence theory of truth" in these matters. In order to make my life-story coherent, why not just rewrite (change, rather than reinterpret) the past? Yet we cannot easily convince ourselves that something did or did not happen when we know or sincerely believe the contrary. If certain theories of the unconscious are to be accepted, we often try to deny the past but the truth constrains us nonetheless, taking its toll in indirect ways. In some cases the constraints are strictly practical: just as I cannot pretend to have added salt and expect the soufflé to turn out well, so I cannot pretend to a talent or capacity I never had and then expect to put it to use. Many of our plans go awry (and stories have to be rewritten) because we make mistakes about the past, about what happened and what we have done. The past *does* constrain us; it does have a fixedness that allows reinterpretation only up to certain limits.

The fact remains, however, that it does not confront us, at least in our everyday, "pre-scientific" experience, as something isolated and standing on its own. Fixed as it may be, its role is to figure in a larger arrangement whose future aspect is not fixed but projected or protended. This means that the whole can very well change, and the parts change not in themselves but in their relation to the other parts of the whole they make up.

IV

Temporality and Historicity

1. The Problem

The time has come to move our investigation in a direction which will contribute more directly to the philosophical understanding of history. We began by proposing that the historical past has a certain status prior to and independently of its thematization in historical inquiry. Our proposal was that it has this status by "figuring" in the general structure of human temporality along with the present and the future, and that this structure is a narrative structure. We explored this structure at the level of ordinary experience and action, attempting to display its essential features and in particular to demonstrate its narrative character. We have limited ourselves so far to the temporal unfolding of experience as lived by the individual, and action as performed by the individual. Thus if we have succeeded in shedding light on the pre-thematic past, it is only the individual's past that we have considered; if the past has been shown to figure in an overall temporal structure, this is a structure belonging to the individual's experience, action, and life.

But the historical past is not limited to the individual's past, and may even be thought of as defined, at least in part, as what lies beyond the scope of the individual's memory. Furthermore, historical accounts are arguably not primarily or directly about individual's experiences, actions, and lives, but only incidentally. The historical past, we could say, is the social, not the individual, past. If the foregoing account of time and narrative is going to prove fruitful for our understanding of history, we shall have to find a way of extending

100

it beyond the individual to the larger social context. We must ask whether there is a pre-thematic social past which, by analogy to our account of the individual, is a function of a larger social temporality. And, having done this, we shall have to demonstrate the narrative character of this social temporality. We shall try to show, in fact, in this and the ensuing chapters, that there is a narrative social time which bears the same relation to social experience and social action as does individual temporality to the experiences, actions, and lives of individuals.

But what exactly does it mean, in this context, to move beyond the individual to the social? Obviously we cannot entirely leave the individual behind, since society is composed of individuals. Further, it may be thought that our way of proposing the topic commits us to retaining the individual, and the individual's experience and action, in a central position. It will be recalled that we explained our inquiry initially by invoking Husserl's concept of the life-world and then drawing an analogy from it.[1] Scientific questioning and theorizing about nature, Husserl argued, take place within a human context in which nature is accessible to us prior to and independently of our scientific picture of it. Is it not the case, we asked, that independently of historical inquiry, the historical past is accessible to us in a similarly prescientific and pre-thematic way? And can we not better understand history as a disciplined inquiry, and the historical past *as* portrayed by such inquiry, if we interrogate the pre-theoretical historical world and our pre-theoretical manner of living and acting in that world?

But this phenomenological question, it can be argued, is implicitly still a question *about* the individual. If the historical past is pre-thematically "accessible," it is to the individual that it is thus accessible. It is in his or her experience and action that this past "figures" as background in the context of a three-dimensional temporality. The question can then be restated as: what pre-thematic significance does the specifically historical past have, what role does it play, in the life of the individual?

Seen in these terms, the first step must be that of distinguishing the specifically historical past from the specifically individual past, even though both are to be considered in relation to the individual. Provisionally we can envisage different ways of doing this, some of which have already been mentioned. So far we have discussed the past only

---

1. See Introduction, above.

insofar as it lies within the experience of the individual. What lies outside the individual's memory includes not only what occurred before his birth, and which thus could not possibly be remembered, but also what simply lies outside his direct experience. In another sense of "historical," however, the individual can be witness to and thus personally remember historical events, and of course the individual can also be actively involved in them by performing actions deemed historical. In this second sense, historical actions and events are those of general social significance; and much that lies beyond the scope of one's memory, as well as much within that scope, of course, is certainly not historical in this sense. If the historical past is accordingly not merely the non-personal past, but the socially significant past, then our task of relating it to the individual is more clearly indicated if also more complicated. For the individual's relation to society in general should be elucidated before turning to society's past as an element of that relation. Social existence and social time must be examined in a general way before the social past in particular can emerge and be understood in its proper place.

Can all these questions be addressed in a way which is consistent with, but also appropriately enlarges, the investigations completed so far?

Two of the authors on whom we have drawn in our discussion of temporality, Husserl and Heidegger, have addressed some of these questions from the perspective of their own concerns. At roughly the same time, the late 1920s and early 1930s, the term *Geschichtlichkeit*, historicity, began to figure importantly in their work. It is clear that both were seeking something like a pre-thematic role for history which would both bear on their central philosophical preoccupations and provide for a philosophical understanding of history as a discipline. Since we are at least partially indebted to them for our view of temporality, it will be useful for us to examine briefly and evaluate critically their excursions into the domain of history. We shall see that it is possible to learn a great deal, both positive and negative, from their approaches to the topic and from their conclusions.

2. Husserl and Heidegger on Geschichtlichkeit

If we turn our attention to Husserl first it is for systematic rather than chronological reasons. The chronological picture is in fact somewhat confused. Heidegger's *Being and Time,* in which the concept of historicity figures prominently, was published in 1927, and it was only in the period after 1934, while writing *The Crisis of European Sciences . . .,* that Husserl made historicity a central concern in his own work. Husserl had certainly read Heidegger's successful book, and while he had many criticisms of it, he may in this instance have been influenced by his pupil. A more complicated but probably more accurate picture of the lines of influence here would point to the key role of Dilthey, even though this pilosopher had died in 1912. We have already noted Heidegger's homage to Dilthey at the beginning of his chapter on historicity, a chapter he says is dedicated to furthering the appropriation (Aneignung) of Dilthey's work.[2] It is significant that 1927 was also the year which saw the publication of volume seven of Dilthey's complete works, from which we have quoted extensively, and which contains the author's late manuscripts on the *"Aufbau der geschichtlichen Welt."*[3] Husserl was acquainted with this volume at least through the work of his assistant Ludwig Landgrebe, and of Georg Misch, who published significant studies of Dilthey from a phenomenological perspective in these years.[4] Husserl had always respected Dilthey, in spite of earlier criticisms, and his respect seemed to grow with the years. It may well have been the latter then, rather than Heidegger, who pushed Husserl's thoughts in the direction of history.

It is also possible to argue, as I have done elsewhere, that Husserl arrives at a concern for historicity by following out the implications of his own earlier investigations, and would have been forced to take history seriously quite independently of any outside influence.[5]

But it is not our task here to sort out and answer these questions of influence. We seek simply to understand what these two thinkers have to say about historicity and how it relates to their respective theories of temporality. The first thing to note is that the two approaches differ as their authors' respective phenomenologies differ, a difference we have already encountered. Husserl, we noted, makes "consciousness" the focus of his investigation and takes the rela-

---

2. Heidegger, *Being and Time,* p. 377 (reference is to the German pagination).

3. See Dilthey, *Gesammelte Schriften,* vol. VII, pp. 277–78.

4. L. Landgrebe, "Wilhelm Diltheys Theorie der Geisteswissenschaften" in *Jahrbuch für Philosophie und phänomenologische Forschung* 9 (1928); G. Misch, *Lebensphilosophie und Phänomenologie,* Bonn, 1930.

5. See my *Phenomenology and the Problem of History* (Evanston: Northwestern University Press, 1974), especially chapter II.

tively passive phenomenon of perception as his paradigm. Heidegger begins his phenomenology with our active "dealings" *(Besorgen)* with the world and prefers to speak simply of *Dasein* (human being) rather than consciousness.

Husserl's preoccupation with perception is a manifestation of his close ties to the epistemological focus of modern philosophy, a focus Heidegger explicitly repudiates.[6] While it is true that Husserl rejects a purely passive account of perception, and portrays the latter as an intentional activity of consciousness, perception remains a "passive synthesis," relatively speaking. Husserl is far from describing all consciousness in such passive terms, but for him the paradigm of *active* consciousness is the activity of scientific cognition, that is, the project of arriving at grounded and coherently interconnected judgments about what is. Consciousness is portrayed by Husserl as animated by concern for this sort of theoretical understanding, and as oriented teleologically toward its achievement. If such a consciousness is active rather than passive, it is nevertheless contemplative rather than practical: It seeks to know rather than intervene in or change its world.

It is consciousness conceived in *these* terms whose historicity Husserl gradually discovered in the course of his later years. He had long recognized that his phenomenology must deal with the problem of intersubjectivity, and he finally arrived at a published formulation of this problem in the *Cartesian Meditations* (1929). He recognized there that the individual ego stands in an essential relation to other such egos—essential, that is, in the sense that the community of such egos plays a constitutive role in the very appearance and givenness of the world. This communal interrelation finds its concrete manifestation in particular cultures and societies.[7]

During this same period Husserl developed his "genetic" phenomenology, in which consciousness is portrayed not only as temporal but also as cumulative and developmental in its acquisition of a world and of its knowledge of the world. It is in this context that Husserl writes the sentence that we quoted earlier, that "the ego constitutes itself for itself, so to speak, in the unity of a *Geschichte.*"[8]

These themes were not drawn together, however, until the period

6. Heidegger, pp. 59–62.
7. Husserl, *Cartesian Meditations*, pp. 132–33.
8. Ibid., p. 75. See above, chapter III, p. 74.

of *The Crisis*. . . . Prior to this, Husserl seemed to believe that the individual consciousness, in its pursuit of theoretical understanding, could simply transcend its concrete social situation and go directly to the truth. What he finally saw in the 1930s was that the very pursuit of theoretical truth is conditioned and determined by history. Husserl's recognition of this is manifested in his famous treatment, in *The Crisis* and related texts, of the natural sciences, of mathematics (geometry in particular), and finally of philosophy itself. Husserl saw that even if it is the nature of consciousness to engage in the pursuit of truth, the individual always inherits this pursuit as an ongoing activity of the society in which he or she takes it up. The incipient scientist also builds on the results already obtained by others. Thus a cognitive endeavor such as science, while it is pursued by individuals, owes its undertaking in each case, as well as its capacity to progress, to the social context in which it exists. This is no less true of philosophy than of the other disciplines.[9]

While the cognitive life of the individual owes its birth to the social context, and depends on the same context for its success, there is a negative side to this dependence. For the concepts and methods taken over from the tradition can equally function as prejudices which skew the individual's perspective on his subject matter, leading him to grasp it and understand it in a one-sided way and overlook other aspects which make up the phenomenon in its fullness. This can happen in any field, where theoretical progress often requires not building on but criticizing and rejecting what is handed down. This is what has happened in philosophy, which has taken over from modern science its conception of the world and then failed to understand subjectivity because it has tried to explain it causally as an element within that world. Even Kant, who recognizes the constitutive role of subjectivity, still conceives of the latter purely in relation to a scientifically construed world. Hence the need for a return to the life-world in which subjectivity has its home prior to science and in which the activity of science, and every other cognitive activity including ultimately philosophy, has its point of departure.[10] While the sciences do not need to comprehend themselves philosophically in order to succeed at their task, it is philosophy's

---

9. See Husserl, *The Crisis*. . . , especially appendix six (pp. 353–78) on the "Origin of Geometry."

10. Ibid., pp. 103–189.

task to understand them and this means tracing them back to their origins. But philosphy must likewise comprehend itself, and must accordingly circle back upon its own origins in the life-world.

It turns out that these developments engender considerable difficulty for Husserl's whole philosophical program, but this need not detain us here.[11] Of interest to us for now is solely the concept of historicity itself. What we have seen is that this concept arises for Husserl as a feature of the individual consciousness engaged in a cognitive project. Such a consciousness does not stand passively before a pregiven world and then undertake on its own a theoretical cognition of that world. For any given individual, the enterprise of cognition exists as a project before he or she takes it up.

Would not the first such individual be an exception? If Husserl does think a "first" such individual conceivable, his fleeting reference, for example, to "some undiscoverable Thales of geometry,"[12] suggests he is at a loss how to treat such a figure. Though he mentions the "origin" of geometry, what he really describes is the situation in which geometry already exists, as a precondition for the individual's engaging in it.

The engagement of the individual in the project thus presupposes his prior situation in the community and the existence of a tradition of inquiry in that community. In taking up the traditional project the individual takes over its questions, goals, concepts, and methods. While the ideal pursuit of a discipline would simply build on the work of predecessors and continue in cumulative and additive fashion, in fact mistakes are made and past work needs to be criticized and undone. This regression involves not only providing new, corrected answers to old questions but, just as often, attacking the old questions and posing new ones in their place.

In sum, the individual's engagement in the ongoing tradition of a socially constituted endeavor is essential to what individual consciousness is about, and its relation to that tradition affects everything it does: certainly its active pursuit of truth but also, at least possibly, even its more passive perception of the world.

We have already had occasion, in chapter III, to refer briefly to Heidegger's chapter on historicity and its relation to the problem of authenticity.[13] We must examine it now with more specific reference

---

11. These difficulties are explored in my *Phenomenology and the Problem of History*.

12. Husserl, *The Crisis*, p. 369.

13. Chapter III, pp. 94–95 above.

to how it moves beyond individual to social experience and social temporality.

In describing authentic existence Heidegger has stressed the future and the prospect of death. As if to compensate for this emphasis on the individual's destiny, he introduces his chapter on historicity by turning to the individual's birth and origins. It is here that he takes up Dilthey's expression *Zusammenhang des Lebens* and invokes again the "wholeness" of Dasein's being, speaking now of a "reach" encompassing birth and death. Dasein *is* this reach, at least if it is authentic: it is the temporal self-integration of itself. Heidegger calls this its *Geschehen*, the term which lies behind *Geschichte* and *Geschichtlichkeit*.[14]

Thus we see the context in which Heidegger's turn to history occurs. If Husserl's focus is the individual consciousness pursuing theoretical understanding, Heidegger's is the individual Dasein pursuing its pretheoretical self-understanding in the struggle for authentic or temporally integrated existence. Dasein is historical because it is temporal in this sense, not temporal because it is "in history," he says.[15] That is, its connection to the social past arises as a function of the temporality of its own existence.

How is this so? That Dasein is social, in the sense that *Mitsein* (being with others) is constitutive of its being, has already been affirmed by Heidegger in an earlier section.[16] Social existence is part of Dasein's "thrownness," its factual embeddedness in a particular situation not of its choosing. While social existence had been treated primarily as the medium of inauthentic existence (that is, the average and impersonal *das Man*, the interchangeable everyone and no one) here it is seen as offering models of authentic existence. My fellows and predecessors constitute a heritage which I can take over. As we saw in the previous chapter, the individual's connection to the heritage may be automatic and unthinking, but it can also be authentic and resolute.[17] I can live out my fate authentically, not as a blind, predetermined course of life but as a mode of existence freely and consciously chosen. Authentic existence can take the form of repetition *(Wiederholung)* which is the explicit appropriation of past possibilities.[18] In other words, I can have heros, emulate them, and be loyal to their memory—but it is I who choose them.

---

14. Heidegger, p. 375.
15. Ibid., p. 376.
16. Ibid., pp. 117–25.
17. Ibid., p. 384.
18. Ibid., p. 385.

How does all this relate to history as such? Heidegger clearly thinks that his conception of historicity has implications for history as a discipline. These derive primarily from the fact that both subject and object of historical research are to be conceived in the terms of the analysis of Dasein. But seeking and acquiring knowledge of the past is only one way, and by no means the only way, of *being* historical in Heidegger's sense. If we try to summarize what Heidegger actually means by historicity, what is perhaps hardest to see is just how it constitutes a link between the individual and the social *past*. If *knowledge* is not the original link to the past, what is?

Much of what Heidegger says in his chapter on historicity can be looked at simply as a reformulation of his general theory of temporality as the sense of Dasein's being. When he speaks of *Geschehen* ("happening") as lying at the root of historicity, he defines this in terms of the underlying integration that links past, present, and future for the individual. It is this underlying integration, rather than an external connection linking separate moments spread out over time, which establishes the *Zusammenhang des Lebens* and constitutes an authentic existence. Nor is this "resoluteness" a momentary "resolution." It is lived rather as a thoroughgoing constancy (*Ständigkeit*) in the sense of a loyalty to one's own self.[19] It is this, rather than the continuity of a substance persisting through time, which makes up the true unity of the self. Only the fragmentation of inauthentic existence cuts off the dimensions of time from each other, splinters the temporal into a sequence of moments and calls forth an act of gathering together or restoration (*Zusammenholen*).[20] Only in inauthentic existence are we cut off from the past so that we have to reestablish our links with it.

But all this seems only to concern the past, present, and future of one's own life—the stretch between one's own birth and death. It is true that Heidegger draws, as we have seen, on his earlier theory of *Mitsein*, suggesting that the lives of others provide models for the factual content of our authentic existence. Thus the social dimension of Dasein appears as quite important to its authenticity, and Heidegger introduces into his discussion a conception of the relation between the self and others which is one of solidarity, loyalty, and emulation. To the integration of past with present Heidegger thus adds the integration of self with others in his discussion of histor-

---

19. Ibid., pp. 390–91.
20. Ibid., p. 390.

icity. Thus the charge that Heidegger never gets beyond the isolation of the individual before his own death is incorrect, as David Hoy has shown.[21] There is no doubt that Heidegger is here compensating for his tendency to link the social with the inauthentic.

But to what extent does he balance his emphasis on the future by displaying the role of the past? If others are important, why specifically *past* others? The kind of temporal integration that Heidegger envisions for the individual seems not to extend in any necessary way beyond the bounds of the individual's life. If others are important, why will contemporaries not suffice?

The only hints toward an answer to this question are provided when Heidegger begins his chapter by linking *birth* to death and when he refers briefly to the concept of "generations."[22] To be born is to have parents, and to belong to a "generation" is to stand in relation to previous (and subsequent) generations. Though he does not say it, Heidegger apparently conceives the paradigm cases of those models for our "repetition" to be our parents. Heidegger considers essential here not the biological sense of the sequence of generations, but the fact that traditions, styles of life, ideals, and values are not just handed *over* to us by others but are first of all handed *down* by our elders when we are young. Heidegger leaves implicit the idea that social existence is generational, that a family persists through time in a way that differs not only from the persistence of a thing but also from the temporal integrity of an individual. It might be thought that Heidegger has touched on only half the problem, since the individual, while linked to his elders, must also free himself from them in sometimes violent and rebellious ways. But Heidegger does admit briefly, in somewhat more genteel terms, that the "repeating" relation to the past may involve a rejoinder *(erwidern)* to it and even a disavowal *(Wideruf)* of it.[23]

Hence it seems clear that Heidegger has something like the parent-child relation in mind. It is true that the elder-younger relationship, which can crucially involve the dialectic of emulation and rebellion, can be replicated in other contexts than the family. For example, in the context which Heidegger knew well, the German academic community, the professor who supervises a doctoral thesis is called the

21. David Couzens Hoy, "History, Historicity and Historiography in *Being and Time*" in *Heidegger and Modern Philosophy,* ed. Michael Murray (New Haven: Yale University Press, 1978), pp. 339–40.
22. Heidegger, pp. 384–85.
23. Ibid., p. 386.

Doktorvater and eminent figures have tended to establish dynastic empires of their students, for whom they become venerated and protective figures. But there are significant instances of youthful rebellion as well, as exemplified precisely in the relationship between Husserl and Heidegger. Academic colleagues, of course, are engaged in a common cognitive endeavor, so we find ourselves here in the realm of the historicity described by Husserl. Heidegger, by contrast, seems to be saying that the relationship of older to younger generations needs no particular project in order to exist—no project except living itself, which is the only purpose, it could be argued, of the family. Heidegger's treatment suggests that like Freud he believes the family relationship to be primary and that later, quasi-generational relationships in specific contexts are replicas and reenactments of the primal family drama.

3. Historicity and Narrative

These and other differences between the two notions of historicity must not hide from us the deep similarities. It is time now to emphasize these in order to arrive if we can at a unified notion of historicity. We shall see that there is such a unified notion and that it can be articulated in terms of the narrative character of human time.

For all the differences we have discovered between the theories of Husserl and Heidegger, at bottom both represent the individual in terms of understanding, indeed, a quest or struggle for understanding. One can also speak of a quest for truth. If Husserl's paradigm is the search for theoretical understanding, and Heidegger's the individual's pre-theoretical understanding of his or her own being, both represent ongoing endeavors in which the individual is engaged. And for both, such an endeavor is obviously constitutive of or essential to what the individual *is:* individual consciousness, individual Dasein.

To speak of an endeavor is to speak of a process ongoing in time, and we have already seen how each of these thinkers deals with human temporality. The cognitive quest would be an instance for Husserl of the protentive-retentive consciousness of time, though it is properly characterized as an activity rather than as the sort of passive experience Husserl uses in his discussion of time. This means that, as we have seen, its temporal unfolding would be organized for the individual as a means-end structure and a temporal span involving a retained beginning and a projected end, corresponding to the individual's undertaking the project and his accomplishing his goal or goals. Internally the project would be articulated into steps and stages, interlocking subordinate means-end structures and the like.

Dasein's self-understanding is likewise laid out in temporal terms according to Heidegger, as we have seen. The projective character manifested in particular projects (including the kind of project Husserl envisaged) outlines a future which in turn organizes the present world into interlocking complexes of significance, all accomplished on the background of Dasein's thrownness or facticity, that is, its finding itself in a particular situation. This projective structure, which accomplishes projects and organizes the world, is actually the self-projection of Dasein onto time which constitutes its understanding of its own being. Heidegger is consistent in his emphasis on the active: Dasein's activity is ultimately its structuring of itself and this, rather than any passive contemplation, is its way of understanding its own being.

We have seen how this projective-retrospective structure is a narrative structure insofar as it involves the reflective and deliberative stock-taking we have associated with the term *Besinnung*. This is easiest to see at work in a cognitive endeavor of the sort that serves as Husserl's paradigm. Even though not every cognitive project involves the peculiar step-wise progression we find in a deductive system, we can see how frequent in any such project is the need to assure oneself of what has been accomplished and what yet needs to be done. To carry out such a complex project requires telling its story to oneself, and the action is intertwined with the telling.

Heidegger's conception of self-understanding is situated at the level of the life-story, as discussed in the last chapter, and it too involves, in its own way, the prospective-retrospective concern for the whole. We have seen how this can be conceived as a special sort of relationship between authorship (or narratorship) and the course of life.

What, now, do the two discussions of historicity add to this picture? First, as we saw, both thinkers root the individual to an intersubjective context. Both discussions of historicity presuppose that the relation with others is somehow essential to the individual's being. There are doubtless many aspects of this relation, but one has already turned up in our discussion of the narrative character of human temporality. This is the idea that narrative involves an interplay of three points of view, not only those of character and storyteller but also that of audience. We have seen that this last point of view is present even in the individual's organization of his or her experience, action, and life. But we saw that this audience's point of view, and the interrelation it involves, is always somehow quasi-intersubjective and reflects or corresponds to the genuinely intersubjective milieu of story-telling. This means that at the level of everyday experience and action, the narrative which organizes the temporal flow often addresses itself to others and often seems to require that address.

Thus concretely, when we recount to others what we are living through and what we are doing, such recounting, rather than the adventitious communication of an already prepared and clearly formulated message, is actually constitutive of the content of what is said, and through it constitutive of the temporal organization itself. Most people have had the experience that they do not quite know what they mean or intend until they try to communicate it to others. The content is all the more affected, of course, when the speaker is met by rejoinders, questions, and criticisms. Thus telling the story of my action or experience to others can organize or reorganize it for me; telling the story of my life can serve to make a sense of it I have not been aware of before.

The social connection among persons, conceived in this way, is one of reciprocal communicative roles in the constitution of experiences, actions, and lives. Others are encountered by me, not only as audiences or sounding-boards for the sense-constitution of my own ongoing experiences and projects, but as engaged in their own narratives as agents and story-tellers, narratives to whose construction I may contribute in my role as audience and possibly critic. This is at least one way to conceive of the social horizon of the individual's existence.

Now the concept of historicity, as put forward by Husserl and Heidegger, adds a crucial element to this picture. It affirms that my connection with the actions and experiences of others can take a special form, apart from the relation of reciprocal narration, a form we can describe as the relation of predecessors and successors. What is indicated is a priority, not only of time but also of accomplishment. In the case of the ongoing scientific project I take up the work already accomplished by others. The end of another's work becomes the beginning of my own. The other need not have finished his or her work, of course, but some conclusion has been reached which serves as my starting point. This is true whether the other's result can be used as a basis for my own, and built upon, or whether I must begin by undoing his or her work and starting over. In either case the work of others, rather than simply existing alongside my own, becomes its background and prior condition.

Heidegger seems to suggest something similar when it comes to arriving at an authentic mode of existence. Others can serve as models because their lives already constitute an accomplishment while my own is still in question. To be sure, everyone's life, at whatever age, is constantly "in question" in Heidegger's sense, and it may be one of the illusions of youth that the lives of the old are accomplished, just as it may be an illusion on the negative side that they are set in their ways. But the illusion, if it is that, may nevertheless be important in these cases. The point is not that others are "older" as such but that their life (or work) represents a background for living (or work) that I have yet to do.

Thus the social world is not composed simply, as A. Schutz seems to suggest in his *Phenomenology of the Social World*, of my "contemporaries," whose experiences overlap in time with mine, together with a rank of "predecessors" who lived before me.[24] Rather, those with whom I have direct contact in life and work are differentiated in a way which indeed often corresponds to the older-younger distinction but is more accurately characterized as a relation of staggered and overlapping narratives. A significant class of my fellows is made up of those who, in different respects, are predecessors or members of a prior generation. Those around me are at different stages on their way, and some of them offer to me the possibility of my inheriting or taking on and continuing what they have done.

But they in turn stand in a similar relation to those before them. Thus my social existence not only puts me in contact with a co-existing multiplicity of contemporaries; it connects me with a peculiar form of temporal continuity, which we can call the relay-form or handing-down form, which runs from predecessors to successors. This sequence extends beyond the boundaries of my life, both into the past before my birth and into the future after my death.

It must be emphasized that this account of historicity reveals what we have been looking for all along: a *pre-thematic* role for the social past in the individual's experience and action. We place the emphasis here on the pre-thematic; we are not claiming, nor do Husserl and

24. Schutz, *The Phenomenology of the Social World*, p. 208. Schutz in later works introduces some of the distinctions I make here. See A. Schutz and Thomas Luckmann, *The Structures of the Life-World* (Evanston: Northwestern University Press, 1973), p. 91.

Heidegger apparently assert, that an explicit preoccupation with or investigation of one's social past is a necessary condition of the on-going present of individual temporality. For the most part it constitutes merely an implicit horizon or background for the present. It will be remembered that in many cases of action and experience, the merely personal past has this same pre-thematic status. But just as the latter occasionally requires a *Besinnung* and a narrative recounting in order to maintain or reconstitute itself, so the social past may be called up explicitly as part of a larger picture into which present concerns and activities can be placed, and in terms of which they are understood. But even this does not constitute a thematic interest or focus on the past, or any particular part of it, for its own sake. The past is involved only in so far as it figures in the larger context which includes present and future.

A good illustration of this is the habitual backward reference that can be found in the professional journals of practically every discipline from philosophy to physics. The author of an article sets out to answer a particular problem, to be sure. But this problem is not snatched out of the air. It is taken up because the new results of colleagues X and Y have made its solution pressing, or because it has repeatedly resisted solution by others, or because it has been wrongly or only partially solved. A brief history of the problem and its attempted solution is presented before the author gets down to the business of solving it himself. (See the beginning of this study for an example of this pattern.) Naturally such a capsule history need not span great lengths of time or many generations of researchers. Nor must the colleagues referred to be literally older. But within the story of the problem at hand they are predecessors; their prior work is cited in explanation and justification of the work to be done.

If an activity such as inquiry needs to be told in order to be performed, the telling thus takes its author beyond the account of his own activity (the story of his project's initiation, prosecution, and conclusion) to include the prior and presupposed work of others. And if, in the larger context envisaged by Heidegger, one's life likewise needs to be told in order to be lived, what life story does not include a reference to those who went before?

What all this shows is that for the individual, his or her own narrative, whether of work or other particular projects or of life, exists within a larger temporal context which is itself narrative in character and which involves other people in a predecessor-successor relation. The importance of configuration for narrative obtains here as well: just as any part of a story acquires its significance from the narrative whole to which it belongs, so any particular story depends for its sense on the larger narrative context of which it is a part. Can this larger context be considered a larger story, or merely a succession of stories? We shall return presently to the notion of a larger story, but we can note for now that even if we can only speak of a plurality of stories, it is no "mere" or unrelated succession that they make up. They are linked in the peculiar relay-form, as we have seen, and their content is joined by the common concerns and interactions of the individuals involved.

Such a narrative context, connecting the individual with a larger social past, can be seen as contributing essentially to the sense, for the individual, not only of what he or she is doing but even more strongly of what the individual is. Husserl conceives of the ego as constituting itself in the unity of a *Geschichte*. This term can be translated as "story," as we saw, and used to refer to the narrative unity of the individual's own stream of consciousness. But to the extent that the paradigm of consciousness is the quest for theoretical understanding, and this personal "story" is linked to the "history" of that quest, the individual understands himself as *being* essentially the inheritor and continuer of a tradition. Especially in *The Crisis*, this is the individual's "self-constitution."

Heidegger does not use the term self-constitution, but he does view selfhood as an achievement, and it is clear that self-interpretation and self-understanding are its means. But the resolute, authentic self must in each case have some concrete content. The chapter on historicity tells us that this content is derived from our connection with those who go before us. Thus the individual's concrete sense of self, which will presumably be different for each individual, is nevertheless essentially linked to the social past.

We can sum up the notion of historicity by saying that what the individual *is* is thus a function of his or her place in a historical setting. This is not a "straightforward" affirmation of the sort that might be made by a historical determinist, who calls the individual a "product" of history or the inevitable result of historical forces. Instead it is a phenomenological assertion about what the individual is "for himself." It means that the individual's self-understanding of himself passes through history. There are varying degrees of explicitness to this understanding, of course. At the limit the historical past is operative only in the manner of a vague horizon for the individual; at the other extreme would perhaps be that "proud traditionalist" we mentioned earlier, who seems at times to emerge from Heidegger's sometimes confusing portrait of the authentic individual.[25] In either case the temporal "grasp" or "reach" that constitutes the individual's narrative self-understanding reaches back to include a continuum of predecessors in its scope. These make up a tradition, since their essential function is to pass along or hand down what the individual takes up in the way of projects and ways of existing.

4. A New Problem

Having outlined the notion of historicity derived from Husserl and Heidegger and having related it to our conception of temporality and narrative, we must now turn a critical and evaluative gaze upon this notion. We must ask ourselves just how much it accomplishes, and what it may overlook, in our attempt to understand history.

The introduction of historicity into the thought of these philosophers stems from the recognition that to understand what the individual is we must move beyond the individual to the social and in particular to the social past. Both accounts thus begin with the individual. But it can be argued that they also retain throughout the individual's perspective and end with the individual as well. Does this permit them a sufficient understanding of history itself as a phenomenon?

What Husserl and Heidegger ask is: to what extent and how is the social past implicated in what the individual does and is? In our terms this means: to what extent does the story of my action or my life require reference to the prior actions or lives of others? In answering this question we learn something about the way individuals interact, and we discover a peculiar form of temporality (what we called the relay-form) which governs the interconnected actions and lives of different individuals. But what we learn is still something *about* particular actions and individual lives, namely that the social and historical past is somehow constitutive of them.

But is *history* about particular actions and individual lives? Historians often write about them, and we certainly think of the historical process as being made up in some sense of the things that individuals do. Yet we also think of history as being properly concerned not primarily with individuals but with groups: peoples, nations,

---

25. See chapter III, p. 94 above.

classes, etc. And historians tend to deal with individual actions and lives only to the extent that these tell us something about the groups which such actions affect and to which the individuals belong. If we identify the historical process with what has generally interested historians, then it consists of the events, activities, and careers of groups, spread out over time.

At the beginning of this chapter we raised the question of how to move from individual temporality and the individual past to the historical. We spoke of moving beyond the individual to the social past. Certainly the notion of historicity succeeds in doing this, since its proponents recognize the intersubjective character of human existence and describe a peculiarly intersubjective mode of temporal development. But to what extent do they touch on social *entities* such as groups and peoples which are at the heart of historical accounts and presumably of the historical process itself? Have they a place for such entities? Do their accounts *leave* a place for such entities? To the extent that our account so far has dealt with the social, everything it says could be conceived in terms of one-to-one relationships between persons; that is, both the role of audience to a particular narrative, and predecessor to a course of action or an individual life, can be fulfilled by individuals. Thus everything so far which goes beyond the individual is either a simultaneity of such relationships or a series of them spread out over time.

An account which does justice to what is genuinely historical, by contrast, would speak of what is proper to groups as such. And if we wish to keep our focus on the connection between time and narrative in relation to history, something needs to be said about the temporality of groups, and about the manner in which narrative organization can be said to characterize that temporality. Clearly the notion of historicity, as discussed so far, does not give us this, and it is this we must seek here.

But do the terms of our discussion so far really permit us to do this? Indeed, does such a project even make sense? It could be argued that Husserl's and Heidegger's concerns remain ultimately with the individual, not merely because that is where their interest lies but because what they say is made possible by a method (the phenomenological) that is linked in principle to individual experience. And could not the same be said of our own whole approach, which is derived not so much from what Husserl, Heidegger, and others said, as from their method?

We have insisted throughout that ours is a "first-person" account.

Following the example of Husserl and other modern philosophers we have used the first-person "I" and spoken of "my" experience, "my" action, etc. It is "for 'me,'" that is, from the perspective of the experiencing subject or agent, that time has the prospective-retrospective structure we have described. And it is the individual who plays the narrator-character-audience roles in our narrative interpretation of temporality and in our discussion of the problem of authorship. It is thus altogether consistent that history as the social past should appear, if at all, on the horizon of the individual's experience. As we saw, it is for the individual that history has the "pre-thematic" status we have sought all along. Indeed it is hard to see how the notion of the pre-thematic could have any meaning except in relation to what is thematic *for* the individual subject.

To be sure, such a first-person account, though it may also be termed "subjective," is not about the contents of an isolated, individual soul. Phenomenologists rightly insist that the *intentionality* they ascribe to consciousness makes it an opening onto a world and that phenomenology treats of the world as much as of consciousness. This means that it should be able to enlighten us about any sort of entity of which the individual could possibly have consciousness.

If this is so, can it not then enlighten us about entities such as social groups? Not doubt it can, but it seems to me that its method would still unacceptably limit its options in dealing with this topic. Groups would have to be discussed with respect to their being *for* the conscious individual subject. This does not mean, of course, that they could be treated only as "objects" in the narrow sense. Social groups are thematic objects of observation and investigation for sociologists and anthropologists, who aspire to a detached and "objective" stance. But if we sought a pre-thematic awareness, a more flexible phenomenological approach would ask how such groups figure in the world of any individual, whether in themselves or functioning as the horizon or background for experience and action which is explicitly directed somewhere else.

Interesting as such an investigation might prove, it can still be argued that it would tell us about the existence and the temporality of social groups only in a very *indirect* way. The real focus of such an inquiry would still be the individual and the individual's world.

On the other hand, any *direct* approach to the nature of social groups, one which would consider them *apart* from their status *for* the individual, would have to abandon the phenomenological approach we have used so far. But to abandon that approach, it seems, is to give up the chance of applying to social existence as such any of the descriptions of temporality and narrative that have emerged from our earlier investigations. For these are, as we have seen, linked to the first-person account. Thus, whether phenomenological or not, any approach to the group seems necessarily to be a *third*-person account; the group is approached as an *it* either as an object of investigation or in its relation to a subject.

Is there any way to escape this consequence? We might begin by taking a second look at a possible phenomenological approach to groups. We said such entities would have to be considered as objects *for* the individual or at best as something which figured in the world *of* the individual. Thus an I-it relation would seem to be the starting point of such an investigation. But we could invoke Buber's famous distinction between I-it and I-thou; we have already made use of this distinction in effect in our discussion of intersubjectivity and its role in historicity. Since groups are composed of individual persons, would the I-thou relation not be a more appropriate starting point than the I-it? That is, should such a phenomenology not approach groups via the *second* rather than the *third* person?

The obvious objection to this is that while groups are composed of individuals they are not themselves individual persons but collections of them. At the same time groups are individual entities, distinct from one another, and it does not seem inappropriate to ask, phenomenologically (returning to the first-person perspective), whether "my" relation to a group is less *like* my relation to a thing than it is *like* my relation to another person. A group, for example, like a person, is something I can not only experience and observe but also communicate and interact with. Here it may be thought that the second person plural (I-you) rather than the second person singular (I-thou) is at issue. Nevertheless groups do become personified and we deal with them and speak of them in many of the same ways in which we deal with and speak about individuals. We communicate with companies and institutions. We are held responsible for our conduct by the state, which can accuse us of violating its law. We think of the state and of companies and institutions, as performing actions for which we hold each of *them* responsible. Parliaments debate and make decisions, nations declare war on others, classes revolt, etc.

About such personifications of groups one can of course always ask if they are not merely *façons de parler*. In fact we communicate not with groups but with their representatives, and the actions and other personal traits we attribute to groups could be said to reduce ultimately to those of the persons that make them up. A phenomenologist may reply that his concern is not ontological, that is, that he is interested not in whether groups really *are* large-scale persons but in the fact that they appear so, that we refer to them and treat them as such.

It might be thought that we should favor such an approach because it permits in effect a subjectivization of groups. By treating the social group as an analogue of a person we might be able to find in it a temporality or organization of experience and action at least similar to what we discovered "from the inside" in the individual. The trouble is that in adopting a quasi-second-person approach to the group, the subject of the phenomenological first-person account is not really viewing the group from the inside at all but again stands over against it. Though it is treated as a quasi-person rather than a thing, the group is still interrogated as something (or someone) that exists *for* me or figures somehow in *my* world.

Obviously we are in search of an approach to the social group which will permit something like a view "from the inside." But the answer should be obvious! I am precisely inside a group by being a member of it. What is clearly needed is an analysis of the group from the point of view of membership or participation in it. The interesting thing is that such an analysis need not even give up the "first person" perspective: in calling on these grammatical categories we have almost forgotten that the first person (like the second and the third) can be plural as well as singular. It is often in using the pronoun "we" that each of us as an individual expresses his or her membership in some particular group. It is in each case *I* who *say* "we." When this happens, a new subject emerges for the experiences and actions in which I am engaged. What our earlier analysis of action and experience did not take into account was that my being engaged in an action or experience does not necessarily make it merely *my* action or experience; that is, it does not necessarily make *me* the sole or even the proper subject of it.

On the other hand, a we-subject cannot be considered in abstraction from the individuals that make it up. Thus this approach meets one desideratum that we mentioned earlier: that the individual's role not be forgotten. We also complained about discussions of social groups which are really discussions about the individual. Analysis of the *we*, of the various circumstances in which individuals say "we," for example, would be a discussion of individuals which is really a discussion about the group.

But this signals that a certain methodological shift is required if the group as *we* is to come into our view. Clearly the phenomenological perspective, that of the first person singular which views everything as it exists *for* the individual or figures in the individual's world, obscures one of the distinctive characteristics of the group, which is precisely that the individual can be a member of it. As a conscious subject I am not a "member" of the things I see or use, or of the other persons I encounter, or of my world. All these leave me, as it were, intact as a subject and as an individual. But as one who participates in a group and says "we," my individuality defers to or effaces itself before a subject larger than itself. Has phenomenology a place for this? Husserl often says that the overall matrix for phenomenological analysis is the complex *ego-cogito-cogitatum*. Intersubjectivity enters the picture for him only by raising the problems of the *cogitatum cogitans*. This may be too rigid a framework for some of Husserl's successors, such as Heidegger or Merleau-Ponty. But do any of them make room for a *cogitamus*?

We decided that in order to do justice to the historical we had to say more about the temporal existence of groups. We now see that in order to do this we must not so much change the object of our analysis as change the subject (as it were) from singular to plural, from *I* to *we*. But in order to do this in turn we much raise certain methodological questions about how this subject is to be approached. It is to these questions that we turn in the next chapter.

V

From I to We

1. In Search of the Trans-Individual Subject

How do we initiate an investigation of social reality, centered on the group, whose point of departure is neither the phenomenological *I* nor the straightforward treatment of an *it*, an item in the world? This is the question which arose in the last chapter as we surveyed some of the defects of the concept of historicity. What we proposed was an investigation which is still first person but is plural; that is, we plan to explore what is involved in the phenomenon often expressed when we use the term "we." Let us take a preliminary look at some of the problems involved.

We are proposing to treat the group not as object but as subject. Does this mean we are treating groups as analogues of persons? As we pointed out, groups often do take on subjective or personal characteristics for us. In ordinary speech and in many forms of political and journalistic discourse, we sometimes ascribe to groups such thing as actions, attitudes, traits of character, even emotions, which seem properly to apply to individual persons. Nations act, classes feel outrage, families mourn, etc. What is the status of such talk? Do groups as such have thoughts and intentions, and act according to them, as persons do? Do they have feelings and experiences? Are some groups just persons "writ large"? Such notions have been taken seriously by thinkers of the past, such as Plato, Rousseau, and Hegel. But most theorists today find them uncongenial and far-fetched.

Even those who argue for "holism" over "individualism" in the current methodological debates about social science and history are far from approving any personification of social groups.[1] The ques-

---

1. See the collection *Modes of Individualism and Collectivism*, ed. John O'Neill

tion in these debates is whether social reality can be accounted for solely by reference to facts about individuals. Individualists hold that since societies are ultimately composed of individuals, any complete explanation of social events would have to trace them to the behavior of those constituent parts. Holists argue that society consists not merely of individuals but also of the relations among them (institutional and economic relations, for example) and that the "behavior" of individuals cannot even be understood apart from those relations. Thus any description of how individuals act will presuppose certain "societal facts," to use Mandelbaum's term.[2]

In these debates it is the individualists who generally want to hold on to mental or intentional terms, and who see in holism the threat of a mechanistic and deterministic explanation which reduces individuals to mere cogs in a social machine. They tend to be advocates of *Verstehen* rather than *Erklären* when it comes to dealing with human events; they prefer a Collingwoodian "reenactment" which looks for the reasons *why* people act rather than laws which would link their behavior causally to its antecedents. And it is individuals whose actions we understand in this way, either *qua* individuals or as Weberian ideal types. We can do this because we are individuals ourselves, can observe other individuals directly, and are capable of imagining ourselves in other situations.

These theorists are thus the champions of liberal individualism against what they see as social engineering. None of them wants to take the mentalistic and voluntaristic properties of individuals and apply them to societies conceived as macropersons. Indeed, they might think such an application even more dangerous to individuality than they do social mechanism. The choice and freedom of the individual person might seem even more threatened if the latter is conceived as the tool of an over-arching personality carrying out its own designs.

For their part the holists, though not always the determinists or mechanists portrayed by some of their opponents, have no interest in this version of holism. Of the notion of a "group mind" Ernest Gellner says: "I take it no one is advocating this seriously."[3] Anthony Quinton, in arguing for a form of holism (or at least against individualism), asserts without argument that attributing mental predicates to

---

(London: Heinemann, 1973); see also W. H. Dray, *Perspectives on History* (London: Routledge & Kegan Paul, 1980), pp. 47–66.

2. O'Neill, ed., pp. 221–34.
3. "Explanation in History," ibid., p. 251.

a group is "plainly metaphorical" and "always an indirect way of ascribing such predicates to its members."[4] The implication is that ways can always be found of translating such attributions into statements about individuals.

There are no doubt many reasons why the idea of a communal subject is not taken seriously today. One of them, however, is surely the resolutely third-person perspective from which the problem of social reality is viewed. Discussions such as the debate between individualists and holists are primarily epistemological and methodological discussions about how society can be known scientifically. They often turn on questions of what can be directly observed: individual behavior can be, some say, but institutional and economic relations cannot. The argument also turns often on basic ontological commitments about the nature of society: it *is* composed of individuals and their behavior; all else is merely a conceptual addition.

Such considerations of what *is* and what can be known leave to the first person only the role of (single) scientific observer standing over against society which is his or her object.

If we propose to consider society as subject rather than object, we are not suggesting straightforward ontological claims about what society *is* or about how it is known by an observer. We propose instead an investigation which is *methodologically* anchored in the first person. Stated in this way our proposal is familiar: it could be said that modern philosophy, from Descartes on, has been characterized by just such an approach. Here the human subject is not simply treated as an item in the known world about whom various claims are advanced, including claims about his ability to know. Rather, all knowledge claims are initially suspect: they are suspended until they can be warranted in the direct experience of the knower. Descartes insists that each of us consult his own experience and draw everything from that.

But this reference to "each of us" reminds us that of course the methodological first person of modern philosophy is precisely *singular*: it is the *individual* who is enjoined by Descartes's skepticism to place all knowledge provisionally in question. Subjectivity is firmly anchored to the particular.

Yet this is not quite true. In the eyes of some thinkers, at least, the epistemological subject of modern philosophy at some point be-

---

4. Anthony Quinton, "Social Objects," *Proceedings of the Aristotelian Society* 76 (1975–6), p. 17.

comes detached from the individual and acquires a more generalized status. It is true that before this happens the subject must graduate from a position of epistemological priority to one of metaphysical priority as well. Descartes was a realist who believed that the independent reality of the world could validly be affirmed on the basis of his subjective method, even if he had to go beyond the evidence of the senses to the rationally determined evidence for the existence and nature of God. Others were less than convinced, and difficulties about evidence for the world's external status led from Descartes's realism to various forms of idealism. The world was reduced to the contents of mind(s) in Berkeley and Leibniz, or conceived by Hume and Kant as having the status, as far as we can know it, of a mental construct.

It was Kant who introduced into this picture the distinction between the transcendental and the empirical subject when speaking of the mind which constructs the world it knows. This distinction is notoriously controversial in Kant, but some interpreters have seen it as affirming that when genuine knowledge takes place it is not you or I, or any particular person, who knows, but a universal subject in which somehow all share. Individuals, so the argument goes, only represent so many fleeting, changing perspectives or subjective impressions. But to know scientifically is to attain to a single world, to arrive at nature as a set of universal and necessary laws. When you and I know a scientific or mathematical truth it is the *same thing* we know and thus the *same thought* we think, whatever the differences in our subjective states or personal histories which make us distinct individuals. In individuality lies error; when we think the truth we are all one. Thus Kant is linked with Averroes's interpretation of Aristotle in which the Universal Thinker is God who thinks all true thoughts, either on his own or through us. Spinoza, though not an idealist, had similar views about the relation of God as thinker to the individual soul. All these conceptions came together in the early stages of German idealism.

Thus the first-person approach characteristic of modern philosophy does lead by this path beyond the individual. But can this path be of help to us? There are two reasons why it cannot.

The first is that its very argument is suspect. It is based on the questionable epistemological premise (an ancient one, to be sure) that in order to know something the mind must be or become like its object. Thus a universal object known requires a universal subject. It further confuses the specific identity of what is thought with the numerical identity of the acts or occasions of its being thought, and makes the further illegitimate move from these to the universal identity of the subject who thinks. These arguments for a universal subject make the same error as does psychologism, but in reverse: While the latter argues from the particularity of thought to the non-universality of its objects, the former postulate the universality of objects and conclude that the subject must be universal as well. Some of the best efforts of twentieth-century logic, semantics, and epistemology, beginning with Husserl and Frege, have been devoted to sorting out the universality of objects of thought and of meaning itself from the particularities of thinking, and while it is generally difficult to discern any real progress in philosophy, here at least some of the worst confusions have been exposed.

Such logical attacks may have little effect on the underlying appeal that the idea of a suprapersonal subject has for many people. It responds to certain concerns in the mystical tradition (a sense of the oneness of all things and especially minds) and provides a novel solution to the problem of how to conceive the relation between God and his creatures. Its critics are quick to point out that this solution raises as many questions as it answers. But in any case, its relevance to a conception of *social* reality is hard to see. Even if it were entirely free of conceptual difficulties it would still not be applicable to social groups. It moves from the individual thinker directly to a universal thinker which presumably encompasses, in its special way, all humanity without differentiation. But social groups are particular, and are to be distinguished not only from the individuals who make them up but also from each other. Further, whatever the relation may be of individual to group and of individual to individual within the group, it is surely not conceivable simply in terms of the unity that comes of thinking the same thought. Social groups engage not only in thought but in action and interaction.

It can also be argued that in order to think the same thought, individuals must first communicate, for which a common language and a common tradition are only necessary conditions. Even where these conditions are present, individuals do not always understand one another, and communication must work to overcome the difference between individuals.

Thus there are good reasons for saying that the move from individual subject to social group is not merely *different* from the move from individual to a putative universal subject; it is also *prior* to any such move, a condition of its possibility, which must be considered before any such leap to the universal makes even the remotest sense. Even a preliminary consideration of the matter convinces us that in a variety of ways (as language, culture, tradition, for example) society stands *between* the individual and the supposed universality of thought or reason. This does not mean that it constitutes a hindrance or barrier which we need to cast aside; it can be conceived instead as the intermediary which enables the universal to appear.

If these arguments remind some readers of Hegel's attack on Schelling in the Preface to the *Phenomenology of Spirit*, this is no accident. Similar arguments were brought forward by Merleau-Ponty against the whole "intellectualist" tradition, for thinking it could avoid or bypass the problems of intersubjectivity and communication by making the abrupt shift to a universal thinker.[5] Merleau-Ponty was contrasting the intellectualist approach with phenomenology (in this case Husserl's and his own) which always regarded intersubjectivity as a problem. And it is certainly true that Husserl, even if he adopted the distinction between the transcendental and the empirical ego, did *not* use the former to indicate a transindividual subject, some of his more superficial commentators to the contrary notwithstanding. Husserl's transcendental ego is singular (it is simply you or I, considered in a very special way), it constitutes itself in the unity of a history, and it has the problem of communicating with other transcendental egos.

But this brings us back to the point we reached at the end of the last chapter, where we were forced to conclude that Husserlian phenomenology, indeed more generally twentieth-century phenomenology, could not overcome its resolutely first-person-*singular* point of departure. The same could be said, in a slightly different way, of that strain of modern philosophy which we have examined that tries to transcend the individual but hold onto its first-person point of view. The "transcendental" subject at which it arrives is still singular, still an *I*. We are still in search of an account which centers methodologically on not the *I* but the *we*.

2. Moving beyond Phenomenology: Common Experience and Common Action

We have raised certain doubts about the capacity of Husserlian or Heideggerian phenomenology to liberate itself from its first-person-singular approach. But if we look closely at both thinkers we may find hints about how to move beyond them.

---

5. See Merleau-Ponty, *Phenomenology of Perception*, pp. 346–65.

To begin with, both seem to want to extend their first-person-singular accounts of existence and temporality to entities beyond the individual. Heidegger in one passage extends the notion of *Geschehen* (the root of his concept of historicity, as we saw) to "the community, the people" *(Gemeinschaft, Volk.)*. This *Mitgeschehen* or common destiny *(Geschick)* is not a mere collection of individual fates, he assures us, but derives from our "being together in the same world" and establishes itself "in communication and in struggle."[6] But we are not given any further details on how this occurs, and it remains a hint and nothing more. The remainder of the discussion of historicity, as we saw, centers on the relation of history to the authenticity of the individual's existence.

Husserl points in a similar direction at the end of his discussion of intersubjectivity in the fifth *Cartesian Meditation*. Having dealt with "the first and lowest level" of intersubjectivity or "communalization," he says we can move on to "higher levels,"[7] some of which take on the form of "personalities of a higher order."[8] This term, which in effect associates subjective characteristics with social groups, turns up in other Husserlian works as well (*The Crisis*, for example[9]), and in some of his unpublished manuscripts Husserl reveals that he takes this notion very seriously. He ascribes not only personality but also subjectivity, consciousness, unity of consciousness, faculties, character, conviction, memory, and, interestingly, even "something like corporality" *(so etwas wie Leiblichkeit)* to social groups.[10] He assures us that such talk is not merely metaphorical and he opposes any attempt to reduce the social "person" to a mere collection of individuals.

Yet Husserl, like Heidegger, gives us very little concrete analysis of such phenomena, and what he says likewise remains a series of hints. As we have suggested, the problem for both may be methodological. When he introduces the notion of "personalities of a higher order," Husserl speaks of them as "spiritual objectivities"

---

6. Heidegger, *Being and Time*, p. 384 (reference is again to the German pagination). John Haugeland "Heidegger on Being a Person," *Nous* 16 (1982), pp. 16–26, proposes an interpretation of *Dasein* as a "primordial institution" and a "unit of accountability" which permits of being applied to groups. Haugeland's proposal is promising, though I find it hardly in accord with Heidegger's text or intentions.

7. Husserl, *Cartesian Meditations*, pp. 128–29.

8. Ibid., p. 132.

9. Husserl, *The Crisis*, p. 188.

10. See *Husserliana*, vol. XIV, *Zur Phänomenologie der Intersubjektivität, Zweiter Teil*, ed. I. Kern (The Hague: M. Nijhoff, 1973), pp. 200–04, 404.

which "are constituted within the objective world."[11] But for him this means that they are constituted by (or for) the ego within its world. Both Husserl and Heidegger are so much tied in their own procedure to the individual's reflective self-awareness that they are unable to follow through analytically on what they both regard as important.

Nevertheless, the seeds for such an analysis are present in their work. If we return for a moment to what they say about historicity, we can find those seeds. Both, we recall, believe that intersubjectivity is essential to the individual subject. Husserl, for his part, arrives at his conception of historicity by considering the individual consciousness engaged in a cognitive project such as science, mathematics, or philosophy itself. Historicity consists in the fact that the undertaking already exists before any given individual takes up and takes over what is handed down by others. Engaged in such a cognitive or theoretical enterprise, the individual's accomplishments are conditioned by, and thus both limited by and made possible by, the accomplishments of others.

But this description of what we called the relay-form or predecessor-successor relation, important as it is, misses something crucial about activities like science. These are often characterized by an intersubjectivity which is not only successive but also simultaneous and cooperative. They are collective endeavors in which individuals work in teams. This means that they not only have a shared objective but also distribute tasks among the individuals who participate. The proper analysis of such an activity, even from the point of view of the individual participant, would look different in some important respects from actions as we have described them up to now. To arrive collectively and cooperatively at a given scientific result is entirely different from a collection of individuals arriving at it singly. Asked who carried out the action in question, the individual participant would have to answer: "We did." How do we analyze such action and how do we characterize its temporality?

As we noted, like Husserl, Heidegger presupposes intersubjectivity when he turns to his analysis of historicity. What he calls *Mitsein*, or being with others, had been dealt with in an earlier chapter of *Being and Time*. Heidegger's treatment of this phenomenon is closely tied to his concept of the "worldhood of the world." The entities of our world, he argued there, are not primordially

---

11. Husserl, *Cartesian Meditations*, p. 132.

encountered as "things" or "objects" for our perception and cognition. They are first of all the equipment and complexes of equipment involved in our everyday dealings and projects. Our encounter with other persons must be understood in this same context. Persons are not items of equipment, of course, but they are not things or objects of our perception either. Opposing the standard epistemological problem of "our knowledge of other minds," Heidegger affirms that others are encountered primarily, and for the most part, "through" or "across" equipment as a function of the workworld in which we are engaged together.[12]

What Heidegger's treatment thus suggests, though he does not draw out this implication, is that the interlocking complexes of equipment he discusses are linked to interlocking complexes of persons who are engaged in common projects. Collaborative or collective endeavors are ever more characteristic of the everyday workworld invoked by Heidegger than they are of the cognitive and scientific domain envisaged by Husserl. Again the distribution and coordination of tasks, organized around the achievement of a product or result, characterizes action which is properly ascribed to a group rather than to an individual or a mere collection of individuals. When I say "We built this house," my use of *we* is in this case not reducible to the series of statements: "I built the house, and you built the house, and he built the house . . . etc." Other uses of *we*, of course, are so reducible. When *we* go to the store, even though we go together, it is still true to say that each of us singly goes to the store. But if *we* do *the* shopping, again the reduction does not work. The job is done by our collaborative endeavor.

Let us recall that we are after a treatment which takes social groups seriously but does so "from the inside." Collective or collaborative endeavors give us examples of action whose true subject is not an individual but a group. And we can attest to this not from the outside, treating the group as an item external to us in the world, but from the internal perspective of a participant. What Husserl and Heidegger both tacitly acknowledge is that much of our contact with others has this character. But they do not (and perhaps cannot) provide us with a further analysis. How can we proceed?

The examples we have coaxed from the texts of Husserl and Heidegger are of common *projects* or collective *actions*. Let us recall that at the beginning of this study we differentiated action from

---

12. Heidegger, *Being and Time*, p. 120.

passive experience, and throughout our discussion of temporality we maintained this distinction. In keeping with that procedure, before considering in more detail the notion of common action, we should ask about the nature of common or collective experience. Since we associated Husserlian phenomenology with the description of passive experience, we can look first to it for clues. They are to be found precisely in what Husserl calls the "first and lowest level" of intersubjectivity.

The basic situation which Husserl seeks to account for in the fifth *Meditation* is what Schutz later called the face-to-face encounter between individuals[13]—described of course from the first-person-singular point of view. We shall see that with a slight shift in standpoint, results can emerge from this discussion which lead beyond Husserl's own procedure. This simple and straightforward one-to-one encounter already contains the means for understanding groups as such.

What clearly emerges from Husserl's analysis is that this encounter of two subjects essentially involves a third element, the common surrounding world. The other is in *my* world, but as a consciousness he is also *for* the world and the world for him as well as for me. We share at the very least, then, this particular place in which we stand and face each other. The simplest way of summarizing Husserl's account of intersubjectivity from *my* perspective is that I encounter *another* perspective on *the* world, a perspective which is not my own.

As is usual with Husserl, the theory of perception is at the center of his account. In perception, the object perceived is both a unity and a multiplicity of ways of showing itself. In my own experience, these showings or profiles are spread out over time, and they are coordinated with my movements, my possible changes of standpoint in relation to the object. In intersubjective experience a common object (or, in general, the common scene of our encounter) likewise has a multiplicity of ways of showing itself, but in this case they are simultaneous: I see it from *here* while you see it from over *there*.

The kinesthetic-spatial system of changing perspectives is something the normal perceiver learns to reckon with in moving about the world. But this familiar system includes the actual and possible view of others as well as one's own. In the encounter with another person I do not *have* his experiences, of course, but I am *aware* of them and of

---

13. Schutz, *The Phenomenology of the Social World*, pp. 163–67.

how they fit in with my own in relation to the surroundings we both perceive. There is a single system of interlocking perspectives on the common world which establishes itself in every face-to-face encounter, and it is a system of which both participants are aware. Like the multiplicity of actual and possible modes of givenness that belong to me as perceiver, this system belongs strictly to us. We can use the good Husserlian scheme: subject–modes of givenness–object given, to describe this situation, but the subject in this case is not *I* but *we*, not *cogito* but *cogitamus*.

Every face-to-face encounter seems in this sense to establish a *we*-relationship and a *we*-subject shared among its participants. Husserl indeed used the term *Vergemeinschaftung* (establishment of a community or communalization) to describe such a situation. But can such a minimal relationship be relevant to the existence and nature of social groups?

It is true that face-to-face encounters can be fleeting and meaningless. Obviously a great deal will turn on the character of the common object or objects which play so crucial a role in this scheme. Simply sharing the same space, provided the parties are aware of each other in doing so, does constitute a common experience. But an object or event which becomes the focus of attention for several persons can change their attitude toward each other. The pedestrians on a crowded street hardly consider themselves a group. But a traffic accident, which suddenly forces their attention to a single focus, makes them into a group which the members recognize as such. Even if they do not rush to offer assistance, individuals begin speaking to one another, comparing their impressions and speculating about the origins and further effects of the accident. Their existence as a group may be further prolonged, of course, if they become legally involved as witnesses. But that is less important for our purposes than the sense of participation that individuals attach to the scene itself. Spectators at a theatre or sports event are similarly united by the common spectacle to which they are witness.

It must be stressed, of course, that for our purposes what counts is the attitude of the members of the group toward the group and toward each other *as* its members. Collections of individuals can be "grouped" in any number of ways by an external observer, ways which may or may not involve their awareness of their membership. The pedestrians on a given street at a certain time may constitute such a group. So may all despositors at a particular bank, all mesomorphs, and all those who are considered security risks by some government department. The fact of belonging to a group may be unknown or a matter of complete indifference to its members. We are thinking here of groups that exist *for* the individuals involved who consider themselves members. The pedestrians on the street are transformed from the former to the latter sort by the intrusion of external circumstances. For the latter, let us use the term *community*.

Such transformations are relevant to larger contexts if we sufficiently extend our notion of common experience. Groups united by nothing but their geographical ties to a common territory may be transformed into a community if their territory is invaded or threatened from outside. What was merely a factual situation becomes the basis of something new. Similarly, Marxists believe that the existence and opposition of classes, which is an objective fact in capitalist society, can be transformed into class consciousness when the individuals perceive that they do belong to a group which is united in being oppressed. Racial and linguistic minority groups, and women, in the recent history of some western countries, have been similarly characterized by this sort of "raised consciousness." In these cases members belonged to their groups, objectively speaking, all along, and were not unaware of it either. But now they perceive that it is *as* a group that they are oppressed or threatened or under attack. The external threat or opposition becomes the common object of a common experience. These in turn refer back and "belong" to a common subject: *we*.

In characterizing certain social groups in this way we are not here making a simple, straightforward claim that group-subjects objectively exist. We are saying that individuals, in their sense of and use of "we," certainly *take* them to exist and that their taking them to exist in a sense makes it so. In saying "we," the individual identifies himself with the group and thus, in a Husserlian sense of the word, *constitutes* the group as comprising those who similarly, in the relevant context, say "we."

We mentioned that all this requires an extension of our notion of experience. It is precisely the notion of a common subject that corresponds to this extension. An individual will say that "we" experienced certain events, suffered this or that humiliation or outrage, even though he or she as an individual had no such experience directly. Furthermore, and significantly for our purposes, the *we* with whose experience the individual identifies can both pre-date and survive the individuals that make it up. The relation among the individuals involved may be the relay-form of predecessors and successors invoked by Husserl and Heidegger, but all identify themselves with a *we* which persists as a subject throughout.

This already suggests that the temporality of group existence differs significantly from what we treated under the heading of historicity, and this will have important consequences for our understanding of historical time. Before we take up this topic, however, we need to turn from common experience back to the theme of common action with which we started.

We turned to common experience partly to demonstrate that and how the *we*-subject can exist even there; for its involvement in collective action is in some ways more obvious. We have already touched on some of the main features of such action. Instead of a common object we have a common objective or result to be achieved. The common project is "articulated" into sub-tasks distributed among the participants, such that the proper agent cannot be any of the members singly but only the group as such.

Again what is crucial is that members identify with the group in attitude and action. It is they, by their participation, who create and sustain the *we*-subject. At the same time this subject transcends their individual existences; it is "we" who accomplish the action, says the individual, even though his contribution is small and other contributions are not even known to him in detail. And the individual may join in a group united by a project already underway, as in Husserl's example of the continuity of science. In this case the *we* survives and succeeds the individual as well; indeed in one sense the accomplishment of its common objective ("the full truth") lies in the indefinite or even the infinitely distant future.

We can relate common experience and common action to each other in several ways. The intersubjective unity of a common project is both more concrete and more fragile than that of a common experience. The spectators at a football game or at the traffic accident, or the victims of an attack or threat, are fused by their common object, but they take the object to exist independently of themselves. For the participants in a common project, such as a barn-raising, their common objective is literally created by their participatory activity. For spectators and observers, their *we*-relationship seems called forth and sustained in being by an independent object. For the participants in a common endeavor, the object is called forth and sustained by their we-relationship. Thus the latter is not at the mercy of its object, as we might say; but at the same time it receives no support from outside, and is dependent on its own internal cohesiveness for its sustained existence.

Another way in which common experience and common action are related is that the one may influence and produce the other. In the case of those groups created by the common experience of threat or danger, the group thus constituted may then act to defend itself; the annihilation or removal of the external threat becomes the common objective toward which all efforts are collectively bent. In the other direction, obviously the prosecution of common action creates the occasion for common experience. In a general way we can say that common experience is a necessary but not sufficient condition for common action: in order for collective action to occur, a group must exist whose members recognize each other as such and are aware of a common situation they all face. But such a group can exist without collective action resulting; oppressed communities may be perfectly united, but only in their suffering, with no prospect, or no perceived prospect, of acting as a group.

It must be pointed out, too, that the existence of an outside force opposed to a particular group is not sufficient to transform it into a community. It may have the opposite effect, whether by design or not, of separating the individuals in the group from each other and preventing their reciprocal consciousness of the unity of their situation. This is a point made by J. P. Sartre in his analysis of the emergence of groups from what he calls their "seriality." It is a good Marxist point, in keeping with Sartre's stated allegiance. The capitalist system of production, according to Marx, alienates workers not only from the product of their labor but also from each other and their Gattungswesen. According to the Marxist concept of "ideology," furthermore, religion and many of the other trappings of society have the function of distracting the gaze of the proletariat from their actual and common plight. Sartre extends the point to the mechanism of representation in parliamentary systems. Like many Marxists, he believes that elective representation produces a false sense of participation and leaves the electors systematically serialized and unaware of the possibilities for community that exist among them. The parliamentary system is in this view a perfect instrument for an economic system whose interest is served when industrial workers in different segments of society (and even in different countries) do not recognize their fate as a shared one related to a common opponent.[14]

But Sartre's requirements for what constitutes a genuine transcendence of seriality are arguably too strict. He takes as the paradigm case the storming of the Bastille on July 14, 1789, and calls it "the dissolution of the series in the group-in-fusion."[15] A group, in this case "the city" of Paris, which had been defined only from the outside as a group by the actions of King and militia against it, now finds its synthetic unity in itself and is fused in one action. For Sartre, this and similar revolutionary groupings are far from the random actions of amorphous mobs; they are conditioned, by the combined circumstances leading to them, to be structured and efficacious in the attainment of their goal.[16] Nevertheless they are fragile and momentary, destined to dissolve in their turn into a new seriality. For Sartre, groups seem to be either serial in character, unified by external circumstances only, or fusions of such intimate character that the individuality of their members is all but obliterated. In such cases individuals are "swept up" into what is not so much a we as a collective I. As is the case in other aspects (and other phases) of Sartre's philosophy, one wonders whether he has not posed too sharp an alternative. Though he often invokes the concept of dialectic, he is presenting us here in effect with a very non-dialectical either-or. We must ask whether the "fusion" of a group or community in common experience and action is not possible in such a way as to preserve rather than obliterate the individuality of its participants.

Another loose end left over by our discussion of the constitution of communities is the possibility that common experience cannot only not lead to common action but in fact can lead to conflict and opposition. It could be said that conflict, no less than common action, presupposes common experience. To take an example used by Sartre, that of famine, the common object, which is the inadequate food supply, establishes a very clear we of reciprocal awareness: we who are the contenders for this short supply. But instead of organizing ourselves cooperatively for purposes of sharing it, we may fight like dogs over what little there is.[17] This sort of struggle is something

14. J. P. Sartre, *Critique de la raison dialectique*, Tome I (Paris: Gallimard, 1960), pp. 386–466.

15. Ibid., p. 391.

16. Ibid., p. 393.

17. Ibid., p. 385.

much more intimate than what is suggested by Sartre's term "seriality." We are not just side by side, each pursuing separate ends unrelated to each other; we are locked in a face-to-face encounter which can certainly be called a common experience.

It seems that in our attempt to describe the constitution of a *we*-subject in relation to common experience and common action, two interrelated questions have arisen which must be answered before we can go on to a fuller description of the temporality of such groups. First, how is the common experience of conflict related to the common experience of a genuine community? Second, is there a way of describing the union of different individuals in a community such that their individual existences are not submerged in a single subject but somehow preserved? We are not denying that groups-in-fusion do come into existence, that individuals can be swept up into a common action in which all become as one. But such groups are ephemeral, their actions often irrational and dangerous, and their status as genuine communities probably illusory. How do we distinguish such phenomena from what we have been seeking to describe, a group subject that is not merely a larger-scale *I*, but is genuinely plural and yet can persist as a temporal unity sustained from within by its members?

These questions are related if only because they bring before us the range of possible relationships that can obtain among a plurality of individuals, from all-out conflict at one extreme to total, undifferentiated union at the other. In criticizing the epistemological concept of the "transcendental" subject, in the first part of this chapter, for not permitting the diversity-within-unity appropriate to the social world, we recalled Hegel's criticism of the German idealists. In Sartre's notion of the group-in-fusion we seem to be faced with the social equivalent of that epistemological concept, not a plural subjectivity, but the reproduction of singular subjectivity at a higher level. Once again we are put in mind of Hegel, because the problem of social unity-within-diversity, and of its connection with conflict and opposition, is one of the chief motivating concerns behind that philosopher's work.

In some well-known pages of his *Phenomenology of Spirit* Hegel gives us a description of how a genuine community might arise. Not only does he relate such a community to its opposite, conflict; he suggests that it arises out of conflict and preserves certain elements of conflict within itself. A brief examination of these pages will prove helpful for us for several reasons.

The passage in question marks the first appearance in Hegel's book of its true subject: *Geist* or spirit; and Hegel, in his first reference to spirit, describes it in terms familiar to us: "an I that is We, a We that is I."[18] This signals a concern for the first person plural which is not only substantive but also methodological. Hegel's approach can instruct us on how to move beyond the singular methodological focus of Husserlian phenomenology by employing a procedure which, by a well-known and confusing historical coincidence, is called precisely: phenomenology. Furthermore, as we said, Hegel tells us how a spiritual subject or community might arise; that is, he is telling us a story, a "likely story," not about particular historical events but applicable as a conceptual description to many of them. Thus Hegel's own account is a kind of narrative. But it also describes, as we shall see, a process that has an internally narrative character, not only for Hegel who tells it to us but for the "characters" of his "story." In short, Hegel's account tells us something important about the relation between time and narrative at the social level, and is thus capable of casting light on history.

3. Hegel's Dialectic of Recognition

Hegel's account of the "independence and dependence of self-consciousness" is too well known and too much commented on to require a detailed exposition here. It is best for our purposes, in any case, to try to extract the essentials of the account in our own terms, not attempting to accommodate ourselves too much to Hegel's notoriously difficult language. Thus the following runs the risk of being impressionistic, personalized, and perhaps slanted by an overall framework which is not Hegel's but ours. But such has been the fate of Hegel's extraordinarily fecund train of thought; at least we have the excuse that we are not the first to have exploited it in this way.

Hegel begins the *Phenomenology* (in the Introduction, that is, not the Preface) with a critique of the shift we spoke of earlier whereby, in modern philosophy, epistemology precedes metaphysics.[19] He attacks just that first-person-*singular* standpoint of which we have already spoken. But his intention is clearly not to abandon but to surpass that standpoint, without giving up everything about it. Even

---

18. G. W. F. Hegel, *Phenomenology of Spirit*, p. 110.
19. Ibid., pp. 46–57.

skepticism, so much a part of Descartes's innovative procedure, is not so much rejected as corrected and improved.

In wanting to surpass the first-person-singular standpoint Hegel is of course very much continuing, not rejecting, the modern tradition; for that is just what his modern forerunners wanted to do. But for them the problem was to bridge the gap between consciousness and the external world. Hegel was enough a follower of Kant to believe that the latter had solved or dissolved *that* problem. But Kant left unsolved the real problem of transcending the *I*, not toward the external world, or for that matter toward the illusory Universal Subject, but toward the other *I*. For Hegel this is not just a philosophical but also a social, a political, a historical, and a religious problem all at once: he believed that the isolation of egos in modern philosophy was a reflection of isolation of persons from each other in real life, a fragmentation of society and a loss or lack of community.

Hegel does not ignore the relation between the self and the external world. He deals with it, but precisely in order to show how it is taken for a real problem only to reveal itself as a false problem when the genuine problem of transcendence appears. One way of describing the peculiar itinerary of the *Phenomenology* is that it is the description of a series of mistakes and of the subsequent unmasking of those mistakes. Learning from our mistakes we call learning from experience—which is exactly how Hegel uses the term *Erfahrung*: phenomenology is "the science of the experience of consciousness" (Hegel's subtitle) in just this sense.

The external world at issue is an object not only of perception and knowledge but also of our desires and needs.[20] We need nature in order to survive. Desire is the practical side of consciousness; its object is at a distance, but in this case a distance which is to be overcome not by knowledge but by possession and consumption. According to Hegel we are engaged in a kind of struggle with nature, for cognitive and technological mastery, both to know it and to make it serve our needs. But the real issue in this struggle is ourselves and our own lives: in the process we learn what we are capable of and what we need to survive in the world. The real issues are finally self-knowledge, self-preservation, and self-mastery.

Transcendence toward nature thus reflects back upon the self. The struggle with nature turns out to be about something other than what it seemed to be about. Not that this struggle is illusory, or that it ever

---

20. Ibid., pp. 105–110.

really ends. But even where it is more or less satisfactorily resolved it is the self (Hegel calls it self-consciousness) which is its outcome. The self asserts its ability to stand on its own; its *Selbständigkeit* or independence.[21]

Hegel may be suggesting that the self-certainty and self-centered-ness of modern thought is a function of the increased "mastery and possession of nature" envisaged by Descartes and realized in the growth of science and technology. But the situation is de-stabilized when one of these confident selves encounters another one. To me the other may seem just a part of the surrounding world I must master to serve my own needs and maintain my independence. But trouble begins if he takes the same view toward me. The existence of each of us as an independent or self-standing self is challenged by the other. We are caught up in the struggle over the independence and dependence of self-consciousness.

As our last sentence indicates, Hegel is now describing a situation in which it is appropriate to use the *we* of common experience. Each of the parties to the situation is aware of the existence of the other in relation to a third element, the common surrounding world which defines their relation to each other. But their common experience is an unstable one; it is a problem crying out for a solution. The ensuing pages of the *Phenomenology* describe various false conceptions of how to solve this problem, which derive from mistaken conceptions of what the struggle is really about. But Hegel seeks to render these mistakes understandable and suggests that they must be made before the real outcome, and the real point of the struggle, can be revealed. If the "I that is We" of a genuine community is possible, it must somehow incorporate in itself the false solutions Hegel describes. It must be the outcome of an experience that learns by its mistakes.

Before we examine Hegel's account of that experience (his famous drama of life-and-death struggle and enslavement) we need to ask a question of the sort that often occurs to readers of the *Phe-nomenology*: just what, concretely, is Hegel talking about? He seems to envisage a conflict among individuals with a strong sense of themselves and of their own independence, who struggle through until they finally establish a true community: a *we*. But such charac-ters—warriors, masters, rebellious servants—are clearly adults. Has each of them not already experienced the original community of the

---

21. Ibid., pp. 109–110.

family? In the life of the individual, is it not the case that the familial *we* precedes everything else?

Hegel does not provide an answer to these questions in chapter IV of the *Phenomenology*, but from what he says elsewhere[22] it is clear that he considers the family something less than a genuine community, even though it has a crucial dialectical role in the life of both individual and society. The family is a natural, not a social, grouping, and as a child the individual is too dependent on the family, his identity too much submerged in it to permit him any genuine individuality. Thus the family is too much like the Universal Subject, or a Sartrian group-in-fusion, to suit Hegel: it is the obliteration rather than the participation of individuals. In the case of the child, of course, we cannot speak of the obliteration of individuality, since it has not yet developed. There is evidence, too, that Hegel considers the Greek *polis*, the model for what he calls Ethical Substance, to be too much like a family to be a genuine community. For all his admiration of the ancient city, he represents it as a kind of childhood state of Western history. If he occasionally romanticizes it, as do so many of his contemporaries, he probably recognizes at the same time that he is expressing the kind of nostalgia we feel for lost childhood. This nostalgia is paradoxical, because most of us would not voluntarily return to childhood again even if we could. We long for its security but want to retain our independence as adults. Such longing *may* gain the upper hand (and have tragic consequences) if we allow ourselves to be swept up in a putative *volonté générale*. The result can be a Terror in which we lose not only our independence but also our heads.

Independence comes not within the family but by breaking out of it. There is a prototype of the master-slave struggle, even the struggle-to-the-death if Freud is right, between the child-adolescent and his or her parents. This familial conflict, like the struggles Hegel describes, is ultimately over mutual recognition, but it can never achieve this goal, since the difference of generations and the parent-child relation can never be overcome. The one thing parents cannot give children (or children parents, for that matter) is recognition as independent and self-sufficient persons. If we seek that, as all of us do, we must look elsewhere.

---

22. Ibid., p. 268. See also Hegel's *Philosophy of Mind*, tr. W. Wallace (Oxford: Clarendon Press, 1971), pp. 255–56.

Hegel is thus affirming what was later asserted by Claude Lévi-Strauss in opposition to some of his fellow anthropologists: namely, that the fundamental social unit is not the family but the relationship that is established between members of different families.[23] It is here that nature is transformed into culture. If this view is correct, it would count against what seems to be Heidegger's tendency to regard the succession of generations within the family as foundational or paradigmatic for historicity. Hegel differs from the anthropologists, of course, because what counts for him in the establishment of society is not intermarriage but the confrontation of self-conscious individuals over the issue of dependence and independence. In the one case new families are established; in the other, if all goes well, communities. It must be said, too, that typically Hegel regards the intra-family relation as *aufgehoben*, not simply abandoned. In genuine extra-familial social relations certain aspects of family life are preserved: certainly its contentiousness and animosity, but also, again if all goes well, the capacity for a harmonious bond.

Alas, it is clear, as Hegel's celebrated "story" gets underway,[24] that all goes well only rarely—and when it does not, the results can be murderous. What may first occur to the individuals whose independence and self-sufficiency are challenged by each other is to eliminate the challenger. But what the latter challenges is not merely the fact but the legitimacy of my independence. If I eliminate him there is no one left to acknowledge that legitimacy. Recognition, not victory, turns out to have been the real point of the struggle. If I win I get only existence, not the acknowledged right to exist; if I lose, of course, I get neither.

Faced with these prospects, enslavement may seem an attractive alternative for both parties. The loser at least keeps his life, while the winner gains not only independence but recognition as well. It is to be recalled, too, that the original struggle was over the unrestricted use of nature to satisfy our needs. The servant's acknowledgment of his master's domination is expressed in the labor he is forced to perform for him.

But this relationship turns out likewise to be unstable and unsatisfying, again because the point of it is other than it at first seems. The master may wonder if he is truly legitimized since his recogni-

23. C. Lévi-Strauss, *Structural Anthropology*, tr. C. Jacobson and B. G. Schoepf (Garden City: Doubleday & Co., 1967), pp. 48–49.
24. Hegel, *Phenomenology of Spirit*, pp. 111–19.

tion comes from one who has now been reduced to a mere extension of his own will. The servant, though he suffers and feels this reduction, nevertheless remains self-conscious, if only because he constantly fears for his life. And it may dawn on him as well that it is he who works on and transforms nature for the satisfaction of human needs. A growing sense of this actually exercised power over nature may raise in the servant's mind a suspicion that this power could be turned on the master, who now appears increasingly superfluous to the whole process. The stage is set for a rebellion.

There are many more subtleties to Hegel's amazingly compressed presentation than we have been able to include here. But these are the essentials of what is thought by some to be a schematic but dynamic account of most of what has happened, and indeed is still happening, in the history of human relations. The life-and-death struggle continues in our large and small wars and on the streets of our cities. Where it is replaced by domination, according to Hegel, something genuinely new and different supervenes. In institutionalized form, political or economic domination, or both, is the structure of most social arrangements, past and present. But these arrangements are inherently unstable, whether they ever actually explode or not. When they do, they can revert to the pattern of death and destruction or they can fall into their own cycle of domination and counter-domination.

On the other hand, something again genuinely different can happen if there occurs what had actually been the point of the whole struggle: the mutual recognition of the parties to the conflict, the acknowledgment by each of the other's right to exist and to enjoy the fruits of their labor. Each sought this recognition from the other all along, but failed to realize that it had to be mutual, that recognition had to come from one who himself was granted the legitimate status of an independent existence. Instead of disputing their territory or exploiting each other for its use, the parties now cooperate in its enjoyment. The details of how this cooperation is to be worked out are less important to Hegel than the reciprocal respect which lies at its base and renders it possible. Mutual recognition is far from a guarantee of the permanence of the community it founds. Indeed, we can say that in a very important sense such a community contains the seeds of its own possible destruction. These are precisely the self-conscious, self-assertive, independent-minded individuals who make it up. Without them it would not be a genuine community. Like children, the docile and self-effacing, or the merely stubborn and petulant, do not qualify: at most they will rationalize a subservient status by the ideologies of stoicism, skepticism, or the Unhappy Consciousness. The individuals Hegel has in mind, who have demanded their independence all along, may be impatient with the capacity of the community to assure it. Precisely such individuals have the capacity to tear it apart.

Yet only the community really is capable of assuring it. Here the dialectic becomes even more paradoxical than usual. Without independent individuals there can be no genuine community; yet without a community there can be no genuinely independent individuals. And the reason for this is that genuine independence is that which is legitimized and recognized by others who are equally independent. Outside the community, or in breaking away from it, individuals can only be independent-minded, can only demand independence. Only the community can give it to them.

This doctrine of the correlation of independence and community explains for us why Hegel presents his views in the way he does. He gives us what are essentially the three main kinds of relations that can exist among independent-minded or self-conscious individuals: struggle to the death, domination, and community. But there is a certain order among them. All-out conflict is the most direct and immediate way in which independence is pursued. Domination answers to the real motives of the conflict (a life of recognized independence) better than the conflict itself, and so represents an advance. But community secures recognized independence for all, not just for some, thereby making the recognition genuine, so it in turn surpasses domination.

This three-step progression by no means imposes any temporal order on events. Any of the stages can persist indefinitely, and one may degenerate to a "previous" stage rather than progress. But Hegel wants to provide the means for distinguishing qualitative social change from a mere sequence of events, and his notion of a progression simply postulates the genuine end of social relations and seeks to distinguish what serves that end from what only seems to serve it. As for mapping his story onto historical events, this is always tentative. In view of other parts of the *Phenomenology* and of Hegel's philosophy, it is likely Hegel believed that genuine community was possible, if at all, only in the modern world after the individual had asserted his demand for independence. As we noted before, we may long for the ancient city as for a lost childhood, but it represents only the abstract idea, not the reality of community; it was not and could not be composed of genuinely independent individuals.

But there is a danger in reading Hegel's text exclusively in this historical way. He was undoubtedly saying something important about the past, the present, and especially the future of his own (our own) society, but he was also articulating a dynamic schema of social relations in general. It is unlikely that he is telling a single story about the possible emergence of the European community. No doubt, in his sense, many communities have emerged and dissolved again, just as many wars have been fought and many people enslaved.

Most important, Hegel is making certain claims about the internal dynamic structure of any such community. If we suppose that one is formed as Hegel describes it, through the mutual recognition of its members, it is not necessary that those members actually have passed through a life-and-death struggle and a period of domination. But it *is* necessary that these remain permanent possibilities for the individuals involved, and that their mutual recognition consequently represents the surmounting and surpassing of those possibilities.

But does it represent this *for* the individuals involved? Do they themselves consciously regard their union as a rejection and surpassing of violence or domination, as a laying down of arms that may always be taken up again? I *think* this is what Hegel *must* have meant. At least implicitly, the internal dynamics, actual and potential, of the group must be apparent to its members. Hegel describes spirit as "this absolute substance which, in the complete freedom and independence of its opposed members—i.e., different self-consciousnesses existing for themselves—is the unity of the same."[25] In other words, says Hegel, spirit is precisely "an I that is We, a We that is I." The group is constituted by individuals who are aware of and assertive of their independance *(I)* but who voluntarily and freely associate *(we)*. There is no blind allegiance, then, or the submergence of the individual in a mass movement. The establishment of community in Hegel's sense is something that happens not just *for us*—to take up a distinction current throughout the *Phenomenology*—that is, for us who look on and describe the process; it occurs for those involved and can only occur with their full awareness. Their awareness, their voluntary and conscious association, is what makes it so.

---

25. Ibid., p. 110 (slightly altered translation).

If this is so then the community as envisaged by Hegel is not the sort of macro-person that acts and pursues ends which are unknown to or even contrary to the ends of its constituent members. The latter is an idea that is often associated with Hegel, though it is found earlier in Vico and in Adam Smith's idea of the Invisible Hand. Hegel does indeed speak elsewhere of the "cunning of reason" in using individuals to achieve its own ends. Even in the struggle for independence, throughout conflict and domination, an end is really being "sought" that is different from that envisaged by the participants, an end *we* (who describe) in retrospect can see but they cannot. What Hegel calls civil society, in the *Philosophy of Right*, also corresponds to such a stage. Where community is lacking and conflict abounds, it is understandable that the overall results of the conflict will often be those envisaged by no one involved. But this is because there is no common endeavor and thus no common envisaged result. In a genuine community such endeavors and envisaged results do exist for the members involved. To be sure, here too the results may be otherwise than envisaged; but they need not be. The idea of the individual's being duped or used by an agency larger and more powerful than himself is the farthest thing from Hegel's idea of the individual's participation in a genuine community. Such an agency, which is indeed larger and more powerful than any of its members, does exist: it is the *we*. But it exists by virtue of the active and associative participation of its members.

4. Group, Time, and Narrative

The foregoing discussion of Hegel was introduced here because his text provides us with the means, we claimed, for answering two crucial questions that arose in our discussion of groups: 1) How do we conceive of a communal subject that is genuinely plural, i.e., which preserves the individuality of its constituent members? and 2) What is the relation between the common experience of conflict and the common experience of community and participation? Hegel's conception, as we read it, ties together the two questions and the answers to them. Common experience among self-conscious or independent-minded individuals always contains the potential for conflict; the establishment of community is the explicit overcoming of conflict even while the recognition of conflict's abiding possibility is preserved. This is to say that the community is established when each individual acknowledges the independence of the others and gets the same acknowledgment from them for himself.

But Hegel provides us with even more than this. His account of the establishment and continued existence of the community tells us something about its temporality and turns out, as we hinted earlier, to be a narrative account. Thus with Hegel's help we can take up what we postponed in the second section of this chapter: an examination of the temporality and narrative character of the *we*.

In our discussion of common experience we spoke of the role of the common object, which refers back to the intersubjective or *we*-subject. If we consider the object as a temporally extended event, or the experience of it as temporally extended, then the unity of the experience, as with the individual, must be procured by a projective-retrospective grasp. In the reciprocal awareness of the individuals, this grasp is effected by a group in relation to this particular experience: "we" experience this object or event together.

As we saw, such common experience may not lead to common action; it may lead to nothing at all, of course, or it may lead to conflict. Where it does lead to or pass over into common action, and provided the individuals are not swept up in a mass undertaking which obliterates their individuality, what happens? Individual actions are conceived by participants as part of a common project; for those who perform them, their meaning is derived from the project, which is the undertaking properly speaking of the group and not of the individuals. Whatever the group may be "in itself," or to an external observer, for the participants it is postulated as the subject which gives meaning to their behavior, the agent whose action is the overall framework of the subactions they as individuals perform.

Hegel's account of the constitution of a community in fact turns on the notion of a common project. He begins his account with the general idea of a common surrounding world as object of both experience and desire. The life-and-death struggle is fought over this common world, and the master-servant relation is organized for its exploitation. Thus the domination of nature, for purposes of habitation and the satisfaction of needs, remains constantly at issue in the confrontation among persons, and the establishment of a community is envisaged by Hegel as the sole satisfactory way to deal with this issue.

This is part of what Hegel means when he speaks of spirit as "the action of all" and "the universal *work* produced by the actions of all and each, as their unity and identity."[26] Elsewhere he says, "action by one side only would be useless because what is to happen is to be brought about by both."[27] Spirit is the "unmoved solid *ground* and *starting-point* for the action of all";[28] that is, the mutual recognition which constitutes the community makes common action possible.

But there is more to the common project than concerted action directed toward an external object or the external world. Hegel claims that the community is both the starting point *and* "the purpose and goal" of common action.[29] We can take this to mean, I think, that part of the common project is that of the group's self-maintenance. Insofar as it is more than a spontaneous upsurge of momentary common sentiment, insofar as it engaged in a sustained and articulated pattern of common action, the group needs constantly to guard itself against the centrifugal tendencies which inhere in it because of the independent-mindedness of the individuals that make it up. Depending on the size and complexity of the group, and the nature of its common task or tasks, this will require various degrees of organization and institutional arrangements to which group members must commit themselves as part of their commitment to the community and its common cause, causes, or projects.

What all this shows is that for Hegel the community is constituted in and through common experience and especially common projects. The mutual recognition of its members does not take place in a vacuum, where the members have nothing to consider but each other; nor is it instantaneous or atemporal. It organizes itself in relation to a world and projects itself over time. The group looks "backwards" (in a perhaps metaphorical rather than strictly temporal sense) to its own origins in the individuality and cross-purpose of its members, which have been surmounted by their mutual recognition and reconciliation. It looks forward to the carrying-out of its common tasks and it projects its own continued existence as the condition for this continued activity.

To speak simply of "the group's" doing all this, of "its" looking forward and back, etc., is still to risk the kind of abstractness Hegel

---

26. Ibid., p. 264.
27. Ibid., p. 112.
28. Ibid., p. 264.
29. Ibid.

wants to avoid, and to resort to an over-personification. But if we take the attitude of participants, there is nothing abstract here: it is *we* who do all this: it is not my land or territory but *ours*, not *I* who act but *we*, not *my* but *our* projects that have to be carried out, not *my* continued existence but *ours* as a group that has to be assured, etc. The group in Hegel's and in our sense, as a community that is sustained from within by its members, exists when and only when it has members who say and use the "we" in just these senses.

When this happens, the *we*-subject could be said to display the same temporal structure of experience, action, and life that we found associated with the *I* or individual subject in earlier chapters. We spoke of the temporal-narrative organization not only of experiences and actions (chapters I and II) but also of the self who experiences and acts (chapter III). As we saw there, each implies the other: to experience or act I must already be a unitary self; yet I am a unitary self only in and through my experiences and actions. The self is a unity *of* experiences and actions. The unity of the former involves, as we saw, somewhat different organizing principles from those involved in the unity of the latter; but in each case a temporal sequence is brought under a specifically temporal form by virtue of a narrative prospective-retrospective grasp.

If we now make the shift to the group, we can say that events of common experience and actions undertaken in common are constituted when *we* gather together sequences of events or sub-actions by projecting onto them a structure comprising beginning, middle, and end. The group itself, as *we*-subject, is constituted as the unity of a temporally extended multiplicity of experiences and actions. In all these cases, though *we* always stand at some particular point in a temporally unfolding event-structure, we retain whatever has gone before and project what is yet to come. In a kind of collective reflection, *we* act or experience in virtue of a story *we* tell *ourselves* about what we are going through or doing. It can be seen that the roles of agent (*we* act), narrator (*we* tell), and audience (to *ourselves*) turn up again, this time in a plural form.

Thus here, as before, the temporal structure or organization of experience and of action is not different from a story that is told about it; rather, the experience or action is embodied in and constituted by the story that is told about it. Likewise, the group's temporally persisting existence as a community, and as a social subject of experience and action, is not different from the story that is told about it; it too is constituted by a story *of* the community, of what it is and what it is doing, which is told, acted out, and received and accepted in a kind of self-reflective social narration.

These are the general features of a theory of community which accounts for its temporal existence by appealing to the same notion of narrative structure that we used when discussing the temporality of individual existence. Development of this theory should permit us to work out a notion of social or historical temporality which answers to the needs that have emerged in the course of our discussion; such a theory permits us to envisage historical time centered on the group, not the individual; yet it makes possible an account of that temporality from within rather than from without, that is, a view of the community not as an object or entity in the world but from the perspective of the communal experience itself. Thus the group and its temporal-narrative mode of existence can not only be described *as* a plural "first person," but also be approached by a method which is itself a first-person (plural) procedure.

What has been proposed so far, however, is exceedingly schematic and overly abstract, from several points of view. Our theory can be made concrete, and its contribution to an understanding of history made evident, only if we address ourselves to a series of critical questions:

1. What we have described as a communal narrative structure has been derived from a comparison to what we said earlier about individuals. There is a danger that in replacing the *I* with the *we* we are not paying sufficient attention to the plurality of the plural subject and how this plurality functions concretely. In other words, we must again avoid the tendency to portray the group simply as a person "writ large." When I tell myself a story in order to act it out, it is one person who is performing this reflective act of narration. If we say, by contrast, in the case of the group, that *we* tell, *we* listen, and *we* act, it is legitimate and appropriate, precisely because of the plurality of the group, to ask: who tells, who listens, who acts? We must not forget that what was only a quasi-intersubjectivity of narrative structure in the individual is a real intersubjectivity in the group.

2. What kinds of groups are envisaged here? We have already excluded groups that exist by external classification alone, and restricted ourselves to those that are constituted by the mutual recognition and conscious participation of their members. But what kinds of groups does this include? We claimed that Hegel's theory applies to different sorts of groups. We saw that for him it probably does not

include the family. There is some indication in the *Phenomenology* that he takes the *Volksgeist*, or spirit of a people, as his paradigm for a community.[30] If we take seriously the historical projection of his theory, of which we spoke earlier, it seems he was considering the various national-cultural groups that figure in the standard history of the West: the Jews, the Greeks, the Romans, etc. It is likely that there is a connection between the "We that is I" which is identified as the key to the emergence of *Geist* generally, and the *we* that functions methodologically, in such a crucial and mysterious way, in the *Phenomenology*: Hegel could be seen to be addressing his European contemporaries and saying: *we* constitute a community in virtue of what we have been through together, up to and including the French Revolution and the conquests of Napoleon. Because of our common experience the past now has a significance *for us* that it did not and could not have for those (including ourselves) who lived through it. Hegel links mutual recognition with reconciliation *(Versöhnung)*[31] and may be urging that the contentious history of modern Europe be transformed dialectically from a bloody struggle and a see-saw of domination into a new community.

Thus it is clear that Hegel's notion of community is meant to be applied to the peoples and nation-states of European history. This raises two questions: 1) does it genuinely apply to them, that is, do they really function as communities in Hegel's (and our) sense? and does it thus help us to understand them? and 2) does it apply only to

---

30. Ibid., p. 265.

31. Ibid., pp. 407–408. In the terms used by Jean-François Lyotard in *The Postmodern Condition* (tr. G. Bennington and B. Massumi. Minneapolis: University of Minnesota Press, 1984), this is Hegel's version of modernism, i.e. the attempt to subsume particular social narratives under a "grand narrative" or "metanarrative." Other versions include capitalist progressivism and Marxism. The "postmodern" is defined as "incredulity toward metanarratives" (p. XXIV). If such narratives are taken as straightforward claims to historical truth, they may well deserve our incredulity. But I am suggesting here, and shall argue further in the next chapter, that such narratives are advanced as part of the project of community-building, and their validity is ultimately a question of whether their advocates succeed in persuading others to join in the community they project. Hegel's philosophy of history may aim too high, its universal project may indeed be unrealizable. But it should be read as a moral-political appeal, not as a putative science.

The same could be said of J. Habermas' *Theory of Communicative Action*, (vol. I, tr. T. McCarthy, Boston: Beacon Press, 1984) which can be seen as a recasting of Hegel's dialectic of recognition and reconciliation. While rejecting the "philosophy of identity" as a *theoretical* stance, Habermas nevertheless projects an ever-widening and ultimately universal sphere of consensus which finally merges with the conditions of communication itself. While he sees particular communities with their "life-worlds" as among the conditions of communication (conditions that in this case can be transcended), Habermas neglects, in my view, the role of communication—and in particular narrative construction—in the *constitution* of communities.

them, that is, is it applicable to groups of other sorts which exist within and perhaps cut across the lines established by our standard notion of history? This is perhaps another way of asking a question which often comes to the surface in studying Hegel: are his conceptual insights applicable outside the framework of a closed conception of world history which has been superceded by events?

3. Is it possible that our notion of community is not only overly schematic and abstract but also somewhat idealized as well? Following Hegel we have stressed the role of conflict and potential for conflict, but have described the community as existing when conflict is overcome. But are there not in fact many communities in which conflict persists and is itself constitutive of the group's identity? Is it not the case that a community is often characterized not by a single story of its origins, unity, and tasks, on which all agree, but by rival and conflicting stories?

Another way in which our account may be over-idealized, again perhaps because of Hegel's influence on it, is in suggesting that a community exists by the conscious and voluntary association of independent individuals. Are there not groups which are significant in the social world at large, significant for history, and important for us as individuals, which we simply grow into or find ourselves belonging to without having made any explicit choice?

These are all questions that can only be addressed by a much more concrete and detailed elaboration of our theory. It is to this task that we turn in our final chapter.

VI

Time, Narrative, and History

1. *Individual and Community* in concerto

In the previous chapter we began elaborating a theory of social existence and temporality which is centered on groups. We proposed instances of experience, action, and life whose subject is not the individual but the social group, and argued that the narrative structure of these phenomena, earlier associated with individual experience, could be projected onto the social plane. With Hegel's help we envisaged a form of association in which a genuine group-subject is formed, but not in such a way as to submerge or obliterate the plurality of individuals that make it up.

It was primarily in connection with this last point, however, that certain questions were raised which must be answered if the proposed conception is to prove fruitful in a concrete way. By addressing ourselves to those questions we shall be able to render our theory more comprehensible and free it from a certain abstractness which has attached to it so far. In particular, we wish to show that it can be applied to actual groups in our social world in such a way as to cast light on their temporality. This in turn will permit us to return to the theme of historical time and draw out certain implications for a pretheoretical understanding of history.

In different ways, each of the questions raised at the end of the previous chapter bears on the relation of the individual to the group. In order to avoid the abstractness that comes of simply considering the group a "big subject," it is necessary for us to drop back to

153

individual experience and interrogate it with respect to such concepts as participation and membership.

It should be noted first that it is obviously abstract to speak simply of the individual as member of *the* community or *the* group, and then seek to identify the latter with some particular social or cultural formation such as "a people" or "a state." Clearly, as individuals we count ourselves members of many different sorts of groups. In order to understand adequately the nature of membership or participation, we had best begin by considering the different kinds of groups with which we identify ourselves.

In the narrowest and closest instance of social groups, we identify with our families. We may discount the sense of family membership we have as children, in keeping with our discussion of Hegel, and even the relation of parents to children. But as adults we enter into marriage and may thereby establish or join a larger or extended family. In identifying ourselves with it we distinguish "our" family from others. Families have always had multiple functions: they are economic units, they provide affective support and protection for their members, they may own or control property and engage in commerce, etc. Thus families are posited by their members as *we*-subjects in the sense that they are the persisting subjects of common experience and agents of common projects, including that of their own self-maintenance. In many cases the identity of an extended family derives from an identifiable foundation, such as an especially important marriage of "founders."

Families generally involve a fairly close proximity and frequent direct association among members. The same is true of work undertaken by groups and group-organized leisure-time activities. Any of these, however, can also be extended in the same way that some families are extended; that is, they involve the participation of members who have very little, very infrequent, or even no direct contact with each other. Nevertheless, the *we* is extended by each participant to all the others, known or unknown. Firms, universities, labor unions, professional associations, and the like may all have this feature. It is clearly characteristic of those larger religious, political, and cultural communities of which we count ourselves members.

Everyone knows, of course, that membership in these smaller and larger groups is an important feature of any individual's life. But discussions of experience and action usually center on the individual alone. What is overlooked is that a large part of the experience I have as an individual, and of the actions in which I engage, is not merely mine alone, and by nature could not be, since my own action or experience is only a functioning and dependent part of a larger phenomenon whose genuine subject is the group. This is to say that *for* the individual, much of what goes on in the social world is the actions and sufferings of groups, not as an external spectacle played out before the individual's eyes but as a function of his or her participation.

It must not be thought that these groups, from the more intimate ones immediately surrounding us to the larger-scale and more remote, simply fit inside one another like a series of concentric circles. Groups criss-cross one another, and participation in one may not be compatible with participation in another. Family may conflict with profession, class with country, religion with civic duty, etc., to mention only the most obvious of such conflicts. Nor do we participate in or belong to these different groups with equal degrees of awareness. Though we are restricting ourselves here to groups to which individuals *consciously* belong, the consciousness of belonging to any particular group may be stronger or weaker and may wax or wane with changing circumstances. Nor is the strength of our identification necessarily a function of the closeness, intimacy, or size of the group. A person may consider himself above all else a Jones, or above all else a worker, or a scientist, or an American, or a Jew. Individuals may or may not be forced to weigh the strength of their loyalties, and many are never forced to decide where their primary allegiance lies. But it is clear that many of the moral conflicts and dilemmas facing individuals have their origin in the individual's sense of belonging to different groups at the same time.

Granted the diversity of groups that most individuals are involved with, we need to explore further the nature of the individual's identification with and participation in any one of them. Our claim is that the group is posited by its members as subject of experiences and actions in virtue of a narrative account which ties distinct phases and elements together into a coherent story. But whence comes this account, and how does it function? In the case of the individual, we spoke of the implicit or explicit telling of a story, serving the practical function of unifying an action or experience. When *we* act, does it make sense to say simply that *we* tell such a story to ourselves?

This is where the diversification of functions, already remarked in the case of communal action, becomes a feature of the narrative structure itself of groups and their communal existence. In our view such existence would require that a "story" be shared by the members of the group, such that its formulation and eventual reformulation would be constitutive of the group and its common undertakings. But such a story can be told by an individual or individuals *on behalf of* the *we;* indeed using the *we* as the subject not only of action and experience but of narration itself. Such is the social function of leaders and spokesmen and women. Theirs is the rhetoric that unites the group and expresses what it is about, where it has come from, and where it is going. Such leaders may spring up spontaneously or their function may be elaborately institutionalized, but their role is the same: to effect the group's collective *Besinnung* on its own nature and activity.

Here the literary theorists' distinction between the author and the implied author can be useful.[1] The political or religious leader invariably presumes to speak in the name of the community itself, not his own name. He or she may tell the story, but it is "our" story that is told. Such has been the practice of political orators from Pericles and Cicero to Abraham Lincoln. "Four score and seven years ago our fathers brought forth on this continent a new nation," says Lincoln in his address at Gettysburg in 1863. "Now we are engaged in a great civil war, testing whether that nation . . . can long endure." Thus he accounts for the meaning of a collective action by placing it in a story with a past and a future: a myth of origin or foundation, a glimpse of a future placed in jeopardy by a present crisis or turning point, etc. Throughout, it is not Lincoln but *we* who speak—to ourselves.

But such a story must be shared if it is to be constitutive of a group's existence and activity. Other participants may not tell the story, but they must believe or accept it as the genuine account of what the group is and what it is doing. Thus, in the relation between formulating and communicating, on the one hand, and receiving or accepting a narrative account, on the other, the group achieves a kind of reflexive self-awareness as a "subject" that is analogous to what we found in the individual. As with the individual, so with the group, the more complex and extended the undertaking, the greater the need for collective stock-taking or *Besinnung*, which may require revision of the narrative account to meet changing circumstance.

Here we may take up the objection that our account idealizes the cohesion of groups; for at precisely the point where the need for

---

1. This distinction was introduced by W. Booth, *The Rhetoric of Fiction*, pp. 70–71; and elaborated in structuralist fashion by G. Genette, "Frontières du récit," *Communication* 8 (1966) and S. Chatman, *Story and Discourse*, pp. 146–158.

collective *Besinnung* arises, rival accounts often present themselves. Is it not the case that much communal activity at all levels, from the smallest and most intimate to our huge modern nation-states, consists in the clash of incompatible story-lines, a battle over which account of who *we* are and where *we* are going is to be accepted?

There is no doubt that much of the communal rhetoric which addresses a group as *we* is putative or persuasive rather than expressive of a genuine unity and an already accepted sense of communal activity. In some cases such story-telling attempts to create a community where none existed before. The rise of the socialist movement in the nineteenth century and its appeals in the form of tracts such as the *Communist Manifesto* attempted in effect to transform a supposedly objective group (the proletariat) into a community. We have mentioned Hegel's use of *we* in the *Phenomenology* and suggested he was appealing to his contemporaries to form a community based on a certain awareness of its past history.

In a sense Hegel's use of *we* is no different from many an author's use of the term in writing a book, including the present one. The author bravely and hopefully envisages a community of readers, each as clear-minded and discerning as the author himself, jointly addressing themselves to the task of investigating some problem— say, the connection between time, narrative, and history. The author leads the way, occasionally (for example, at the beginning of each chapter) reminding his readers what "we" have accomplished and what remains to be done. He imagines them vigorously nodding their heads at each turn in the argument. Yet they are not necessarily merely docile listeners; occasionally one of them may be permitted to raise an objection which the author neatly demolishes and which by coincidence facilitates his move to the next point and his further advancement of the investigation toward its conclusion.

Needless to say, the existence of this envisaged community may be entirely confined to the author's mind. Even if anyone did read his book, they may have rejected his whole approach by chapter two and in reading on may only be sharpening their pencils for the attack. Hegel's community, too, and even those of Marx and Engels, may never have formed in the manner envisaged by their putative leaders, and they may retain only the status of an ideal.

The same persuasive rhetoric can also be employed in cases in which a fairly cohesive community already exists, but in which there are rival versions of what it should do. It is as if there was agreement over the story up to now, but dispute over how it is to continue.

Insofar as there is unspoken agreement on all sides that members address each other *as* members of a community there must be some sense of a common story, at least as regards the past. Nevertheless, disagreement may even arise over how to interpret the past. Americans, whose political rhetoric assumes a shared history and often appeals to a quasi-mythical act of establishment by "founding fathers," nevertheless have profound disagreements about the nature of the principles involved in that foundation: over the relation of church and state, the balance of rights and duties, etc. In a more general way, in many Western countries at least, "conservatives" are distinguished from "progressives" by the kind of story they tell of the *whole* of their country's history: whether it is the steady application of basic and unchanging first principles, or whether it is a forward progress toward some goal not attained but only envisaged in its foundation. Thus differences concern not only the present and future but also the past and indeed the whole story which encompasses all three temporal dimensions.

These can be rival versions of the same story, but they can also be the basis for factions so sharply divided that they threaten the unified existence of the community from which they spring. Communities of all sizes and durations *can* disintegrate, and their existence can be a fragile one which hovers for a long time on the brink of fragmentation. Separatist movements formed of religious and linguistic minorities, which have threatened the integrity of many modern nation-states in recent times, are cases in point. Individuals identify themselves as Basques or Corsicans or Québecois or Kurds rather than as members of the "official " group to which they supposedly belong; and in doing this they subscribe to a story about their community, usually involving its repression at the hands of others, which differs from the official account of their minority group's status within the larger state.

These considerations bring to mind the importance of opposition in the formation and maintenance of groups, something we have noted before. Hegel suggested that the independence and integrity of the individual is won in a struggle with others, at least initially. We have already noted that an external threat can often constitute the common experience which fuses a group into a community: individuals recognize that it is *as* a group, not merely as individuals, that they are threatened. The threat of a group's extinction and its organization into an active force which counters the threat figure importantly in the account a community gives to itself of its own origins or foundations and in some cases its continuing *raison d'être*. Such an account is a story of oppression or exploitation and liberation, triumph over adversity, etc. Typically the story is told from the middle and becomes a tale of suspense: the threat is still there, we may succumb to it yet, unless we rise up as one and defeat it once and for all. That quintessential element of narrative, the crisis or turning point, is the stuff of communal life.

Hegel's dialectic of dependence and independence is thus replicated at higher levels. Communities are formed in which individuals mutually acknowledge one another. But *as* a community we stand in opposition to another group whose threat may have occasioned our mutual recognition in the first place. The struggle to the death may ensue, in which groups try to annihilate each other; or they may seek domination and enslavement. Or again, mutual recognition may occur between groups. It is mutual recognition at this level which is at issue in our large modern states, composed of so many religious, cultural, and other sub-groups, and which these states find so difficult to achieve.

Do communities require external opposition in order to survive? History seems to suggest that they do. If it is true, Hegel's projection of a grand reconciliation among opposed historical forces would have little chance of success. We interpreted his *Phenomenology* as attempting on one level, at least, to constitute a community by telling a persuasive story of its origins and destiny, and we can look at his more grandiose philosophy of history in the same way. In the latter case it is not so much the spirit of modern Europe as the spirit of humanity as such he is attempting to forge. Seen in this light the failure of Hegel's philosophy of history is not a theoretical but a practical one; it should be understood not as a putative science but as a kind of world-political rhetoric, and its problem is not that it makes false predictions or implausible claims about the end of history, but that it is not able to constitute a community of humanity by telling a persuasive story about it. And the trouble may not be merely that Hegel's works are somewhat lacking in popular appeal. Humanity as such seems to be a group with which most individuals have a hard time identifying themselves. Hegel wanted to avoid the abstract leap from the individual directly to the "Big Subject" by insisting on the intermediate role of social and other communities. But he wanted to get to the Big Subject eventually nevertheless. The question, however, is whether the nature of the community is not such that it must always remain plural, that is, whether communities do not always constitute themselves and define themselves in opposition to each other.

Hegel apparently did believe what we have denied earlier, namely, that social groups fit inside one another like a series of concentric circles, each of which constitutes the truth of the ones inside it. For all his insistence on concreteness and conflict, Hegel was still a philosopher of identity. In his mature philosophy he seemed to think that the state could encompass all the lower levels of spirit (family and civil society) and be the vehicle for expressing the religion and thought of the Absolute. In our view there is no doubt that spirit in Hegel's sense exists in the social world, but it exists in many forms and there seems little hope that these forms will one day converge.

We have tried in this section to address several different senses in which our account of the social subject was overly schematic and abstract. There remains the objection that our portrayal of the relation of the individual to the group is too voluntaristic or contractarian. We have spoken of a community's "story" which is "accepted" by its members, and in relying on Hegel we may have placed too much emphasis on the independence, or autonomy (*Selbständigkeit*), and self-consciousness of the individuals involved. Is it not true of some of the most important groups we belong to, such as cultural or religious communities, that their existence and continuity long predate us, and that we are members from the moment of our birth because of our place, time, and circumstances?

But this is to overlook the distinction made earlier between objective membership and membership by participation. It is certainly true that one is born into certain communities. But part of the process of growing up is recognizing that this is so and then accepting or rejecting such membership. Such a processs of "ratification" (or its opposite) need not take place all at once, in a conscious decision; it may develop quite gradually through a slow shift of attitude and through a series of actions and decisions which seem initially to have nothing to do with the issue of group membership, but which in retrospect place a certain distance between oneself and the group in question. Gradually we come to an awareness of which groups we count ourselves as belonging to and which not.

This is not to deny that "objective" origins or objective group-memberships influence or properly characterize our conduct. An Irish Catholic may still think and act like an Irish Catholic long after he has left the church and declared himself an atheist, and even though he may vehemently deny it. And a member of "Lump-enproletariat" may think and act in a way that is thoroughly typical of that group even though he has no awareness of belonging to it and has never even heard the term. Thus one can objectively belong to a group and not know it or admit it; or one can know it but consider it a matter of indifference or indeed reject it. We are certainly not denying that groups composed in this way can play an important role in society and history, but we would not characterize them in any subjective terms. Only groups distinguished by the active and conscious participation of their members qualify as *we*-subjects in the sense of this discussion, and this because they are so characterized precisely by their members.

This may seem either overly bold or curiously hesitant from an ontological point of view, depending on how it is understood. We are saying that the *we*-subject exists insofar as individuals take it to exist and act accordingly. Is this to say that it exists because some people either think it does or act as if it did, or both? Surely thinking and pretending are never enough to bring something into existence. Are we then saying that it exists only "in the minds" of the participants and thus has no objective existence at all? The existence and identity of a group-subject seems nothing but a series of overlapping projections made from different but concurring points of view, those of the individuals involved.

This may be so, but we could say the same thing precisely of the individuals themselves and their existence and identity. We did say something like this, in fact, in chapter III. The self is the unity of a series of overlapping projections made from different temporal points of view. It is a story-in-the-making which may in some cases fall apart for lack of coherence. In this sense the identity and existence of groups are no less and no more stable than those of individuals.

This is yet another way in which the two can be considered analogues of each other. We must not forget, however, that groups *contain* individuals, as well as being in some ways analogous to them. What we have said about groups in this and the previous chapter permits us to add some important observations to our discussion of the individual in chapters I–III. We noted there the quasi-intersubjective nature of the narrative structure of action, experience, and life; story-telling involves a character and an audience to whom the story is told. As we always stand in relation to other people, it is never clear whether we are telling primarily to ourselves or primarily to others the stories that make up our lives. Both are involved in different measures.

In this and the previous chapter, we have insisted on the importance to the individual of belonging to and identifying with groups. This has two implications for our notion of the coherence of life: One is that an important part of the *individual's* reflection on that coherence will involve questions of which groups he or she chooses to belong to, which to reject, etc., the other is that the answer to these questions determines in large measure the audience to whom one is addressing oneself, implicitly or explicitly, in composing the narrative of one's own life. Life indeed involves, in Goffman's words, a "presentation" of self to others; but it is in each case to a select group of others that I as individual feel a real need to explain and justify myself. These are precisely the ones with whom I stand in relation of mutual recognition and with whom I thus form a group.

But this works in diverse ways. As we noted earlier, as an individual I belong to different groups at once. It is as a family member that I "present" myself to my family, as a citizen to my fellow citizens, etc. The groups to which I belong provide different contexts of justification and narrative explanation, different expectations about courses of action I must follow and attitudes I may adopt. Groups which have existed long before I came along have their institutionalized or conventionalized roles, and my membership in the group involves an acceptance of those roles. MacIntyre is quite right to say that we "find ourselves" in such roles.[2] He might better have stated his view by saying simply that we *are* in these roles, and in the groups from which they derive, right from the start of our lives. It is precisely when we "find ourselves" in them, that is, when we not only are in them but realize that we are, that the question of our adherence arises for us. From then on we have chosen, explicitly or by default. It is true that our conduct is determined by the roles and standards of the community or the communities to which we belong. But we as individuals are ultimately responsible for our belonging. To which group or groups I shall belong as an individual is part of the problem of coherence that I must deal with in the course of life. These, then, are some of the ways our account of communities reflects back upon our earlier account of individual existence. The implication of all of

---

2. See chapter III above, p. 92.

this for the theory of communities, in turn, is that it explains the sense in which communities are composed ultimately of individuals who, in a more or less explicit way, choose to belong to them and are conscious of doing so.

2. *Communal Narrative and Historical Time*

Let us try to sum up what we have been saying in the previous section and then turn to some of its implications for history. At whatever level of size or degree of complexity, a community exists wherever a narrative account exists of a *we* which has continuous existence through its experiences and activities. When we say that such an account "exists," we mean to say that it gets articulated or formulated, perhaps by only one or a few of the group's members, in terms of the *we* and is accepted or subscribed to by the other members. It is their acceptance that makes them members, constitutes their recognition of the others as fellow members, and determines their participation in the action, experience, and life of the community. To be a participant or member in this sense, and to posit a *we* as group-subject of such a communal story, are really the same thing.

In this sense, where such a community exists it is constantly in the process, as an individual is, of composing and re-composing its own autobiography. Like the autobiography of an individual, such a story seeks a unifying structure for a sequence of experiences and actions. An individual's life-story is provided by birth and death, of course, with the limits of beginning and end. Most communities, too, trace themselves to an origin or foundation; we have mentioned the "founders" of families and of nations and we could find corresponding phenomena elsewhere, from the divine establishment of religious communities to the organizational meetings of the most humble and small-scale local groups or clubs. Every such community is likewise faced with the constant possibility of its own "death"; if it is not threatened with destruction from without, it must deal with its own centrifugal tendencies toward dissolution or fragmentation from within. As we said before, whatever else a group may be about, it must see to its own self-maintenance. The prospective death of a community, like the death of an individual, is usually an open eventuality of uncertain date. It may not be lived and anticipated with the same degree of inevitability as the death of an individual; but the sense of finitude and fragility is part of any community's existence because of the latter's dependence on the attitudes and interests of the individuals that make it up.

We have already made the point that it is at least partly in response to the problem of self-maintenance that conventions, constitutions, laws, and hierarchical structure become important. As has often been observed, no community is established by such arrangements; on the contrary, a prior community must exist which establishes them. But they may well play a role in the community's continuity, provided they are accepted as the channels for collective existence and activity.

It is institutional arrangements of this sort that can release a community from its dependence on particular leaders. It is obvious that individual persons are often the source and sole assurance of the existence of a community. As its spokesman and agent, the leader embodies the subjectivity of the group by speaking (the "royal we") and acting on its behalf. The actions, experiences, and even the thoughts of this individual, as long as he or she is operating in an "official" capacity, are no longer merely those of an individual but are transposed to a communal scale. But the same can also be true of that individual's death, which can become at the same time the death of the community. Typical if the story of many communities is the early crisis of how to survive the death of its founder or founders; solutions included apostolic succession, the establishment of a dynasty, the agreement on constitutional arrangements for transfering power, etc.[3]

Thus, like an individual, a community at any moment has a sense of its origins and the prospect of its own death as it seeks to articulate its own internal coherence and integrity over time. Such articulation involves an interplay of formulation and acceptance, as we saw, on the part of the participants. It may also take the form of a kind of negotiation among participants or even between parties to different versions of the group's story. Changing external circumstances or internal crises may be the occasion for a sort of collective *Besinnung* in which participants are reminded of their past, formulate or refor-

---

3. The death of the founder can also, of course, be the catalyst, the violent attack from without or within which fuses the community. See R. Girard, *La Violence et le sacré* (Paris: Grasset, 1972) which takes up themes already treated in James G. Frazer's classic, *The Golden Bough: A Study in Magic and Religion*, 3rd ed. (New York: St. Martin's Press, 1966).

mulate present problems and projects, and orient themselves toward the future.

This description of social existence now permits us to formulate a conception of historical time and the historical past which corresponds to what we have been searching for in this inquiry. It reveals a pre-thematic temporality and accordingly a pre-thematic past which pertain specifically to the social and not merely to the individual.

In order to get at this conception of temporality let us revert initially to the first person singular. As a social being my own identity is partly a function of the groups with which I identify myself and which constitute communities of reciprocally recognized individuals. As we have seen, for me these groups may vary in importance, and my membership in more than one may be a source of conflict for me. Questions of identification, adherence, rejection, participation, conflicting loyalties, etc., are part of *my* life-story; they figure importantly in the implicit autobiography that I am constantly composing and recomposing, and in which the coherence of personal past, present, and future is at issue. It is I who am the hero of *this* story, I who am the subject of the actions and experiences spread out over time. It is I who am constituted in the unity of the story they make up when I tell it to myself.

But my adherence to a community injects me into a different temporality with a different subject.[4] (If I now shift to the first person plural, it should be noted that I am not using the "we" with which I as author address the putative readers of this book, but rather the "we" the members of a community would use in addressing each other.) Now it is our actions and experiences which are spread out over time. The experience we are having, the action in which we are engaged, is the temporal configuration of which the present phase is a dependent part. At any moment we stand in a certain "place" in the life of our community and from that place the future prospects and the past background make up the temporal horizons of this particular present. Like time at the personal level, these horizons are not empty, receding without differentiation into the distance; they are filled in precisely with the events we (as a group) have experienced (or will experience), with our experiences themselves, and with the

---

4. The notion of different temporalities is advanced by Claude Lévi-Strauss in *The Savage Mind* (Chicago: University of Chicago Press, 1966), p. 260.

sequence of our communal actions. Since they are attached to the *we* as their subject they are part of the life of the community in question and refer ultimately to the life-story of this community encompassed by its birth and prospective death. In this way the broad outlines of our description of the temporality of experience and action, and our account of the coherence of life, will hold true for the community as lived "from the inside" by its members who in reciprocal recognition constitute a *we*.

This structure was referred to as a "different temporality," and this must be explained. It is different from temporality at the individual level, but the difference is clearly one of content, not of form. Taking the place of the *I*-subject is the *we*-subject. In place of the events, experience, and actions of the individual life are those of the community. And the coherence which can become an issue in collective *Besinnung* is the coherence of the community's life taken as a whole.

The events that make up a community's life may be an economic crisis, a struggle for leadership, the failure or success of some collective project, etc. It is the sequence of such strictly communal events that figures in the narrative account of the existence of the group to which the individual member subscribes as a function of his or her membership. The individual's participation in the event or action itself may be minimal and is usually partial, unless the individual has some important representative function. It is nevertheless the *we* of which the individual counts himself a part that remains the legitimate subject of the experience or action in question.

To be sure, the same events may figure in the life of both a community and an individual and constitute an important part of that individual's life story. The Great Depression was an event in the lives of many individuals, as well as in the lives of different communities, from families to nation-states to the larger international economic community. But the event will have a different significance at each of these levels, even though all levels are interconnected as is the economic system itself. For the individual the experience of this phenomenon is connected with other personal experiences, such as maturing, getting an education, or choosing a career. Even the individual's participation in a collective action (such as enlisting and fighting in a war) is an element in his own life-story. But one can distinguish an individual's part in such an action from the action itself, and it is the latter, as *our* action when *we* are faced with a common situation, that belongs in the life of the community. In such cases, individuals, as an expression of their membership in the community, will speak of *our* experience, *our* action, etc., even of events in which they were not directly involved.

One obvious class of communal events that lies outside the range of the individual's own experience and involvement consists of those that occurred before his birth. The life-span of the community in many cases exceeds that of any of its members, and their membership and participation implicates them in a *we*-relationship with others who are in principle not accessible to them. It is certainly not the case that we use the *we* only in relation to contemporaries. "We know more now than we did in the nineteenth century," say the astronomers about their own community and its collective endeavor, past and present. The events, too, of communal life may have dimensions that do not fit within an individual lifetime, such as the Industrial Revolution or the ascendancy and decline of the Roman Empire. Even actions such as the conquest of the American West or the colonization of the New World are far beyond the span of the individual's experience.

This is not to say, however, that the difference between individual and community "temporalities" is necessarily one of *scale*. Important communal events, such as the Paris Commune of 1871 or the Arab-Israeli Seven-day War can be very short-lived indeed. What makes them communal is not their scale but the reference to the *we*, both internally, as we might say, and externally. That is, they constitute actions or experiences which are communal by their nature, involving a collection of mutually recognizing participants; and as events they take their place in a temporally configured sequence of other events that have the same communal reference. The Seven-day War, whatever its many significances for the individuals involved, is a turning point in the early life of the state of Israel and of the post-war Middle East.

It is events of this sort, and the configured sequences they make up, that constitute what we can call the pre-thematic complex of historical time. The communal event of the present, in which *we* participate as subjects of experience or action, gets its sense from the background of comparable events to which it belongs. We participate in them (enjoy or suffer, act in common, and understand what we are doing) to the extent that we place the event in this context. And our placing it there is a function of the overall story *we* tell, and if necessary retell, to each other about ourselves and what we are doing.

Like the personal (or first-person-singular) temporality we described in earlier chapters, this historical temporality is centered in the present. We can use the same spatially-expressed metaphors to describe it: it radiates out from the present, the present is surrounded by or set off by the past and future horizons from which it stands out, etc. All this is to say that *we* (the communal *we*, again, for any given community) live an ongoing communal life projecting a future before us an retaining a past behind us, which is being organized prospectively and retrospectively in a narrative fashion. The past is prethematic in the sense that it is not under scrutiny for its own sake but functions as part of a larger complex. The occasionally necessary shift from a more or less straightforward, unreflective activity to a collective *Besinnung* has the function not of investigating any dimension of time (such as the past) for its own sake but of bringing into focus the whole temporal complex (the "whole story") in which we are engaged.

The narrative recounting and accounting which occurs on these occasions is accordingly, like narrative activity at the personal level, above all practical in character. As before, it has a doubly practical function, that of constituting actions themselves, in the form of deliberation and planning, and the more general function of drawing together any temporally extended sequence, whether of action, experience, or even a whole life, when such a sequence has gone astray or lost its coherence. Discovering or rediscovering the story, picking up the thread, reminding ourselves where we stand, where we have been and where we are going—these are typical narrative-practical modes of discourse which are as prevalent and as important for groups as they are for individuals.

These considerations are enough to convince us anew, with our conclusions transferred from the individual to the social plane, that narrative is not in any way adventitious or external to the actions and experiences of real life but is part of its fabric. Narrative is not only constitutive of the temporal structure of communal events, which take the form of configured sequences with beginnings, middles, and ends, turning points and reversals, departures and returns, suspensions and resolutions, etc. It is also found in the reflective, prospective-retrospective grasp of these sequences which assigns them these configurations by telling about them as they are going on.

3. From Historical Time to Historiography

By now it should be obvious that the foregoing view of historical time and historical existence generally will have certain implications for the understanding of historical inquiry and of historical writing. In the present section we shall examine those implications. The most general point we want to make is that, insofar as such inquiry results in narrative accounts, these must be regarded not as a departure from the structure of the reality they purport to depict, much less a distortion or radical transformation of its character, but as an extension of its very nature. By arguing for the narrative character of human experience, both individual and social, we have been concerned from the start to counter the view of certain theorists, mentioned at the outset, that a narrative account is so utterly different *in form* from the events it portrays that by virtue of this form alone it is constitutionally condemned to misrepresentation. But this does not yet tell us how to understand the relationship between historical events, historical time, and a historian's narrative account of them.

To get at this understanding, the best place to start is with an instance of historical inquiry and historiography that has always occupied a central place in the field: namely, the case of historians writing about their own society, especially about its relatively recent past. This sort of history has of course played an important role in the past development of historiography as a genre and of history as a research discipline. And it is no less important today, wherever historical research is practiced, both inside and outside the academy. When I speak of historians' writing about "their own society" I refer not only to our modern nation-states, but also to significant cultural communities, for example, French Canada, the American South, the Roman Catholic Church, etc.

The first thing we want to say about such historians is that insofar as they are participating members of their own community, in our view they live in a milieu in which a very general story *already exists*. It is by virtue of this story that the community exists, coheres, and continues as a social entity. This story is continually being written and rewritten in the political and social transactions of its members; such a story unites the present with the past in relation to a projected future of greater or less determinateness.

Needless to say it is abstract to portray such a historian, as do some epistemological approaches, as if he or she were to reconstruct the past *ex nihilo* by applying rules of evidence to a heap of documents or ruins. Such a historian always functions in a context in which an account already exists before he or she begins. I refer not merely to the account generally accepted by the academic establishment in which the historian is trained. It is true enough that such an establishment usually exists and dominates a discipline such as history at any given time. I am referring rather to the generalized popular account which exists outside the discipline and which provides the social context in which the historians' discipline is found. This account is pre-thematic in the sense that it is prior to the historians' thematization of it.

I need hardly add that, in keeping with what was said earlier, this pre-thematic narrative context will doubtless contain not just one account but possibly conflicting accounts of major past developments, present circumstances, and above all the future prospects of the community in question. At the same time the community will probably share fundamental narrative presuppositions about itself; its origins, its major turning points, its abiding aims, etc. As we claimed before, without some narrative consensus at this very deep level a community is on the brink of fragmentation.

Thus when something like disciplined historical inquiry gets underway in a given society, it may be confronted with an array of narratives at different levels, in some cases conflicting ones, about its subject matter. It can hardly be unaffected by these narratives, whether or not it thinks it should be. This is not at all to say that any historian will simply retail a standard line, though some do. Historians are often among those who challenge some of the basic assumptions of their communities, up to and including even the basic story which constitutes the community *as* a community in the first place. Clearly the material on which the historian works, to which he turns his attention, is anything but a mass of unrelated events waiting for a story to be told about them, as theorists like Ricoeur and Mink seem to suggest. Furthermore, in the case of the historian concerned with the recent past of his or her community, it is likely that the historian's account will enter into the current and ongoing debates the community conducts with itself about its own nature, temporal coherence, life, and goals. And indeed historians are known to play an influential role, at least in some societies, in just this way. The rewriting of the history of the French Revolution is a classic case of the historiographic component in a continuing communal debate over the nature of French society and the French Republic. And one could cite many more such examples.

Does this mean that a historian's account is just another story to add to those already existing? By arguing for a common structure between a historian's narrative and the others that make up the social fabric, and by denying any basic difference of form, are we asserting that the only difference, if there is any, lies at the level of content? This would be to say, in effect, that historical knowledge is merely part of historical reality. We have argued that historical narrative is not formally condemned to mis–representation; but now we seem to be denying it any special capacity for representation. Even those who agree with the first part might hesitate to accept the second. Are there not after all some formal features of historical inquiry which set it apart from the reality it depicts and from the narratives that constitute that reality?

Two such features can be mentioned. The first has to do with the interest which lies behind narration in each case: the narrative structure and narrational activity within communal existence is, as we have insisted, primarily practical in character; historical narrative, by contrast, is cognitive and seeks an objective representation. The former is engaged in action and has an interest in its outcome; the latter is detached and disinterested, and aims only at the truth. The second difference concerns the temporal standpoints of the narrators in each case. Our "practical" narrator is situated *in medias res*, whereas the historical narrator looks back on actions and events already completed. This gives the latter the well-known (and already discussed) advantage of hindsight over his subjects: he knows how things turned out, knows the difference between the intended consequences and the real consequences of their action, etc.

These differences between narrative agent or participant and narrative historian are operative and important: there is no denying the importance of temporal standpoint and of the difference in attitude (engaged or detached) in relation to a lived or performed sequence of human events. At the same time we should like to emphasize several respects in which these differences are mitigated. And we shall do this not by denying objectivity and hindsight to historical inquiry, but by attributing them to narrative-historical existence.

We have already pointed out at the end of chapter III, with respect to individual action and experience, that the narrativization that goes on there cannot be indifferent to truth where the past is concerned.[5] Indeed, where the issue is not merely the shaping of an open future but the coherence of future, present, and past, it is important to be clear on what really happened; the past may be variously interpreted but it cannot be wished away or forcibly altered by an inventive narrative imagination. So much of one's present

---

5. Chapter III, p. 98 above.

capacities are in continuity with, and sometimes result from, past choices and experiences that getting straight one's past can be seen as a desideratum and even a necessary condition for a coherent life. This is, of course, one of the insights on which much psychotherapy is based, as we pointed out.

A concern for the truth of the past plays the same role in the case of the community. Members often debate the facts of the past, precisely because they are so important in the constitution of the present and the future. This is not to deny that the past is often manipulated, especially where social story-telling is political and persuasive in character. The personal past is often distorted too, deliberately or not. My point is merely that a genuine interest in the truth of the past is compatible with and indeed important for the practical narrative constitution of communal existence. Equally, objectively-oriented historical inquiry and research are not disqualified from playing a role in the ongoing political and social debates of a community; on the contrary, they can and do contribute to them.

We are not commenting here, it should be noted, on the success with which truthfulness about the past is actually attained. Our point concerns the *interest* in or commitment to truth, and we are only saying that this is not restricted to history as a discipline. It is true that the discipline has among other things developed techniques for discovering and evaluating evidence in order to implement its commitment to truth. A justified suspicion that partisanship in the events of the day can distort our view of the past has led to the emphasis on detachment and objectivity. But these in turn, once achieved, can be put in the service of engagement in the present and the shaping of the future.

As for the hindsight which is characteristic of historical inquiry, this too is not exclusive to the latter, at least not formally. Socially constitutive narrative, like the narrative structure of individual life and action, has a prospective-retrospective form. In anticipating the future, it aims at, and largely achieves, that quasi-hindsight that we characterized earlier, borrowing Schutz's term, as the future perfect.[6] Far from waiting passively for things to happen, communities negotiate with the future and understand the present in light of that future.

To be sure, insofar as history restricts itself to the past, it is capable of real and not merely quasi-hindsight. Our point is merely that viewing events and actions in light of what follows them, and of what

---

6. See chapter I, p. 38 above.

follows from them, is not something exclusive to the historian's point of view nor even to the consideration of the past; it is our way of viewing the present as well. More generally, it is our way of viewing time and living and acting in it. By restricting itself to just the past, history indeed avails itself of a special advantage; by cultivating a detached attitude and developing techniques of research it may more greatly satisfy its interest in the truth about the past. But neither in having this interest nor in its retrospective view does it differ in form from the socially constitutive narrative structure of the community.

Thus, as we said, our purpose here is not to deny the objectivity and the hindsight of the historian's point of view, but only to deny that these are formal features that are exclusive to that point of view. The only remark that needs to be made about the historian's approach is that his retrospective vantage point is hardly absolute, especially in the case of the sort of history we have been considering, namely, the recent history of one's own community. Far from dealing with past events which are fixed and whose consequences are clear, historians here deal with events whose consequences are still being felt and are operative in the present. Danto has made the general point that the historian's descriptions of past events derive from an awareness of the later consequences of these events, so that in principle no final description could be achieved as long as time goes on and further consequences unfold.[7] This point may seem abstract when applied to the remote past, but it is certainly important for the recent past, and for one's own society where the historian is himself involved in the consequences of the events under his retrospective view.

But these considerations may raise a much more sweeping objection to our characterization of historiography. By choosing as our paradigm the recent history of the historian's own society, have we not prejudiced the case? We have chosen a type of history-writing which is indeed often closely linked to the narrative constitution of a community. But not all historiography is so closely linked. Historians turn their attention to the farthest reaches of history and prehistory, and to societies not even remotely connected with their own. They construct narrative accounts of the cultural, political, and economic developments of such societies which in some cases are as rich in detail, drama, and narrative skill as are those dealing with familiar events. Is it possible to say of such histories that they are just

---

7. Danto, *Analytical Philosophy of History*, p. 15.

an extension of social existence? Do these cases not prove that historical narrative is an autonomous activity not requiring or presuppos-
ing the involvement of the historian in the society he or she writes
about? Should we not rather view "history-close-to-home" simply as
an instance of historical knowledge which happens to turn its attention to events that are proximate rather than remote in time and
space?

Nothing in this objection, of course, counts against our claim that a
narrative account of events is *formally* not different from the events it
portrays, even if those events are distant from the portrayal. Insofar as
the historian tells us of past actions, experiences, and lives, even if
he does not have access to the stories of those who lived them but has
to construct one out of fragmentary evidence, the reality recounted is
one already lived as narrative. That the historian's account may differ
in *content* we do not deny, of course—but this is equally true of the
most recent and most proximate events.

The objection may seem, however, to conflict with our claim that
the historical account is produced against the background or horizon
of an already-existing story of the events in question. It can be
maintained, however, that the pre-thematic past, that is, that aspect
of the social-temporal complex which is past, extends indefinitely
and is not confined to the content of the story of one's own community. Thus the proximate communities to which we belong, including our present-day political and cultural communities *and* the
community of contemporary historical scholars, besides exhibiting
an internal narrative articulation of their own, are situated for us
within the larger panorama of history reaching back into the remotest
regions and times. When historians turn their attention to the remote
and distant past, even if they are not dealing with a period already
explored by other historians but are discovering new terrain, they are
not venturing into the totally unknown. Rather, they are picking out
something from within a pregiven horizon of more or less clear
shapes and contours. To adapt the spatial metaphor we have used
before, we stand within historical, social time as we stand within
space. It extends in all directions about us. As historians we may
pick out for treatment some familiar landmark, such as a recent war
or famous political event, or we may turn to something hidden in the
recesses among the familiar landmarks, something that puzzles us
precisely because it is for us a gap in the terrain. This is not to say
that the whole of world history lies spread out before us, or that it
constitutes, in Mink's words, a story already written and just waiting

to be told. But certainly in a very general way its narrative contours are there prior to any particular historian's work and provide the framework within which the latter takes place.

These considerations are relevant to a further objection that may be raised to our treatment of historical inquiry. This is the objection that we have spoken of it entirely in terms of historical narrative. Again we could be said to have chosen a weighted paradigm. Not all historiography is narrative in character. Inquiry, research, and writing about the past need not take the form of telling stories about the past, of recounting sequences of the actions or experiences of individuals or communities. In fact, considerable controversy has raged over the role of narrative in history.

Some historians have argued that history should not be narrative in character, since narrative's focus is on the actions and experiences of individuals, whereas what is important in society, and determines the actions and experiences of persons, is deeper-lying social and economic factors. These must be viewed as phenomena of the long term *(longue durée)*, to use Braudel's expression,[8] and be described as static structures or extremely slow changes not even perceptible to persons affected by them.

Paul Ricoeur has argued, by analyzing Braudel's classic study of Mediterranean civilization, that even in this sort of history certain narrative structures and strategies (emplotment involving large-scale "quasi-persons" or "quasi-events," turning points, teleological ordering, etc.) can turn up in altered guise.[9] But Ricoeur's argument is not essential to our response to this objection. Genuinely non-narrative history does exist, and existed long before Braudel and the *Annales* school. Some of the classics of European historiography (Fustel de Coulonge and Carcopino on ancient cities, Huizinga and Pirenne on the Middle Ages, etc.) give us social and cultural cross-sections of a particular period and tell no story at all in the strict sense.

The *first* point to be made is that such histories tell us about the settings and circumstances in which people and communities existed and in which they acted, experienced, and thus projected themselves into time. About these, narrative histories have been written and continue to be written, as of course the anti-narrativists admit. Whether the settings and circumstances described in non-

---

8. F. Braudel, "La longue durée," in his *Écrits sur l'histoire* (Paris, Flammarion, 1969), pp. 41–83.

9. Ricoeur, *Temps et récit*, vol. I pp. 190–304.

narrative histories were known to historical agents (customs, social practices) or unknown to them (long-term trends in population, climate, prices) will of course make a difference; the former would enter into the stories these agents told about themselves, the latter would not. But there are many ways in which historians, looking back on a course of action, will tell a story about it which differs from that told by those who performed it. This can be true of anyone who looks at actions already completed, even his own. Factors come to light in retrospect of which the agent was not aware, including some of which he could not have been aware. The economic history of the *longue durée* joins psycho-history and certain kinds of Marxist history in implicitly portraying historical agents largely as dupes, pushed and pulled by forces of which they were not aware. The fact remains that what they were aware of, illusory or not, formed the basis *for them* of a temporal projection and a self-understanding which took narrative form. However misguided their self-understanding, it is part of the human reality of the past about which historians write. And *when* they do write about it, their narrative recounting partakes of the *form* (at least) of the original narrative accounting which is their object.

A *second* point to be made about non-narrative history is that, like any other history, it tacitly presupposes the background, large-scale historical continuum from which its cross-section is drawn. In other words, it may for good reasons choose to disregard the historical change of its objects, but it cannot deny it. In this sense it shares what we have called the pre-thematic sense of the historical past which places that past in a certain narrative relation to the present of the historian's own time.

Our point here of course has not been to argue for or against narrative history. Indeed, I have never understood why narrative and non-narrative history could not be considered two perfectly compatible and complementary approaches to the past. Our purpose here has been merely to place historiography generally, and especially narrative history, in relation to the pre-thematic sense of history we have been trying to describe in this and the previous chapters.

One further position on narrative in historiography needs to be mentioned briefly. This is the view of certain analytic philosophers mentioned earlier that narrative is merely the literary surface, the manner in which historians write up the results of their research, which is really incidental to the scientific work of discovery or reconstruction.[10] But our whole theory must count as a denial of this view. For what are historians discovering or reconstructing? *Insofar* as the actions and experiences of individuals and communities constitute the objects of their inquiry (and we have admitted these are not history's only objects), historians are dealing with and evaluating narratives from start to finish. Narrative, on our view, lies in the *objects* of historical research, not merely in its own manner of writing about these objects. It may indeed be true that historical research will often penetrate to causal connections among events and actions (particularly psychological or economic connections) which were hidden from the historical agents themselves. But this is not to deny that these agents lived in a narrative fashion; it is just to say that *their* story of what they were doing must be revised or indeed replaced by a better one.

4. Who Are "We"?

In the previous section we argued that historical narrative is an extension by others means, and to some extent with different attitudes, of historical existence itself. To tell the story of a community and of the events and actions that make up its history is simply to continue, at a somewhat more reflective and usually more retrospective level, the story-telling process through which the community constitutes itself and its actions. We are thus making the same point at the social level that we made earlier about the individual: that narrative, far from originating externally and imposing a story on what was previously a mass of unrelated facts, is inherent in the process in the first place—in this case, the experiences, actions, and lives of communities. For the *we*, no less than for the *I*, reflectively structuring time in narrative form is just *our* way of living in time.

This connection between historical existence and historical narration has been made before in somewhat different terms. Hegel, for example, believes it is no accident that the term *Geschichte* denotes both the *res gestae* and the *historia rerum gestarum*: "We must suppose historical narrations to have appeared contemporaneously with historical deeds and events. It is an internal vital principle

---

10. Mandelbaum, "A Note on History as Narrative"; Goldstein, *Historical Knowing*.

common to both that produces them synchronously."[11] Such a view is behind Dilthey's assertion that "we are historical beings first, before we are observers of history."[12] The prospective-retrospective *Besinnung* is the way in which we not only understand ourselves but constitute ourselves. R. G. Collingwood makes a similar point when he writes: "There is not, first, a special kind of process, the historical process, and then a special way of knowing this, historical thought. The historical process is itself a process of thought, and it exists only insofar as the minds, which are parts of it know themselves for parts of it."[13] Neither Dilthey nor Collingwood goes as far as we have gone, and as far as Hegel goes, in attaching this "process of thought" to the *we*. They tend to think of history as the actions of individuals. But they share the idea that historical existence and historical understanding are of a piece.

To speak of a "process of thought" is admittedly to risk falling prey to an "idealist" tendency for which Collingwood and sometimes Hegel are often reproached. These philosophers are often caricatured as believing that history is nothing *but* thought or that there is no difference between what people were doing and what they thought they were doing. Such a view would of course be just as wrong-headed as one which saw no connection at all between action and the agent's intentions, memories, and reflections. But distinguishing between what a person is doing and what he thinks he is doing is not something that only a historian, a sociologist, or a psychoanalyst can do. We make this very distinction about ourselves in retrospect and this is one of the factors that contribute to the frequent revisions of our plans, projects, and narrative accounts of ourselves. These revisions belong as much to the historical process itself as to the retrospective assessments of it by historians.

To assert the unity of historical existence and historical thought is to assert again that narrative is not artificial, not a case of forcing reality into an alien mold. But this brings us back to the question we briefly touched on in chapter II: if narrative is not artificial, is it then "natural"?[14] And does "natural" in this case mean universal, something that inheres in human nature itself, wherever and whenever it

---

11. G. W. F. Hegel, *The Philosophy of History*, tr. J. Sibree (New York: Dover Publications, 1956), p. 60.

12. Dilthey, *Gesammelte Schriften*. vol. VII, pp. 277–78.

13. R. G. Collingwood, "Human Nature and Human History" in *Ideas of History*, vol. 2, ed. T. Nash (New York: E. P. Dutton, 1969), p. 51.

14. See chapter II, pp. 66–68.

is found? This question was raised earlier about individuals. Now it must be raised anew at the social and historical level. Does narrative belong to the *nature* of social existence as such?

Nothing seems more natural to us, indeed, than the narrative structure of human events, personal or social. The idea that events form meaningful configurations, that we shape them reflectively into such configurations by drawing together past and present, that action is aimed toward a future which is the outcome of present and past, etc.—all these, as we said, are just features of our way of living in time. We take them to be natural and invariant features of human existence because we find it hard to imagine it otherwise.

But again, who are "we"?

Persuasive arguments have been made in recent years that the narrative conception of human time and human history is a relatively limited cultural phenomenon. Some see it as an expression of the exaggerated historical consciousness that overtakes European thought in the eighteenth century and extends to our day. The teleological structure of narrative is linked with the idea of progress, as is the idea that the future is subject to our wills and plans.[15] Others take a much broader view of this conception, linking it to the Judeo-Christian tradition as a whole of which recent historical consciousness is just a secularized version.

The idea that events in human life derive their significance and their value from other events in the same temporal sequence, finding in earlier events their origin and in later events their destiny, is characterized as a relatively restricted scheme by Mircea Eliade in his well-known work in comparative religion.[16] Even the Greeks did not share this scheme. In most non-Western religions, linear time is a mere appearance, reality is atemporal or cyclical, and human events are significant only as repetitive commemorations of mythic events that are not situated on the same temporal continuum.

Claude Lévi-Strauss has drawn from his anthropological studies a similar contrast between the Western, linear and developmental conception of human events and the conception he finds prevalent in many non-Western societies. In the latter, time and change are de-

---

15. See R. Kosellek, "Historia magistra vitae" and other essays in his collection *Vergangene Zukunft: zur Semantik geschichtlicher Zeiten* (Frankfurt: Suhrkamp Verlag, 1979). Similarly, F. Furet, "From Narrative History to History as a Problem" in *Diogenes* 89 (Spring 1975): 106 ff.

16. See M. Eliade, *Cosmos and History* (New York: Harper & Row, 1956), especially chapters 3 and 4.

valued if not denied. A primary purpose of social organization is to prevent change or to contain it as much as possible within an interpretive scheme in which its significance can be denied. An action or event derives its value not from its place in a narrative sequence but from its capacity to reflect other events and actions in a timeless symbolic scheme of affinities and oppositions.[17]

What is the significance of these studies for our conception of narrative time and for the question of its "universal" status? It might be argued that these non-Western conceptions reflect not the actual organization of experience but only its interpretation and schematization at a relatively abstract cultural level, that of myth and religion. Lévi-Strauss makes the point that naturally things do change in these societies, but that it is the purpose of the cultural-conceptual system to render such changes harmless.[18] In order to be thus under attack, change must be experienced and appreciated in the first place. We could thus maintain that for such cultures, linear and narrative organization *is* characteristic of ordinary experience, but that this organization does not get projected onto the larger-scale time of long-term social events. The narrative structure could thus be affirmed to hold universally after all, but only at the level of individual experience and action. The "upper story" of our theory, in which this temporal structure is interpreted socially as well as individually, would turn out to reflect a culturally relative phenomenon.

This solution, however, is objectionable both in itself and in its implications. It suggests too sharp a contrast between the structure of experience and the structure of thought. Are we to suppose that these non-Western conceptions are totally without effect on the way people view themselves and their everyday actions and experiences? Or, alternatively, that they are not expressions of a way of experiencing the world and acting in it? Anthropologists such as Lévi-Strauss claim that the conceptual systems they describe cover all aspects of the lives of those who subscribe to them, not merely a part of them. The very idea of separating our thought about the world from our experience of it is itself distinctly Western.

---

17. C. Lévi-Strauss, *The Savage Mind*, pp. 234–35. See further the work of R. Horton on African conceptions of time, e.g., "African Traditional Thought and Western Science" in *Rationality*, ed. B. R. Wilson (New York: Harper & Row, 1970), and "Tradition and Modernity Revisited" in *Rationality and Relativism*, ed. M. Hollis and S. Lukes (Cambridge: M.I.T. Press, 1972).

18. Lévi-Strauss, p. 234.

But the solution we outlined is even more unsatisfying in some of its implications. It suggests that the linear and narrative conception of time is tacitly recognized by everyone as reflecting the reality of human events, and that non-linear conceptions are just so many efforts to deny this reality. From there it is an easy step to the view that the *proper* conception of time and events is one which accepts and comes to term with change, difference, and development, rather than fleeing from them. Frederick Olafson suggests that in considering societies of the sort Lévi-Strauss describes, we might borrow the terminology of Heidegger and say that in them "historicity is present in its 'deficient' or 'inauthentic' mode."[19]

Olafson is reluctant to embrace this conclusion, but one can easily imagine Heidegger drawing it. Any refusal to face up to the finiteness of time, any attempt to flee into the timeless or eternal, is certainly counter to Heidegger's notion of authenticity. In this way the conceptual scheme of whole societies is relegated to the inauthentic. J. P. Sartre is reproached by Lévi-Strauss for doing something quite similar in his *Critique of Dialectical Reason*. If historical existence is an essential feature of human nature, as Sartre believes, what happens to "peoples without history"? Lévi-Strauss attacks Sartre for treating them sometimes in purely "biological" terms, and sometimes as humans but of a clearly deficient sort.[20] Significantly, Olafson's discussion of this topic too takes place in the context of comparing the timelessness of animal consciousness with human narrative-historical existence. Olafson comes to the conclusion that for "peoples without history" the narrative view of time is "waiting in the wings" for the moment when it *will* become operative.[21]

What emerges from this is an all-too-familiar picture. Not to put too fine a point on it, "peoples without history" are being placed on a scale somewhere between animals and the fully human! And it is clear that this is an *evaluative* and not just a descriptive scale. It is a scale of just this sort which has led to certain societies being labelled "primitive," a label against which Lévi-Strauss, among others, has argued vigorously.

The most recent version of this evaluative notion is hinted at in Paul Ricoeur's *Time and Narrative*. Ricoeur's "basic hypothesis" is

---

19. Olafson, *The Dialectic of Action*, p. 113.
20. Lévi-Strauss, pp. 248–49.
21. Olafson, p. 114.

"that between the activity of narrating a story and the temporal character of human existence there exists a correlation that is not merely accidental but . . . presents a transcultural form of necessity. To put it another way, *time becomes human to the extent that it is articulated through a narrative mode.*"[22] But what if we find peoples who do not construe their temporality through the activity of narrating? It would seem that, if there is a conflict between the "transcultural necessity" of narrative form and "peoples without history," this is to be resolved by saying that their time has somehow *not yet* become fully human. One is saved from excluding such peoples altogether from humanity by permitting them the possibility of *becoming* human.

This is admittedly the most blatant possible expression of a conclusion which Ricoeur, Olafson, and the others would probably not want to see drawn from their work. The sentiments it expresses are very much out of fashion. Yet it is hard to avoid drawing this conclusion from what they say. Something very deeply embedded in our way of viewing the world is being expressed in hidden forms in these writings.

Moreover, the view of the world being expressed here is itself a narrative-historical view. The scale from animals to "primitive" societies to "historical" Western society is not merely evaluative but developmental. This is the same conception which led Hegel, in his lectures on the philosophy of history, to treat "China" and "India" as precursors of the Western world even though both continued to exist in his own day as they do in ours. Now "primitive" societies, which exist in the present all over the globe, are relegated to the past by being regarded as leftovers from an earlier stage of humanity. What is in fact synchronous is arranged on a diachronic scale. What is more, the latter constitutes a dramatic story, the *Bildungsroman* in which Western man represents the maturity of civilization and the realization of all that is human. What Ricoeur calls a "transcultural necessity" turns out to be a historical necessity.

When looked at in this way it is understandable that the narrative conception of history should come under attack by structuralist and post-structuralist thinkers as a self-congratulatory and parochial Western point of view wanting to see itself as universal and devaluing anything that does not conform to it. The appeal to "history" is seen as the last gasp of "humanism," the view that man is capable of

---

22. Ricoeur, p. 85.

taking charge of himself and working out his own destiny.[23] A Marxist version of humanism may question the existentialist view that the individual can accomplish this on his own; but it asserts that "man" can do it collectively and that history is just the acted-out story of that achievement. The term "humanism" itself, of course, attests to the putative universality of this doctrine.

One could assert further that it wants this universality so much it is prepared to force it on those who do not accept. One thing that can surely be said in favor of the "historical necessity" of the Western view, and this counts in Hegel's favor too, is that the Westernization of the rest of the globe *is* proceeding apace, and that non-historical societies may eventually be in fact consigned to the past. Unless, of course, the critique from within Western thought succeeds in surpassing what it takes to be intellectual Eurocentrism and cultural imperialism and in replacing them with something else. Unfortunately, we are told very little about what this "something else" might be.

These arguments against the universality and "transcultural necessity" of the narrative conception of time are perhaps less than convincing and in some cases tendentious. In a sense they can never be fully convincing to *us* because *we* are asked to admit the reality of a way of construing and living in time which is alien to us. At the same time the considerations introduced by these arguments are important enough to make us cautious about asserting the universality of narrative time. When we say, then, that historical narrative is just an extention of historical existence, and that historical existence is the social counterpart of the individual's way of experiencing and acting in time, *we* are asserting all this about *ourselves*, not necessarily about everyone. Who, then, are *we*? Perhaps just that community that recognizes itself as sharing a certain conception of and a certain way of living in time, and recognizes that in this it differs or may differ from other communities past, present, or future.

Earlier we characterized this approach to time as a matter of confronting and dealing with the specter of temporal chaos, the meaninglessness of mere unstructured sequence. Questioning the universality of this approach forces us to recognize that narrative may be only *one* way of confronting time and its inherent threat. To

---

23. See the introduction to M. Foucault's *The Archaeology of Knowledge* (New York: Harper & Row, 1972), Barthes' "Historical Discourse," and Lyotard's *The Postmodern Condition.*

say that our way is bravely to face up to time, shaping and fashioning it rather than fleeing from it into timelessness, is merely once again to claim an advantage for our own way of doing things. Perhaps in the end we should be content to recognize, underlying cultural differences in these matters, a genuinely universal human trait: the struggle against temporal chaos, the fear of sequential dispersion and dissolution, the need to kill off Father Time or at least stave off (postpone?) his attempts to devour us all.

In any case, our purpose here has not been to argue for the universality of narrative structure but to claim that *for us* it constitutes the unifying form common to two sets of possible oppositions: it is on the one hand the unity of the *lived* and the *told*, and on the other hand the unity of the *individual* and the *social* or *historical*.

It may be thought that by admitting the possibility that narrative structure is culturally bound, we are undercutting an important part of our thesis. If it is true that the narrative organization of time is proper to a particular culture and tradition, does this not mean that its origin is *literary* after all? Rather than being extensions and reflections of our way of living in time, perhaps the great literary works of our culture, no doubt starting with the Bible, have inculcated in us a tendency to live our lives as stories. This would be the vindication of another aspect of Ricoeur's view (an aspect which, incidentally, is hard to square with his own universalism). Human lives are a heterogeneity of actions, intentions, goals, and circumstances, but they "need and deserve to be told."[24] Fictional and historical narratives render them this service, introducing harmony and order where none was before, providing them with ways of making sense of themselves. But these literary works in their turn affect the world from which they come, Ricoeur asserts, suggesting that they provide the models for narratively constructed lives. This is, of course, another version of the view that life imitates art; it can also be seen as describing a spiralling form of interaction or interplay between the reality of our culture and its representation in art and history.

This view has much to recommend it, but at bottom it rests on the opposition between non-narrative life and narrative form which is entirely poetic in nature and origin. It says that if action, life, history have narrative form, they acquire it from the literary products of our culture. But where do these, in turn, get their narrative form? For

---

24. Ricoeur, p. 115.

Ricoeur the chain of explanation stops here: the poetic act seems autonomous and self-moving.

We argue, by contrast, that action, life, and historical existence are themselves structured narratively, independently of their presentation in literary form, and that this structure is practical before it is aesthetic or cognitive. This is not to say that the literary embodiment of narrative is incidental to the life from which it springs, or that it has no effect on that life. We have said of historical writing that it is an extension of historical existence, its continuation by other means; something similar could be said of fiction in relation to individual existence, though we have not tried to argue that here. The effect of both forms of writing on the culture from which they derive is unmistakable. But what they provide is examples of how the narrative form can be filled in, representations of how to live, both as individuals and as communities. They do not provide the narrative form itself.

But to assert that this form is not created by the literary products of our culture is not to say that it is universal or independent of our community. A community is a great deal more than the products of its high culture. What we have tried to describe here, with the help of the concept of narrative, is our way of experiencing, of acting, and of living both as individuals and as communities. It is our way of being in and dealing with time.

Index

Action: "basic," 33, 43; logic of, 32; temporality of, 30–40; theory of, 31–32
Annales historians, 8
Annals, 12
Anxiety, 82, 87, 95, 97
Aristotle, 14, 33, 47, 74, 79–80, 125
Audience, 5, 45, 57–65, 111–112, 118, 149, 161; implied, 5
Augustine, 15, 42, 75
Authenticity, 82–92, 106–107, 113, 181
Author, implied, 156
Authorship, 82–92, 111, 118
Autobiography, 75–78
Averroes, 125

Barthes, Roland, 8, 13, 16, 50, 57
Beginning-middle-end structure, 10, 12–13, 15, 47–48, 51, 54, 57, 61
Bergson, Henri, 23, 26, 37, 41
Besinnung, 56–57, 63, 74, 78, 82–83, 87, 111, 114, 156–157, 164, 178; collective, 166, 168
Biography, 77, 79–80
Birth, 97, 107, 109, 163
Body: equilibrium of, 28; lived, 29
Booth, Wayne, 7
Braudel, Fernand, 175
Bremond, Claude, 8, 50
Brentano, Franz, 21, 30
Brough, John, 20n.
Buber, Martin, 119
Burke, Kenneth, 7

Capitalism, 133
Carcopino, Jérôme, 175
Causality, 36; in action, 35
Causes vs. reasons in explanation, 31
Characters (in a story), 5, 111, 118, 161
Chatman, Seymour, 13
Childhood, 96
Chronicle, 12, 90; vs. narrative, 59
Cicero, 156
Collingwood, R. G., 11, 123, 178
Communist Manifesto, 157
Configuration, 45; temporal, 24–30

Danto, Arthur, 7, 33, 43, 58, 78, 173
Das Man, 82, 85, 107
Death, 81, 83, 96, 107, 109; of community, 163
Deliberation, 56

Descartes, René, 124, 125, 140
Determinism vs. freedom, 32
Dilthey, Wilhelm, 2, 4, 38, 56, 74–82, 86, 91, 103, 107, 178
Dray, William, 11

Ego, 42, 104, 115; substantial, 25, 74; transcendental, 74; transcendental vs. empirical, 125, 127
Eliade, Mircea, 179
Engels, Friedrich, 157
Epistemology, 104, 124–126, 130
Erlebnisse, 56
Ethics, 32, 73
Existentialism, 82, 92, 96
Expectation, 55; primary, see Protention
Experience, temporality of, 21–30
Explanation: causal, 11; logic of, 32; by reasons vs. causes, 11, 31; vs. understanding, 31–32, 123

Family, 141, 154, 160, 162–163
First person: approach or method, 117–121, 124; singular and plural, 120
Freedom, 36; and determinism 32
Frege, Gottlob, 126
Freud, Sigmund, 110
Frye, Northrop, 7–8, 12
Fustel de Coulanges, Numa-Denis, 175
Future perfect tense, 38

Gallie, W. B., 7, 8
Geisteswissenschaften, 80
Gellner, Ernest, 123
Generations, 109–110
Genetic phenomenology, 104
Geometry, 105–106
German Idealism, 125, 137
Gestalt: spatial, 68–69; temporal, 41–42
Goethe, J. W. von, 75
Goffman, Erving, 162
Goldstein, Leon, 9
Greimas, A. J., 8, 50

Habermas, Jürgen, 151n.
Hardy, Barbara, 16, 65–66, 68, 70
Haugeland, John, 128n.
Hegel, G. W. F., 1, 5–6, 127, 137–152, 153, 154, 157, 158–159, 160, 178, 183; philosophy of history of, 159
Heidegger, Martin, 4–5, 30, 38–39, 57,

80–88, 92, 102–121, 127, 130, 134, 181
Hempel, Carl, 11
Heraclitean flux, 24
Herder, J. G., 1
Hexter, J. H., 7
Historicity, 4, 5, 102–121, 128–129
History: narrative conception of, 7–17;
     non-narrative, 173–177
History, philosophy of: analytic or crit-
     ical, 1–2; analytic, and narrative, 7–17;
     substantive or speculative, 1–2
Holism vs. individualism, 122–124
Horizons: internal vs. external, 23; spa-
     tial, 21–30; temporal, 21–30
Hoy, David, 109
Huizinga, J., 175
Human sciences, epistemology of, 38
Humanism, 182–183
Humanities, 69
Hume, David, 21, 35, 53, 97
Husserl, Edmund, 3–5, 19–30, 31, 32, 34,
     37, 39, 46, 55, 56, 60, 67, 69, 74, 95,
     101, 102, 103–121, 126, 131, 133, 134
Hyletic contents, 26

I-thou relation, 119
Idealism vs. realism, 125
Ideology, 135, 144
Imagination, 91
Implied author, 156
Individualism vs. holism, 122–124
Intentional vs. non-intentional, 26
Intentionality, 118
Intersubjectivity, 104, 111, 121, 128
Irony, 58–59

Jakobson, Roman, 8
Jaspers, Karl, 82

Kafka, Franz, 85
Kant, Immanuel, 2, 97, 105, 125, 139
Kellogg, Robert, 7, 58
Kermode, Frank, 7, 13, 19–20, 25
Kierkegaard, Søren, 82

Landgrebe, Ludwig, 103
Lévi-Strauss, Claude, 50, 142, 179, 181
Life and death struggle, 142–145, 147,
     159
Life-story, 74–80, 111
Life-world, 3, 101
Lincoln, Abraham, 156
Locke, John, 35
Logic, 126; of action, 32; of explanation,
     32
Logical: structure, 52; vs. temporal order,
     50
Longue durée, 175–176
Lyotard, Jean-François, 151n.

MacIntyre, Alasdair, 17, 70, 73–75, 81,
     86, 91, 92–93, 96
Mandelbaum, Maurice, 9, 123
Marriage, 154
Marx, Karl, 157
Marxism, 133, 135, 183
Marxist history, 176
Master-servant relation, 142–145
Mathematics, 50, 105, 125
Means-end relation, 48, 49, 50, 53, 57
Melody, 44, 46, 52, 57
Memory: primary, see Retention; second-
     ary, see Recollection
Merleau-Ponty, Maurice, 5, 24, 28, 29, 30,
     41, 121, 127
Metaphor, 15
Metaphysics, 125
Mimesis, 14–15
Mind-body interaction, 31
Mink, Louis, 7–17, 19, 45, 58, 61, 64, 71,
     89, 95, 170, 174
Misch, Georg, 103
Music, 56, 77
Munz, Peter, 16
Mysticism, 126

Narrative: and history, 7–17; literary
     study of, 7–8; structure, 15, 45–72;
     voice, 58–65
Narrator, 57–65; vs. author, 85; implied, 5
Nature: vs. culture, 66; science of, 66,
     101, 105
Neo-Kantians, 2

Olafson, Frederick A., 17, 27, 66–67, 69–
     70, 181, 182

Past: historical, 100; social, 117
Perception, 104
Pericles, 156
Personal identity, 73
Phenomenology, 3–5, 20, 127, 131; ge-
     netic, 104; Hegelian, 5–6; method of,
     117–121
Pirenne, Henri, 175
Plato, 122
Plot-structures, 12
Political conversions, 76
Post-structuralism, 182
Predecessors and Successors, 112–113,
     129, 134
Pre-thematic Awareness, 3–4, 18, 101,
     113–114
Propp, Vladimir, 8, 50
Protention, 22–30, 34, 36, 37, 41, 47, 48,
     55, 60, 69, 95, 110
Psychohistory, 176
Psychologism, 126
Psychotherapy, 172

Quinton, Anthony, 123

Realism *vs.* idealism, 125
Reality, human *vs.* physical, 19
Reasons *vs.* causes, 31
Recollection, 21–30, 55
Reconciliation, 151
Relativity, historical, 68
Religion, 135, 155, 158, 160
Religious conversions, 75–76
Representation: in action, 35–37; of reality, 10–17, 19
Resoluteness, 82
Retention, 21–30, 34, 36, 37, 41, 47, 48, 55, 60, 69, 95, 110
Rhetoric, 156, 157; political, 158
Ricoeur, Paul, 8–9, 14–15, 45, 64–65, 67, 170, 181–182
Rousseau, Jean-Jacques, 75

Sartre, Jean-Paul, 82, 83, 135, 136–137, 141, 181
Schapp, Wilhelm, 16, 62, 70, 73–74, 83–86, 91, 92
Schelling, F. W. J. von, 127
Schleiermacher, Friedrich, 77
Scholes, Robert, 7, 58
Schutz, Alfred, 37–38, 40, 55, 113, 131, 172
Science: of nature, 1–3, 66, 101, 105; philosophy of, 1
Sellars, Wilfred, 66
Semantics, 126
Sensation, 24
Separatist movements, 158
Skepticism, 144
Smith, Adam, 146
Social time, 101, 102

Sokolowski, Robert, 20n.
Sonata form, 52
Space, 41; experience of, 21–30; objective, 23
Spinoza, Baruch, 125
Stoicism, 144
Story-teller, 5, 46, 111; *vs.* author, 85
Story-telling, 4–5, 12, 18, 161
Structuralism, 5, 14, 50, 182; in literary theory, 8
Successors and predecessors, 112–113, 129, 134
Suspension-resolution, 49

Temporality: of action, 30–40; of experience, 21–30
Text, narrative as, 9
Time: historical, 7; objective, 23
Thales, 106
Truth, 98, 110

Understanding *vs.* explanation, 31, 123
Unhappy Consciousness, 144

Value, theory of, 32
Vico, Giambattista, 1, 4, 146
Virtue, 33

Weber, Max, 123
White, Hayden, 8–9, 11–16, 19–20, 59, 72, 88–90, 95
White, Morton, 7
Wittgenstein, Ludwig, 11
Wright, G. H. von, 38

Zusammenhang des Lebens, 57, 74–80, 86–87, 107–108

David Carr received his undergraduate and graduate degrees in philosophy at Yale University. He has taught at Yale, the New School for Social Research, Washington University, and the University of Oklahoma, and is now Professor of Philosophy at the University of Ottawa.